*The Case
for the South*

William D. Workman, Jr.

THE CASE
FOR THE SOUTH

THE DEVIN-ADAIR COMPANY, *New York*

First printing, December 1959
Second printing, January 1960
Third printing, April 1960

TO DAVID LAWRENCE
WHO BEFRIENDED THE SOUTH BY
TELLING THE TRUTH TO THE NATION

Contents

Foreword

THE South is being scourged by four pestilential forces which impose an almost intolerable burden upon Americans who cherish state sovereignty, constitutional government, and racial integrity. On the one hand are these three: the Supreme Court of the United States, which has wrought havoc in its injudicious effort to play at sociology; the National Association for the Advancement of Colored People, which has recklessly undertaken to achieve race-mixing by pressure; and the Northern politicians and propagandists who pervert small truths into big lies as they purvey vilification and ignorance on a grand scale. On the other hand is the Ku Klux Klan with its unlovely cohorts who substitute muscle and meanness for the intellect which by rights must be the defense of the South.

The man in the middle is the one whose voice needs to be heard, for too long has his quiet but determined resistance to tyranny from either side been unheralded and unexplained. Yet he has a case, a strong case, rooted in American

soil and nurtured in Southern tradition. In plain terms his
case is simply this: He demands for his state the right to ad-
minister its own domestic affairs, and he demands for himself the right to rear his children in the school atmosphere
most conducive to their learning—all without hurt or harm
to his Negro neighbor or to the Negro's children.

White men and black men, or, if you prefer the colloquial,
white folks and colored folks, have lived together in peaceful co-existence in the South for a long time, and can continue to do so to their mutual advantage if the pressures are
removed. The Supreme Court of the United States—away
back in 1896—said: *"If the races are to meet upon terms
of social equality, it must be the result of natural affinities,
a mutual appreciation of each other's merits, and a voluntary consent of individuals.* . . . Legislation is powerless to
eradicate racial instincts based upon physical differences,
and the attempt to do so can only result in accentuating the
difficulties of the present situation."

This book is predicated upon the idea that the formula
italicized above is as good now as it was then, and that it
sets a basis for amicable race relations not only in the South,
but everywhere. And to the extent that the principles laid
down in that formula are ignored, repressed, or suppressed,
so will the cause of racial amity be retarded.

Another Supreme Court of the United States—in May of
1954—saw fit to reject the admonition of its predecessor
Court, and to cast out (by a novel process of socio-judicial
reasoning) the 1896 doctrine which held that the white and
Negro races could be provided "separate but equal" facilities without any hurt to the Constitution of the United
States. There are lawyers, North and South, who challenge
both the legality and the propriety of that 1954 desegregation decision of the Supreme Court, but my concern here is
with the layman's rather than the lawyer's reaction to the
decision.

More particularly, my concern is with the white South-

erner and his reaction to that decision, and with the necessity for having the non-Southerner become aware of that
reaction and the reasons underlying it. After generations of
reliance on the "separate but equal" doctrine as an acceptable and accepted precept of government, the Southerner
found that his present and his future were suddenly turned
topsy-turvy by a federal court decree which proclaimed that
his entire past (with respect to race relations) had been
built on an improper premise. The shock of that abrupt re-
ordering of a traditional way of life was not one to wear off
quickly, nor was it one which gave promise of becoming
tolerable through exposure. Rather, it brought to a head the
long-smouldering Southern resentment against continuing
inroads of the federal government into affairs of local government. It touched off a wave of protest and resistance
which was wide in its scope and varied in its manifestations.

Because that wave shows little signs of receding except
around the fringes of the Southern heartland, it is a matter
of national as well as regional concern to see what underlies,
and undergirds, the Southern position. The hope of portraying some of the factors which go into the composition of
that Southern position prompts the writing of this book.
Much of it has been written on the edge of anger, for there
are emotional factors involved which evoke response from
the pressure-sensitive Southerner, and which frequently pro-
voke his resentment against those who cannot, or will not,
accept the sincerity of his views or the weight of his arguments.

But because it is important that the beliefs and behavior
of Southerners be appreciated, if not shared, by the rest of
the nation, this book undertakes the admittedly difficult task
of explaining, at least in part, why we Southerners think,
act, and react as we do.

For too long, as a perceptive Yankee once wrote, the
Southerner has been denied fair treatment in literature and
in the press. "People have not described him," wrote John

William deForest in the aftermath of the War Between the States, "they have felt driven to declaim about him; they have preached for him or preached against him. Northern pens have not done justice to his virtues nor Southern pens to his vices."

This book aims at remedying that situation in some measure, and it aims also at portraying for Southerners themselves the depth and the breadth of the forces which are drawn up in battle array against the South—forces which in many instances draw some of their sustenance from the very region which they pillory so sanctimoniously. It is well that the Southerner as well as the non-Southerner realize the nature and the number of his enemies, for this is no passing skirmish, but a cold war in which it may prove fatal to underestimate the opposition. Time and truth are on the side of the Southerner, but his faith must be firm and his resistance must be stout if he is to gain the time needed for the truth to become known. The Southerner will find little explanation herein for the animus which seems directed his way by both white men and black men (and a mixture of both) who live far from the Southern scene. But the documentation of anti-Southern sentiment, and the enumeration of the political considerations which inspire it, may reveal the alarming degree to which the South is constantly being used as a remote target for long-range attack by persons who have everything to gain and nothing to lose by economic, political, and social disruption of the Southern region.

This, then, seeks to present the case for the South. But since the South is a land of the black man as well as of the white man, it is, more precisely, a case stated for—and by—the white Southerner. It is presented in the hope that it might contribute to a better understanding of many related problems, both within and without the South, to the ultimate end that a better South might emerge for both races.

1

The South—
Home Guard of the Nation

I t is fashionable these days to talk of the "many Souths" rather than of one South. It is fashionable, too, to refer to the "liberal" Southerner, as opposed to his "conservative" or "reactionary" brother. In all truth, then, there is no hard and fast basis for reference to "THE South" or to "THE Southerner." Yet despite all this, there IS a strong bond of common identity and tradition which ties together a considerable portion of the white South into a homogeneous grouping of individuals whose thoughts, attitudes, and actions reflect a similarity which cuts across geographic, economic, educational, and political lines.

The South of today, as of yesterday, is a family—not altogether a happy family, yet happier than most and certainly closer knit than any other of the regional clans in the nation. It is a big family, both in geographic spread and in diversity of its members; and yet all its members are bound together by a tribal identity which transcends state lines (although they, too, are important family factors). From

Tidewater Virginia to Texas, the family ties of blood, belief, or behavior distinguish Southerners from other Americans, and there is a like-mindedness on ways of life (not just on race relations) which is almost incomprehensible to the Northerner.

Despite a reputation for quick temper, the Southerner is amiable, friendly, and tolerant of all save those who would interfere with his family life. Southerners will wrangle among themselves over their own code of conduct, and practice it with relative degrees of faithfulness, but they will draw together in quick resentment against the non-Southerner who proposes to alter their conduct by compulsion of word or deed. There is a regional consciousness which virtually establishes a "mutual defense alliance" among Southern states. An attack against any one is considered to be an attack against them all.

A major portion of this common bond stems from a heritage which might be termed Anglo-Saxon, Nordic, North European, or Celtic Teutonic. The manifestations of that heritage have remained meaningful and measurable for centuries, and even today they account for some of the Southern character traits which perplex and sometimes exasperate non-Southerners.

An understanding of the Southern character (if the reader will go along with the concept that there is such a central character typical of the white South) comes with study of the Southerner's antecedents back through the centuries.

An interesting facet of any such study is the quite obvious but little-noted diagonal transposition of North European culture to the American South. Through the Colonial and Revolutionary War days, and during the earlier days of the United States as such, the Anglo-Saxon atmosphere was apparent throughout all of the New World which had been settled by the British. It was in this atmosphere that the South developed, and it was this atmosphere which the

South retained as successive waves of immigrants swept into the North, there to dilute the customs and traditions which remained relatively unchanged in the South. Thus the South escaped much of the influx of new ideas, of new peoples, and of new practices which were poured into the melting pot of the North.

The South went through its "melting pot" phase early in the game, with the result that the French and German Protestants, along with the handfuls of other non-British peoples, were absorbed and assimilated into a way of life reflective of Anglo-Saxon traditions. All this took place in the years before the Yankee slave traders had begun to discharge their profitable cargoes at Southern ports. Thus there developed a regional consciousness in the South, stemming from common problems and a common ancestry, while the North remained in a constant state of flux.

In both population and political outlook, the South remained a microcosm of the early America which brought forth the United States of America and which laid the basis for the peculiarly successful form of constitutional, republican government which has given the nation unparalleled prosperity, progress, and personal freedom.

There is a definite correlation between the complexion of the Southern states today and that of the early Americans who wrested their independence from the British Crown. As evidence of that, look at these percentages of nationality reflected in the nation's first census—1790: English—82.1%; Scottish—7.0; Irish—1.9; German—5.6; Dutch—2.5, and French—.6. That same sort of overwhelming identification with Anglo-Saxon (Teutonic) Europe characterizes the South of today. Is it any wonder that differences should exist in the outlook of persons with that cultural heritage as contrasted with those whose national ties are with the Balkan, Mediterranean, African or Asiatic nations?

For one thing, it has meant that the South has continued as the most homogeneous section of the country, that region where, except for the distinct separation of the white and black races, there has been greatest assimilation of all persons into the political, social, and cultural pattern of the existing dominant group. The South has fewer enclaves of non-assimilable population groups than any part of the nation; it has fewer "ghettos," fewer "foreign element" problems, fewer language difficulties, and more harmony in civic and community functions than any area of equal size in the nation.

The South has proved the practical workability and desirability of a population expansion based on what could be called the "national origins" principle. Population characteristics which were reflected among the early settlers of the South still are in evidence, and they stem from long continuation of the Anglo-Saxon culture which developed with the original permanent colonization of the region. The frontier thinking and attitudes which came to characterize Americans of that early period remained characteristic of Southerners for a much longer period of time. Not only did the South retain its frontier flavor along the sparsely settled boundary lands between the settlers and Indians for longer than is generally realized, but a wholly new "frontier" was re-imposed upon the South during Reconstruction days, and thereafter, by force of economic hardship. Consequently, frontier thinking was preserved in the South long after it had evaporated in the wealthier and more populous areas of the North and Midwest.

But, on the other hand, the South was spared the turmoil and cultural upset which accompanies mass influxes of alien peoples. The result has been that from Virginia to Texas people live the same sort of lives, think more nearly alike, cling more tenaciously to the political tenets of early America, and in general reflect a greater mutuality of interest than can be found in any other part of the nation.

The presence of this common background and the absence of unassimilable white minority groups has given the South this additional advantage—it remains today as the most actively non-Communist section of the country. Communism has made little progress among native Southerners, and there are not enough foreign elements identifiable as such to provide a breeding ground among non-natives in the region. Figures cited by Rep. Francis E. Walter, of Pennsylvania, show that of some 5,000 "more militant members of the Communist Party" in America, 91.5 per cent either were of foreign birth, were married to persons of foreign birth, or were born of foreign parentage. The South of today provides barren soil for that sort of Communistic spawning.

The South was by-passed by the great wave of immigrants who swept into this country from southern and eastern Europe, and from the Mediterranean lands, during the years following the Confederate War and up through the wake of World War I. Consequently, the homogeneous and stabilized (in the sense of national origins) peoples of the South find it extremely difficult to realize that, to quote the President's Committee on Civil Rights, in 1947, "one out of every four Americans is still either a foreign-born white or the child of foreign-born white parents. One out of every five white Americans speaks some language other than English in his home."

A contributing factor to the homogeneity of the South is the overwhelming prevalence of Protestantism in the region, save for the heavy Roman Catholic population of Louisiana. The surge of immigrants which swept into the North during the half-century following the outbreak of the War between the States included great numbers of Catholics and of Jews, many of whom banded together by religious and cultural affinities in virtual enclaves. By contrast, those few who made their way South, or who entered initially into the Southern region at the behest of friends or relatives, were rapidly absorbed into the preponderantly Anglo-Saxon culture and, except for purely religious activities, took on the general attributes of the predominant white Protestant populace.

There early developed a crystalization of the South's cultural pattern, with the Anglo-Saxon white man occupying the upper and middle levels, and the Negro slaves, the lower. The freeing of the slaves did little to upset that economic, political, and social arrangement, so that the mores and customs of the South continued with little or no change as the decades rolled by. If anything, the Southern pattern became more distinctive than ever by virtue of the contrast it afforded to the ever-changing kaleidoscope of the North, where vast numbers of immigrants converted every metropolis into a veritable melting pot within itself.

As American history moved deeper into the 19th Century, more and more writers undertook to "explain" the South to the rest of the nation, especially to the East and North. Much of the West had no such need of explanation since that region was in large degree peopled by westward-ranging Southerners, driven by their own restlessness or by the pressure of an expanding slave system which brooked little competition from the independent farmer.

These portrayals of the South and of the Southern character had then, as they have now, a strong flavor of censure and an equally strong dose of incomprehension. The situation, then and now, is reminiscent of the inability of the Roman writers of old to understand their Germanic rivals when those two cultures came into conflict. Note these perceptive, and analogous, words of the noted Danish historian, Vilhelm Grönbech, in his study, *The Culture of the Teutons:*

"The Romans had excellent opportunities of observation, and were often keen observers; the great majority of what the Romans and the Greeks wrote about the Germanic people is right in its way. But every single remark, great or small, reveals its derivation from a sweeping glance across the frontier. We can always notice that the narrator himself stood far outside; he has seen what these people did, but he has not understood why they did so . . ."

But Grönbech can contribute even more to an understanding of the analogy between the Germanic peoples of the early Christian era and the Southerners of many centuries later. Speaking of the Teuton, for which we might substitute the Southerner, Grönbech says:

"Wherever he goes, he carries within himself a social structure which manifests itself in definite political forms as soon as he is thrown together with a crowd of others speaking the same tongue. He is not of that inarticulate type which forms kaleidoscopic tribal communities. However small his people may be, and however slight the degree of cohesion between its component molecules, the social consciousness is always present and active . . ."

Also caught up in the same Teutonic-Anglo-Saxon heritage is the Southerner's trait of according a high degree of respect and protection to womankind and his propensity for keeping them in something of a sanctified isolation.

Another Southern trait traceable at least in part to the Teutonic heritage is the reliance upon custom as a basis for conduct, even in the absence of specific laws. The Roman historian Tacitus noted that characteristic among the Germanic tribes when he wrote, ". . . good habits have there more influence than good laws elsewhere." Set in contrast against that observation is this contemporary (May—1957) expression from one of South Carolina's few white advocates of compliance with the Supreme Court's desegregation decision, a farmer and one-time college professor named J. M. Dabbs, of Mayesville. As if to refute Tacitus, Dabbs says, "We live in a world which, in its essential nature, is moving from custom toward law."

Yet neither of these quotations is as profound as the following statement of Thomas Jefferson, made in a September 20, 1810, letter to J. B. Colvin:

"A strict observance of the written law is doubtless one of

the high duties of a good citizen, but it is not the highest.
The law of necessity, of self-preservation, of saving our
country when in danger, are of higher obligation. To lose
our country by a scrupulous adherence to written law,
would be to lose the law itself, with life, liberty, property
and all those who are enjoying them with us; thus absurdly
sacrificing the end to the means."

To the Southerner, as to his Anglo-Saxon-Teuton forebears, the law springs not alone from the law books but
from the combined law sense of the tribal group. Where the
offense against the written law combines with offense against
custom, reaction is severe and punishment complete, not
only with respect to the penalties imposed by the statute
but—more importantly to the individual in many cases—
with respect to the judgment of the community. The Southerner whose misdeed makes him an outcast within the
group becomes, in fact as well as in name, an outlaw. But
where the law itself runs counter to the sense of the group,
no such lasting stigma attaches to the offender. Through
the years, that attitude has characterized the "moonshin-
ing" proclivities of the Southern mountaineers. The right
of a man to make his own strong drink is rooted deep in the
Anglo-Saxon tradition, and indeed at one time was a measure of a man's hospitality and of his religion. Thus today,
more than a thousand years later, the federal government
still is plagued by the same refusal of many Southern areas,
not all of them in the mountains, to bring the pressure of
community disapproval to bear against convicted moon-
shiners.

So it is with the Supreme Court's arbitrary ruling that
racial segregation is unlawful. In the eyes of the Southerner,
no honor attaches to that decision, and no dishonor to those
who scorn it.

The decision, which is widely regarded in the South as
a mark of oppression, is arousing once again that sort of
reaction which has been described, under other circum-

stances, as "a thoroughly orthodox English revolution, seeking to conserve rather than destroy." A South Carolina historian, the late Dr. D. D. Wallace, used that description in portraying the attitude of the early colonists who rebelled against the inept and dictatorial rule of the Lords Proprietors. It could be as well used to describe the reaction against the British Crown as the War of the Revolution developed, and later still, as the South rebelled against the Northern aggression which provoked and sustained the War Between the States. And it can be used today, when Southerners once more seek to conserve rather than destroy a way of life which they have evolved to their own satisfaction. Today's feeling of revulsion against outside dictation also carries with it this further mark of the "thoroughly orthodox English revolution," the characteristic that it is being led "by most substantial citizens." Here is no attempt of a radical band to overthrow established government or to destroy a pattern of social conduct—rather it is a determined effort to preserve the settled practices which have promoted domestic tranquility in the Southern community through the years. Here is a large-scale manifestation of the like-mindedness of Southerners, and of their tribal allegiance to the precepts and concepts which undergirded the foundations of American society from its very inception.

The flavor of the Southerner has seldom been better caught up in mere words than in these few opening lines of the late Ben Robertson's story of the Upcountry South Carolinians, *Red Hills and Cotton:*

"By the grace of God, my kinfolks and I are Carolinians. Our Grandmother Bowen always told us that we had the honor to be born in Carolina. She said we and all of our kissing kin were Carolinians, and that after we were Carolinians we were Southerners, and after we were Southerners, we were citizens of the United States. We were older than the Union in Carolina, and our grandmother told us never to forget that fact. Our kinfolks had given their personal consent to the forming of the Union, we had voted for it at the polls, and what we had voted to form we had the right to vote to unform."

The Southerner is proud of the past, and is imbued with a deeper sense of history than are Americans generally. Memories of things long past and persons long dead are meaningful in the South, and none are so cherished as those stemming from the glory of the Confederacy and the gloom of Reconstruction. The Southerner understands and in large measure illustrates the verity of what Winston Churchill writes in his *History of the English Speaking Peoples:*

"The cleavages of the great Civil War [of England] dominated English life for two centuries, and many strange examples of their persistency survive under universal suffrage in English constituencies today."

But there is this difference: Both Cavalier and Puritan traditions in England are laced with Civil War recollections, whereas in America the North has long since ceased to remember a war it won with weight of men and materiel. Forgetfulness comes easy to victors who fought and won on what to them was foreign soil. It does not come so easily for the vanquished whose homeland was ravaged and laid desolate, whose manhood was blighted by death and war wounds, whose economy was wrecked by both the war and by the aftermath, and whose leaders were stigmatized by imprisonment and ignoble treatment after giving all they had to a cause in which they believed. And as insult added to injury, the South was taxed by the national government to pension the very Federal servicemen who devastated the South, while being taxed by their own Southern states to provide for the Confederate servicemen who defended their homes and ideals.

Non-Southerners do not have—indeed they could not have—any real appreciation of the purely economic consequences of the War Between the States, and of the lasting effects of those consequences upon both the economy and the regional personality of the South. Aside from the ravages of the war itself, the South was dealt a crippling blow by the freeing of the slaves, a step which (without reference to its moral and social justification) was in effect a wholesale expropriation of valuable property held by Southerners.

Slaves were, under the economic system then prevailing in the South and countenanced by the national government as a legal if not a desirable institution, the means of production. They were the Southern planter's "producer goods," and as such they represented a tremendous proportion of the South's capital investment in the business of agriculture. When it is remembered that prior to the outbreak of the War Between the States an able-bodied slave was valued at about $1,000 or more, some idea may be gained of the terrific loss sustained by Southerners who owned anywhere from one to a thousand slaves. Modern conditions afford nothing approaching an analogy, but the contemporary American might get some vague idea of the economic impact of emancipation if he can visualize the chaos which would result today if the federal government were suddenly to deprive every automobile owner of his vehicle, and every trucker, contractor, shipper, and merchant of ALL vehicles —to a value, in 1860 currency, of some $2,000,000,000.

The economic implications of freeing the slaves was much in the minds of Southerners and Northerners alike in the years preceding the war, and in all fairness to the more responsible Northerners in executive and legislative posts, there was genuine concern over the problem and a sincere inclination to provide slave-owners with some compensation for their threatened loss of property.

It is purposeless now to go into the causes, conduct, or aftermath of the War Between the States, except insofar as such inquiries may give an insight into Southern character traits which are reflected in the current controversy over racial segregation, civil rights, and states' rights. Yet, precisely because those bygone developments *do* mirror a state of mind which characterizes Southern behavior even today, it is worth while noting regional reactions of a hundred years ago.

The continual abuse heaped upon the South and its institutions, notably slavery, aroused in the white Southerner a spirit of defensive defiance which had these consequences:

It prompted a defense of slavery from Southerners generally, even those who previously had looked askance at the practice and whose influence was being felt as a factor leading toward the early curbing and ultimate elimination of the institution.

It drove the "moderates" of that day into one or the other of the opposing camps, and, since white Southerners were both white and Southern, it was inevitable that they should side, almost to a man, with their own people.

It persuaded Southerners that they were the objects of general Northern hatred, for the reason that the purveyors of abolitionist propaganda had the floor while more reasonable men of the North, as of the South, sat quietly by because of diffidence or the dread of having their views misrepresented by persons more interested in the problem than in the solution.

That was the picture then. It is the picture today.

That premise is borne out by these words from a man who studied long and exhaustively into the factors leading up to and following the Confederate War, and whose definitive work, *The Tragic Era*, dramatically documents what the author himself calls "the twelve disgraceful years." Here is what the late Claude G. Bowers, American historian and diplomat, native of Indiana and long-time resident of New York, had to say in July of 1957 on the subject of South-hating propaganda in the Twentieth Century:

"I certainly do find a striking and disturbing similarity in the propaganda by Northern extremists against the South in the 1850's—which culminated in a sectional war that almost eventuated in the disruption of the Union—and the unbridled abuse of the South and its people from the same quarter on the issue of segregation. . . .

"Certainly, in these critical days calling for the unification of the nation against the common enemy in Moscow, no national or patriotic purpose is served by attempts of extremists to array one section against the other, and one race against the other."

The reluctance (in most cases, the refusal) of the Southern white man to entrust the Negro with positions of political authority is based on a multitude of factors, ranging over such broad fields as education, economics, and governmental practice, as well as race itself.

Southerners are the only white Americans who have been subjected to black rule—"misrule" would be the more apt term—and they want no more of it. No other section of the country has ever undergone the same experience, not even during the periods when Texans and Californians lived under Mexican rule before the admission of those states to the Union.

Reconstruction in the South dies hard in the memories and in the records of Southerners. Here was a civilization turned topsy-turvy by force of Northern arms. Here was a land laid waste, an economy utterly wrecked, a political system completely upset, and a military occupation superimposed upon the whole sorry scene. Here was a case, as phrased by Mississippi's post-Reconstruction Gov. James K. Vardaman, "of the bottom rail being on top."

And what happened? Was economic aid poured into this aching void? Were trade concessions granted in an effort to put the region back on its feet? Was there a "Marshall Plan" to rebuild a countryside laid desolate by warfare, and further despoiled by vengeful invaders who blazoned their own "scorched earth" policy across the face of the South?

Present-day Northerners have little cause to recall that the answers to all these questions was a firm "no," but

Southerners have cause to remember. The South had no claim on Yankee generosity after the War, and indeed made no such claim. The people of the seceding states had risked their all in what they considered to be a just cause, and they had lost. The fighting was done, and perhaps there was an expectation that the conquerors would exercise their prerogative of claiming that "to the victor belong the spoils."

But there were no spoils worthy of the name, except for what could be gouged out of a defenseless populace by the swarms of vultures who descended, carpetbags in hand, upon the South, there to join forces with the renegade "scalawags" whose love of money, and of power, transcended whatever love of community they once may have possessed. And undergirding the organized rascality and thievery which permeated the Reconstruction governments of the Southern states was the authority of the federal troops, stationed in military occupation of the "late rebellious" states.

Here was supreme irony. On the one hand was the oft-stated (by President Lincoln, among others) contention that the Southern states had never left the Union at all, that their efforts at secession were ineffectual and unrecognized. On the other hand was the vindictive program of Congressional-directed "reconstruction" which viewed the South as a conquered province, incapable of governing itself except as it complied with the highly questionable mandates of a Republican administration determined to entrench its influence in the South through the medium of newly-enfranchised Negroes.

The story of the 14th amendment stands out as the prime example of this split personality of the federal government. And it is ironic that this amendment, which has served as the anvil on which the Supreme Court has hammered out many of its civil rights decisions, should itself have been adopted in such an uncivil, unrighteous and manifestly unconstitutional manner.

This, in brief, is that story:

The governments of the Southern states were reconstituted after the Confederate War, received presidential recognition, and began participating in national affairs to the extent of helping provide the number of states necessary to ratify the 13th (anti-slavery) amendment to the Federal Constitution. But when the 14th amendment was proposed by Congress in June of 1866, the Southern states (except for Tennessee) rejected it. Not only did the former Confederate states reject the amendment, but so did Delaware, Maryland, and Kentucky. (An interesting footnote to the story is that three of the early-ratifying states, New Jersey, Oregon, and Ohio, subsequently, in 1868, passed resolutions withdrawing their consent to ratification. Another footnote can be added with the notation that the state of California never did ratify the 14th amendment, and has not to this date done so.)

But the Southern states exercised their power to prevent the amendment from receiving the required approval of three-fourths of the then 37 states in the Union. This wholesale rejection of the 14th amendment infuriated the Republicans in control of Congress, and paved the way to passage of the unparalleled Reconstruction Acts.

A major element in the Republican plan of action was the exclusion of Southerners from Congress until the reconstruction pattern could be forced upon the "rebel states," so as to mold them into conformity with Republican desires. Accordingly, acting under the thin cloak of the Constitutional provision which permits each house of Congress to be the judge of its own members, the House and Senate barred Southern representatives and senators from Congress. Here was a clear-cut abridgment of two other Constitutional provisions, one guaranteeing (in Article 1, Section 2) that "each state shall have at least one Representative," and the other declaring (in Article 5) "that no State, without its consent, shall be deprived of its equal suffrage in the Senate."

Riding roughshod over any constitutional, ethical, or moral grounds which would have dictated otherwise, Congress made this stipulation in its Reconstruction Act:

". . . and when said State, by a vote of its legislature elected under said constitution, shall have adopted the amendment to the Constitution of the United States, proposed by the 39th Congress, and known as Article 14, and when said article shall have become a part of the Constitution of the United States, said State shall be declared entitled to representation in Congress. . . ."

Walter J. Suthon, Jr., former president of the Louisiana State Bar Association and law professor at Tulane University, terms that imposition "the most extreme and amazing feature" of the Reconstruction Act. In his well-documented study of *The Dubious Origin of the Fourteenth Amendment,* Mr. Suthon singles out this excerpt from a Wisconsin senator (Doolittle) as typifying the attitude of the Republicans, even the conservative Republicans:

"My friend has said what has been said all around me, what is said every day: the people of the South have rejected the constitutional amendment, and therefore we will march upon them and force them to adopt it at the point of the bayonet, and establish military power over them until they do adopt it."

That sort of thinking is abroad in the North again today, and yet the very individuals who evidence the greatest willingness to compel Southern submission to Northern domination are the very ones who scream loudest about "dictatorship" in the South when Southern whites seek to retain control of their own affairs. Those who call the Southerner "fascist" reveal an ignorance of both the Southerner and the fascist. Nowhere in the civilized world, except in the South, has there been such a fierce insistence upon "states' rights" and local self-government, factors which are in themselves the very antithesis of fascism. True, the South has had, and perhaps still has, its little dictators—on the city, or the county, or occasionally on the state level—but never has there been any broad support for a strong centralist government, which is the essence of totalitarianism, whether termed fascism or otherwise.

There have been times when the insistence upon states' rights operated against the Southerner's own self-interest, as was the case during the days of the Confederacy. Even then, despite the obvious military, political, and diplomatic demands for a strong central government, the Southern states were reluctant to yield their individual sovereignty to the Confederate government. The stubborn refusal of some states to cooperate fully with the Confederate government brought about difficulties which sorely hampered the South's efforts to wage a successful war and establish a stable government of its own.

It is sheer idiocy, therefore, when an individual of official importance and of presumed intelligence such as the editor of the *Christian Century* charges the South with moving toward Naziism through the functioning of its Citizens' Councils. The fact of the matter is that, had the German people manifested the same determination on the local level to resist the establishment of an all-powerful centralist state, there might never have been a Nazi Germany.

Because of that willingness of the Southerner to fight for what he believes, he is constantly on the receiving end of condemnation and pressure from those centralists who masquerade under the name of liberals. Through all the years of American history, the Southerner has reflected an amiability, a friendliness, and a tolerance which has kept him from poking and prying into the affairs of his non-Southern neighbors; but he demands in return that he be left alone to manage his own internal affairs.

He fought an uphill battle against the North during the War Between the States for that very reason—not to impose his will upon the Northerner, but to prevent the reverse from happening. Imbued with the conviction that it was

both right and proper for the South to repel political, economic, and military aggression from the North, the Southerner fought—and lost. And in losing, he laid himself open
to retribution of such vindictiveness that even a hint of a
repeat performance against a conquered enemy would today bring down the denunciations of the entire world on
the nation which attempted it.

But the Southerner lived through his ordeal and at long
last has climbed back to a position of economic and social
well-being more commensurate with his abilities. And with
restoration of that posture in national affairs, the South once
more finds itself pilloried by non-Southerners to whom Southern success seems unbearable. What non-Southerners cannot
get through their heads is the fact that their winning the War
Between the States proved nothing except that they had the
stronger military and economic establishment. The outcome
of that struggle proved who was stronger, not necessarily who
was right.

Southerners then, as Southerners now, wished merely to
govern their own affairs in a manner consistent with the customs of the people and within the framework of a written
constitution which had guaranteed the right to do so to the
several states of the Union. The issue of slavery had both its
defenders and attackers in the South as well as in the North;
indeed, it is said that prior to 1860 there were more anti-
slavery societies in the South than in the North. Many leading men and women of the South sought to rid their region
of the curse of slavery, and they were making progress up to
the time that hostile outside pressures became unbearable.
It was that uncompromising and uncomprehending interference from the North which drove Southern men of good
will, of moderation, and of proven leadership into the front
ranks of the Confederates.

Today, the same sort of pressure has pushed into the core
of real Southern resistance the respectable citizenry, which
is far removed from the fringe elements which dabble in

violence and vituperation. For every hate-mongering crack-pot or bully-boy who hits the headlines with an act of bru-tality or of utter stupidity, there are literally thousands of solid, substantial citizens whose opposition to enforced in-tegration is as constant and steadfast as it is peaceable.

Today, these men (and women) are not in the ranks of the Ku Klux Klan or in the more virulent pro-segregation organizations. But thousands of them are members of the responsible Citizens' Councils which abound in the deep South, and more thousands think alike on the segregation question even though they belong to no group, make no speeches, and attend few meetings.

It is this type of person which makes up the backbone of any popular movement of consequence, whether it be po-litical, religious, social, or otherwise. These people are the leaders in their own communities, and they carry the pres-tige and the influence which goes with community leader-ship. Hundreds among them are influential on state and re-gional levels. The steady, unrelenting resistance which stems from Southerners of this type is no frantic flurry of reaction, to blaze today and die out tomorrow. Theirs is a determined purpose to apply their intellect, their resources, and their undeniable political ascendancy to the maintenance of seg-regated schools until such time as their communities are willing to accept integration—when and if that time ever does come.

The important factor here is the nature of that resistance, not its nomenclature. And the failure of the integrationists to recognize and respect the nature of that opposition could lead to tragic results. Already the integrationists have had to revise their programs repeatedly in the deep South as resistance took on what was to them unexpected depth, breadth, and effectiveness. This sort of resistance cannot be dismissed lightly, nor can it be banished by threat or in-timidated by a show of force.

American history bears out the formidable character of an

aroused citizenry which draws its strength from the ranks
of civic leaders, church members, established business men,
respectable farmers, and others, both in and out of public
life, to whom their fellows turn with confidence and reliance
for community guidance. These people are slow to be
goaded into action, but once prodded into concerted motion
by force of circumstance or by threat of upset to community life, they move with implacable determination to save
the situation.

It was so with the "Regulators" who sought to bring order
to the Southern frontier; it was so with the "vigilantes" of
the Old West, and it was so with the Ku Klux Klan of the
Reconstruction period. In each of these periods of American crisis, situations became so intolerable that the substantial citizenry rose up literally in arms and removed the
threat to the community. But it was also unfortunately true
that self-seeking, brutal men moved in on the heels of those
movements and corrupted what were initially decent organizations into agencies of oppression and misguided violence.
These periods of aftermath have left a lingering and unpleasant odor to such movements, especially to the KKK.
But even that unsavory afterglow cannot erase the fact that
there was a time when these extra-legal and spontaneous
organizations, drawing as they did from the heart of the
community, served a necessary purpose which otherwise
was not being served.

There were other times and other places where the same
sort of developments occurred, frequently without name
and without formal organization. The controlling factor in
every instance, and the difference between success and failure, lay in the type of people who rallied to the cause. It is
so today in the South, where the effectiveness of resistance
to integration lies, not in the names or even in the numbers
of organizations which are formally dedicated to the maintenance of segregated schools, but in the caliber of the people who are informally dedicated to the same cause.

A testimonial on that score comes from a Southern Presbyterian minister, the Rev. Robert B. McNeill, late of Columbus, Ga., writing in early 1957 in *LOOK* magazine.

"As for the klansmen and their threats of violence, we do not fear them, we only pity them. God pity anyone who has to spread fear to be rid of fear, whose self-esteem is so low that he has to flatten someone else to feel that he is upright.

"The White Citizens' Councils are more formidable. They are smart enough to know that physical force will backfire against them. They resort to political and economic pressure to attain their ends. But they, too, will run their course.

"Our greatest concern is with good citizens who create the climate of opinion, in their service clubs, in their coffee-break talks, in business transactions, in political decisions, in church affairs, in the management of the home. The heavy pressure we ministers feel comes from them. They elect the State officials who vie with each other in proposing bizarre methods for strengthening segregation. They furnish a Stars-and-Bars backdrop against which we have to speak cross-centered words of reconciliation. They lay upon us the pressures they feel all the time, everywhere, in the regular concourse of life, as though we were the real disturbers of the peace. There is little indignation expressed over the klan or racial violence, just silence, cold sweaty silence. The klan is the impassioned tip of the community's refined prejudice. . . ."

Whether by accident or intention, this modern-day Georgian is giving paraphrase to much the same thought expressed in 1889 by Georgia's "voice of the New South," Henry W. Grady:

"If there is any human force that cannot be withstood, it is the power of the blended intelligence and responsibility of a free community. Against it, numbers and corruption cannot prevail. It cannot be forbidden in the law, or divorced in force. It is the inalienable right of every free community. It is on this, Sir, that we rely in the South. Not the cowardly menace of mask or shotgun, but the peaceful majesty of intelligence and responsibility, massed and united for the protection of its homes and the preservation of its liberty."

All this, and more, is characteristic of what often is referred to, sometimes disparagingly, sometimes pridefully, as "the Southern way of life."

2

"Uncluttered with Precedents"

IN THE beginning was the Declaration of Independence, which proclaimed the American proposition that governments among men derive their just powers from the consent of the governed, and that the people have the right to alter or abolish any form of government which becomes destructive of their life, liberty, and pursuit of happiness.

Thereafter came open warfare, as Americans fought to achieve the safety and happiness they regarded as just goals of free men. Had they not done so, there would have been no United States of America. It was a spirit of resistance, not of submission, which brought this country into being, and which carried the American Revolution through to a successful conclusion.

The conflict ended in a peace treaty wherein "His Britannic Majesty acknowledges the said United States, viz., New Hampshire, Massachusetts Bay, Rhode Island and Providence Plantations, Connecticut, New York, New Jersey, Pennsylvania, Delaware, Virginia, North Carolina, South

Carolina and Georgia to be free, sovereign, and independent states." Then came the drafting of a Constitution of the United States, whereby the "free, sovereign, and independent states" agreed to enter into a compact which created a central government of limited powers and which reserved to those sovereign states and to their people all the powers not specifically granted to the central government.

Now comes a Supreme Court of the United States, a creation of the Constitution, which abrogates that bilateral contract, which assumes unto itself authority which never devolved upon it, and which has precipitated a constitutional crisis in the relationship of states to nation. And it does so in complete disregard of the sound legal principle, expressed thus in 1880 by Francis Lieber:

"The more a constitution partakes of the character of a solemn compact, the closer its construction must be; for we have no right to construe or interpret otherwise, if there are several parties. Construction of federal constitutions, therefore, ought to be close."

Even more definitive and pertinent to the current proclivity of the Warren Court to twist the Constitution to its own whims is this statement from one of the great constitutional authorities of America, the Michigan jurist, Judge Thomas Cooley:

"A cardinal rule in dealing with written instruments is that they are to receive an unvarying interpretation, and that their practical construction is to be uniform. A constitution is not to be made to mean one thing at one time, and another at some subsequent time when the circumstances may have so changed as perhaps to make a different rule in the case seem desirable. A principal share of the benefit expected from written constitutions would be lost if the rules they established were so flexible as to bend to circumstances or be modified by public opinion."

Yet the Warren Court, with a fine disdain of both the Constitution and the body of law built up by predecessor courts, has undertaken to declare that what had heretofore been accepted as legal equality is sociological inequality. At the same time, the Court bolsters the growing tendency of the central government, through the federal judiciary, to supplant the state governments as the determinant of what is and what is not equality, not only in law, but in education.

Every man, whether layman or lawyer, is entitled to his own view of what prompted the Supreme Court of 1954 to cast aside the accumulated wisdom of earlier courts and to veer off into the tangled underbrush of sociology, where even the best of legal bloodhounds lose the trail of law. My own view is that the Court succumbed to pressures, or blandishments, which persuaded the Justices that a desegregation decision could perform a highly useful function in the realm of international relations and perhaps enhance the position of the United States in its dealings with the non-white nations of the world. One indication which points in that direction is this statement from the Justice Department's brief in the school cases:

"It is in the context of the present world struggle between freedom and tyranny that the problem of racial discrimination must be viewed. The United States is trying to prove to the people of the world, of every nationality, race, and color, that a free democracy is the most civilized and most secure form of government yet devised by man. We must set an example for others by showing firm determination to remove existing flaws in our democracy."

In similar vein, and even more pertinent to the internationalist aspect of the situation, was this statement by the Secretary of State, quoted in the U. S. Government's brief before the Supreme Court in December of 1952:

"The segregation of school children on a racial basis is one of the practices in the United States that has been singled out for hostile foreign comment in the United States and elsewhere. Other people cannot understand how such a

practice can exist in a country which professes to be a
staunch supporter of freedom, justice, and democracy. The
sincerity of the United States in this respect will be judged
by its deeds as well as by its words."

But if the Supreme Court, as I suspect, was in fact influenced by such considerations, it would have done better
to say so openly and to declare that as a matter of national
policy the decision was being promulgated as it was. But instead of taking that course of departure from legal precedent, the Court elected to wander afield into the sociological
morass, taking cover and refuge amidst verbiage which as-
tounded the lawyer, horrified the white Southerner, and
gratified the politically-potent NAACP.

Perhaps the most revealing accolade came to the Court
from the Southern-born but Negro-oriented writer, Lillian
Smith, who said in her emotional little book, *Now Is The
Time* (to give up segregation):

"Chief Justice Warren, who spoke for a unanimous court,
did not clutter his pages with legal precedents."

And so, refusing to "clutter up its pages with legal precedent," the Court ruled that the separation of Negro children
from white children in schools denied the Negroes the equal
protection of the law. Thus did it overthrow both the law
and the custom of generations. Thus did it negate the right
of the states to govern their own educational affairs in the
interests of domestic peace and tranquility. Thus did it
usurp the prerogatives of the Congress, which is charged
with the enforcement of the 14th Amendment and its guarantee of "equal protection of the laws." And thus did the
Court fulfill the prophecies of Thomas Jefferson, who gave
these warnings on several occasions in his later life:

"There is no danger I apprehend so much as the consolidation of our government by the noiseless, and therefore
unalarming instrumentality of the Supreme Court. . . .
The Constitution . . . is a mere thing of wax in the hands

of the judiciary, which they may twist and shape into any
form they please. . . .

"The judiciary of the United States is the subtle corps
of sappers and miners constantly working under ground to
undermine the foundations of our confederated fabric. They
are construing our government from a coordination of a general and a special government to a general and supreme one
alone."

It is quite apparent that insofar as the Supreme Court suc-
ceeds in re-ordering the governmental processes according
to its own notion, the Court becomes an instrument of abso-
lutism. If the Court is allowed to roam freely about the entire realm of government, unrestricted by the once-coordi-
nate branches of government, and unresponsive to the
electorate whose interests supposedly are safeguarded by a
written Constitution, there will shortly and certainly come
an end to the "beautiful equilibrium" which the Constitution established between the central and the state governments.

That equilibrium has frequently been threatened by
proponents of an all-powerful federal government, but the
threat began to become ominous and imminent in 1947
when President Harry Truman's Committee on Civil Rights
submitted its report. In many respects, that report is a
frightening document—frightening in the sense that it poses
a clear and present danger to the concept of balanced state-
federal relationships in the United States. The composition
of the hand-picked committee might have forewarned the
public of the extreme "liberalism" to be found in the committee's report, but it was not expected that the group,
which included a number of respectable and presumably
cautious individuals, should go so far as to recommend bare-
faced "experimentation" with devices whereby the central
government might more effectively invade the sphere of the
states.

There is much sanctimonious talk in the report about the "Bill of Rights" of the American Constitution, and of the 13th, 14th, and 15th amendments which grew out of the Confederate War. But nowhere in the report is there any mention of the Tenth Amendment as being either an element of the Constitution, or of the oft-cited Bill of Rights. The only references to state and local governments arise by way of condemnation and contempt, and the report dwells at length on various proposals by which the Federal government might exert a civil rights authority in the admitted absence of any Constitutional provision expressly vesting the central government with any such power.

One such device (almost a dozen are listed) suggests that the Government of the United States lean, not upon its own institutions, but upon Article 55 of the United Nations Charter, which states in part that the U.N. shall promote "universal respect for, and observance of, human rights and fundamental freedoms for all without distinction as to race, sex, language, or religion," and upon Article 56, by which all U.N. members pledge themselves to "take joint and separate action . . . for the achievement of the purposes set forth in Article 55."

In its devious reasoning, the Committee proposes that the federal government consider the enactment of civil rights legislation to implement those goals set forth in the U.N. Charter, since Article II, Section 2, of the Constitution of the United States has been held to permit Congress to enact statutes to carry out treaty obligations.

In the domestic field, the Committee suggests not only that federal grants-in-aid, or the withholding thereof, be used as a weapon to secure civil rights compliance by public and private agencies, but that study be made of the possibility of "the use of the taxing power to discipline individuals and organizations which are guilty of discriminatory practices. The right of nonprofit educational or welfare organizations to be exempt from property or income taxes and the right of individuals to deduct from their income tax contributions made to such organizations might be deliberately withheld. . . ."

In casting about for "new tools for the enforcement of civil rights policy," the Committee states baldly:

"Experimentation in the use of these powers and this machinery for such a worthwhile purpose is eminently desirable and should be undertaken immediately."

Since those recommendations were made by the President's Committee on Civil Rights, the Supreme Court has made notable progress in usurping, gradually but steadily, additional powers beyond those granted it by the Constitution. So effective has this encroachment been that there has evolved a strong body of opinion outside the South, and a smattering of it inside parts of the South, that any pronouncement of the United States Supreme Court comes as final judgment from on high and cannot even be questioned, much less challenged. Admitting that such a policy generally is, and should be, observed, there nevertheless is always the possibility that the Court itself, which is made up of fallible men, may exceed its own authority and undertake to do those things which are themselves beyond the confines of "due process" in the broader application of that term.

The present impasse over the school desegregation decision brings us face to face with just such an occasion—one wherein the Supreme Court, at least in the eyes of countless Southerners and numerous non-Southerners, has transgressed. The issue here, from an abstract view of purely governmental philosophy, is not so much concerned with how the Court ruled, as with its having moved into a field where its authority is based on non-existent or at best highly dubious grounds. From a strictly legal approach to the situation, the South's contention that the Supreme Court erred would be just as valid had the Court undertaken to tell the states that they could not integrate their schools. A ruling in either vein, for or against integration, would have placed the Court in the position of dictating to the states how their schools should be managed—something the South contends that the Court is without authority to do.

The seriousness of this particular ruling, which has a fundamental effect upon the traditional structure of Southern society, constitutes an invasion so "deliberate, palpable and dangerous" (to borrow from the Virginia and Kentucky interposition resolutions of 1798) that the South feels justified in raising the issue of a conflict of sovereignty at the highest level. Here is no judicial decision, based on judicial precedent or even on legal reasoning, but one which admittedly flows out of and into the sociological concepts of Americans generally, and one which threatens the destruction of a sociological concept long held by citizens in one-fourth of the nation.

Under these circumstances, Southerners challenge the authority of the Court, saying it has no right to intervene in matters which rest within the reserved powers of the States, as safeguarded by the Tenth Amendment to the federal constitution. They ask, as did Dean W. W. Pierson, of the University of North Carolina's Graduate School:

"If a decision is not based on law, is the decision law? If the Constitution is what the Supreme Court says it is, the thoughtful, conscientious, loyal, and law-abiding citizen should read the opinions of the Court rather than the text of the instrument before taking an oath to defend the Constitution. When the court reverses itself, what is the plight of the law-abiding citizen? Does the fact that one decision is later in time give it greater logical validity? Does not the prestige and sanctity of the Constitution suffer in a case of The Supreme Court v. The Supreme Court? If the Court can exercise the constituent power and amend the Constitution in one particular why cannot it do so in any? Could it not on petition of a 'class,' called in a certain ideology the 'proletariat,' declare the body of legislation which prescribed conditions of the system of 'free enterprise' invalid on the ground that competition, even if defined as fair, is a denial of the equal protection of the law?"

What is involved in this constitutional crisis is a conflict of interpretation with respect to the Constitution itself, and a conflict of authority with respect to the enforcement of laws. Submission to federal bureaucracy and subscription to centralized authority have become so much a part of American thinking outside the South that horror is expressed that anyone should question the omniscience of the Supreme Court. Southerners are less inclined to submit supinely to anything done in the name of officialdom, and they retain a spirit of resistance to tyranny, no matter in what guise it comes.

But lest Southerners be termed "lawless," as they already have been by integrationists and conformists, this point should be understood: The people of the South are observing the laws of their states and localities—laws properly, legally, and representatively enacted by the people themselves. The clash is not between the people and the law, but between two opposing sets of laws: those of the central government and those of the local government.

Here is a clash of sovereignty, not a breakdown of laws. The submissionists cry out that the Southern states are "defying" the Supreme Court and "the law of the land." Yet even if it be admitted that there is defiance of the Supreme Court, it does not necessarily follow that "the law of the land" is being flouted.

In the first place, nowhere is it declared that the Supreme Court, or the federal judiciary, shall have dominion over the other two parts of government. The law of the land need not be always what the Supreme Court wills it to be at any given moment of sociological progress. Note what the Constitution itself says on the subject:

"This Constitution, and the laws of the United States which shall be made in pursuance thereof . . . shall be the supreme law of the land."

The Constitution itself, along with the acts of Congress, therefore, stands, or should stand, as a barrier against excessive enthusiasm on the part of any one of the three branches of government, including the judiciary. With respect to that branch, its authority extends only to "cases, in law and equity, arising under this Constitution." If the Supreme Court is empowered to extend and expand its authority indefinitely by the simple expedient of reading into the Constitution whatever justification the Court desires, then the Court becomes, in effect, not only *the* government but *all* government.

The roadblock which stands in the way of any such self-nourishing expansion of the judicial authority, as well as of the executive and legislative authorities, is the Tenth Amendment of the Bill of Rights. Without that amendment, it is doubtful that the American people would long have subscribed to the Constitutional compact of states. The wording of that neglected amendment, too often ignored or abused, needs repetition at every opportunity if ever it is to regain its original luster and its initial importance as a controlling factor in the pattern of American government:

"The powers not delegated to the United States by the Constitution, nor prohibited by it to the States, are reserved to the States respectively, or to the people."

Here is what seems to the layman, as to the lawyer, a clear-cut declaration that those governmental powers which are not specifically enumerated as being within the federal domain shall remain within the domain of the States, or within the hands of the people. But who is to arbitrate when serious dispute arises, as has now arisen, between the authority of the central government (as represented by the Supreme Court) and the authority of the several States, as currently represented by those of the South?

If the Supreme Court itself was contemplated as being the final arbiter of any and all questions concerning interpretation of the Constitution, then it becomes obvious from the outset that there would have been no purpose whatever in adopting either the Tenth amendment, already quoted, or the Ninth, which states:

"The enumeration in the Constitution, of certain rights, shall not be construed to deny or disparage others retained by the people."

If those two amendments were meant to be effective, then it is hard to conceive any idea that the framers of the Constitution had any intention of establishing the Supreme Court as the voice of final authority. Nor, if Thomas Jefferson's words in the 1798 Kentucky Resolution of Interposition are to be regarded, did the framers intend that the central government was to have discretion over the Constitution:

". . . the Government created by this compact was not made the exclusive or final judge of the extent of the powers delegated to itself, since that would have made its discretion, and not the Constitution, the measure of its powers; but that as in all other cases of compact among parties having no common judge, each party has an equal right to judge for itself, as well as of infractions as of the mode and measure of redress."

If the Supreme Court, then, is not the final voice in such disputes, who does have that voice? The answer is that the States themselves are the final determinant—not individually through secession, which was tried and found wanting (in military strength), but collectively through the process of Constitutional amendment.

The present case lends itself to that determination. Here is an issue of transcendent importance to a dozen states or more. Here is a deep-seated division within the national Congress. Here is a judicial innovation of sociologically-based decision which conceivably could lead to similar and

even more far-reaching opinions in the future as the sociological whims of the Supreme Court justices ebb and flow.
What could be fairer, then, than to submit the question to
the entities which of themselves brought this government
into being and gave it a name—the *united* States?

If three-fourths of the states ratify an amendment which
would vest the federal government with control over the
public schools of the nation, then so be it. The States of the
South still would not like it, but they would no longer have
a legal or constitutional basis upon which to resist such a
ruling. And there would be unmistakable evidence through
ratification of such an amendment that the policy of federal
authority over schools had the endorsement of the American
people, speaking though their elected representatives in
their respective state governments. But without the submission of the question to the people, there is no measure whatever of public willingness to have the federal power extended into the realm of public education.

Southerners recognize that the Constitution of the United
States was not designed as an inflexible and unchanging
document, but they subscribe (with Washington and Jefferson) to the proposition that any changes should be wrought
in the manner contemplated by the Constitution itself. That
means that either the Congress or the States themselves
might initiate a constitutional amendment, but it does not
meant that changing sociological doctrines should be read
into the Constitution by federal judges who thereby seek to
effect an amendment.

As evidence of their good faith in the amendment process, a number of Southern States have proposed by formal
declaration that the question of a state's right to manage its
own educational affairs be submitted as a Constitutional
amendment. The way is open to submit that proposition
either negatively or affirmatively to the States, and to abide
by their decision. One version of such an amendment could
vest the federal government with authority to act in the

field of public education. Another version could be worded so as to specifically exclude the federal government from the field, leaving the matter among the powers reserved to the States by the Ninth and Tenth Amendments. In either event, the issue could be settled by constitutional means.

The very existence of the 15th amendment is a powerful argument in favor of this constitutional approach to the problem, as can be seen from the following sequence of events: With the end of the War Between the States, Congress proposed, and the requisite three-fourths of the States (including many in the South) ratified, the 13th amendment, which abolished slavery throughout the country.

Thereafter, with a demonstration of naked force described elsewhere, the 14th Amendment was shoved into the Constitution by forced ratification. This amendment gave the privileges of full citizenship to the former slaves, prohibited any state from depriving them of life, liberty, or property without due process of law, and guaranteed all persons the equal protection of the laws.

Now it must be admitted that there is no more basic right of a citizen than the right to vote, nor is there any field in which he is more entitled to the equal protection of the laws. Certainly the right of suffrage is more fundamental than any real or fancied right to attend racially integrated schools, or even to receive an education, for that matter. So if it was considered necessary to spell out (in the 15th amendment) the right of citizens to vote without denial or abridgment because of race, color, or previous condition of servitude, would it not be even more necessary to spell out in the Constitution any sought-after right to integrated education, or integrated employment? In other words, if so basic a right as that of suffrage had to be established by amendment of the Constitution, then does it not follow that lesser "rights" which are in dispute should likewise be subjected to the amendment process?

If the federal government considered it necessary to

amend the Constitution so as to grant Negroes the right to vote, and later to grant women that same right, is it not equally necessary to amend the Constitution if permission is sought for the federal government to meddle in the school affairs of the various States? And if the Constitution must be amended (as it was by the 16th Amendment) before the federal government can legally drain off the individual's income by way of taxation, must not it be amended to permit the government to take away the individual's choice of applying his local school taxes as he sees fit through his state legislative bodies?

The crucial nature of the 15th amendment, which exists as proof positive of the necessity of adding new concepts of civil rights to the Constitution through the amending process, is further portrayed in words of the NAACP itself. NAACP lawyers before the Supreme Court had this to say with respect to the 14th Amendment:

"The historic background of the 14th Amendment and the legislative history of its adoption show clearly that the framers intended that the amendment would deprive the States of power to make any racial distinction in the enjoyment of civil rights. . . . The framers of the 14th Amendment were men who came to the 39th Congress with a well-defined background of Abolitionist doctrine dedicated to the equalitarian principles. . . . This background gives an understanding of the determination of the framers of the 14th Amendment to change the inferior legal and political status of Negroes and to give them the full protection of the Federal Government in the enjoyment of complete and real equality in all civil rights."

Now, if that be true, then why was it necessary to adopt the 15th Amendment so as to spell out the right of suffrage for Negroes? The 14th Amendment went far enough with its broad and fuzzy terms of "due process" and "equal protection," but if the right to vote was not included within those blanket assurances, how now can it be argued that the right of integrated schooling was included among them?

But the Supreme Court decision tramples not only upon the Ninth and Tenth Amendments to the Constitution, but upon the Preamble to that document. The Court seems not to have noticed that placed third among the six fundamental objectives of the Constitution is the goal labeled, "insure domestic tranquility." Manifestly, that is a matter of as much, if not more, concern to the individual States than to the central government. Through all the years of American history, the states have exercised their police powers—as powers of sovereign bodies—to insure domestic tranquility within their own borders. In the South, where the separation of two large population segments of different cultures and standards has been judged necessary as a means of keeping the peace, segregation has been a matter of law and of custom for the preservation of public peace.

The maintenance of such peace, together with the establishment of a pattern of orderly living, is a major objective of the very institution of government itself. Political custom, social etiquette, economic practice, and all other facets of the social structure are but the outward expression of the will of the community. And throughout all of these accepted codes of conduct, whether of business, of government, of education, of social life, or otherwise, intelligent discrimination and natural segregation make up the very essence of good order. To remove them and to abolish all barriers which stand in the way of indiscriminate mingling of diverse groups would be to invite chaos. To a very large degree, segregation (in the sense of separation of dissimilar groupings on bases of logical and reasonable distinctions) prevents government from collapsing into anarchy.

Now the Supreme Court presents its own peculiar finding that "segregation in public education is not reasonably related to any proper governmental objective," utterly discounting the obvious relationship in the Deep South between racial separation and domestic tranquility. The do-

mestic upheaval which accompanied efforts at forced integration has disclosed the patent absurdity of the Court's
contention and has given rise to the revised phrase that
"justices are blind."

Were the Court not so blind, it could have seen the merit
of restricting itself to determining the school question on the
basis of legal rather than sociological reasoning. An admonition to that effect came indirectly to the Court in July of
1956 from the then president of the American Bar Association, E. Smythe Gambrell, speaking to the Fourth Circuit
Judicial Conference at Hot Springs, Va.:

"The antithesis of a government of laws and not of men,
and the essence of despotism, is a court enforcing not law
but policy. . . . No public policy, however laudable, is worth
the sacrifice of the disinterested judicial function, for without it the whole structure of American civilization would be
threatened. Even a taint of political motivation may impair
the usefulness of a judge and undermine the public confidence essential to the rule of law. . . ."

There is an increasing awareness of Americans everywhere that the Supreme Court is embarked upon a course
which threatens the very principles upon which the nation
was founded. But unless other Americans follow the lead of
Southerners in guarding against the subversion of both the
Constitution and the Congress, they may see the truth of
Jefferson's warnings against the federal judiciary, a body
which he foresaw as "working like gravity by night and by
day, gaining a little today and a little tomorrow, and advancing its noiseless step like a thief, over the field of juris-
diction, until all shall be usurped from the States, and the
government of all be consolidated into one."

The prospect is all the more threatening since substantial
elements of the body politic are aiding and abetting the
judicial design of centralization. The manipulators of minority blocs loudly applaud every court action which weak-
ens the once-firm body of the Constitution. Intoxicated with

the heady scent of political power, these individuals envision more power to come, once they can reduce the Constitution to a malleable and meaningless thing susceptible of any interpretation which serves their own purpose.

Under false banners of self-asserted righteousness and liberality, these manipulators attract the support of little men, the timid men, the insecure ones who fear being submerged in what has so well been termed "the boisterous sea of liberty." These are the persons who rally behind any "progressive" movement which promises them greater security, or larger rewards for less work, or less exposure to the demands of competitive living. These are the ones who flock to "liberal" leaders in the hope that through them they may obtain gains they are incapable of earning on their own. These are the gullible and the misguided—and these are the dangerous ones because they provide the substance upon which would-be Caesars feed.

Dangerous also are the hosts of apathetic and overly-optimistic citizens who see no threat to their own liberties or to those of their respective states. They accept at face value the slogans, the preachments, and the promises of the "liberals," the "moderates," and the "progressives." All unsuspecting, they give comfort to those who would destroy the states by attrition, the Constitution by usurpation, and finally the nation by despotism. Despots never proclaim themselves as such, but make their advances under high-sounding statements to which the sentimental and the senseless can subscribe in all good faith. What looms now is that which James Madison warned against in these words:

"I believe there are more instances of the abridgment of the freedom of the people by the gradual and silent encroachment of those in power than by violent and sudden usurpations."

3

The War of Words—Semantics

THE segregation fight is having its effect not only upon the temper and traditions of the people, but upon their speech as well. The question of semantics looms large in the controversy, as each side seeks to bend words to its own use, or to phrase its purposes and procedures in terms which will induce support, or conversely, damn the opposition with words and phrases which automatically engender disapproval. Then, too, there have crept into the picture a number of terms which carry no loaded meaning, and which may or may not give better definition to points under debate. Such terms as "the non-South" came along to fill a need heretofore met only by an abundance of words.

The word "South" may itself need clarification, although it is subject to enlargement or contraction depending upon the matter under discussion and upon the point of view of the speaker. Generally, it refers to the southeastern quadrant of the United States, extending westward far enough to include Texas. That is the "South" geographically, but in the minds of many people, the term refers primarily to those eleven states which made up the Southern Confederacy during the War Between the States—Virginia, North Carolina, South Carolina, Georgia, Florida, Alabama, Mississippi, Louisiana, Texas, Arkansas, and Tennessee. In large measure, this is the "emotional" South of Southerners who maintain their Confederate heritage in lively fashion.

Four states along the border are sometimes included within the "South," especially by their own residents when they think in terms of respected Southern traditions, such as courtesy, hospitality and gracious living. There is, therefore, a measure of justification for including Delaware, Maryland, Kentucky, and Missouri within the classification of Southern states. Incidentally, it may come as something of a shock for Marylanders to learn that in the Deep South (Virginia through Texas) few Southerners acknowledge Maryland as being one of the states of the South. Kentucky is accepted with about the same degree of feeling that Maryland is rejected, and Delaware and Missouri are so seldom considered by Southerners to be in the family that the question hardly ever arises. West Virginia lost all claim as a Southern state (in the minds of people of the Deep South) when she separated from Virginia and thereby from the Confederacy.

In passing, it might enlighten non-Southerners to explain why the term "Civil War" is frowned upon by dyed-in-the-wool Southerners of Confederate extraction. The term "Civil War" denotes a struggle between factions or segments of a single nation. Unreconstructed Southerners maintain, with ample historic justification, that "the late unpleasantness" was a bona fide conflict between *two* nations—the United States of America on the one hand, and the Confederate States of America on the other. Consequently, the very use of the term "Civil War" tends to belittle the status of the Confederacy and to reduce the war to the level of domestic insurrection. The appellation is used generally these days in both the North and the South, but the self-respecting and history-conscious Southerner will make his references to "the Confederate War," "The War Between the States," or, with grim humor, "the War of Northern Aggression."

The Mason and Dixon line, which initially served only to mark the boundary between Pennsylvania and Maryland, carries little weight these days as a regional marker, even with its extension westward along the course of the Ohio River. Its current role in the segregation controversy is one of implied identity only, as South-baiters (and Southerners, too, for that matter) refer to it as "the Smith and Wesson line," an allusion aimed at pointing up the ready reliance on "shooting irons" south of that line.

But with specific reference to school segregation, the "South" encompasses seventeen states and the District of Columbia, all of which shared the common practice (before 1954) that schools for white and Negro students be maintained separately. In this sense, the region includes Alabama, Arkansas, Delaware, Florida, Georgia, Kentucky, Louisiana, Maryland, Mississippi, Missouri, North and South Carolina, Oklahoma, Tennessee, Texas, Virginia, West Virginia, and the District of Columbia. Acceptance of the Supreme Court's desegregation decision by the border states of Delaware, Maryland, Missouri, Oklahoma, West Virginia, and Kentucky has virtually removed those states, and the District of Columbia, from what might now be called "the embattled South." There remains, therefore, the "heartland" of the South, a vast crescent stretching from Virginia south and west to and including Texas, or at least East Texas.

And this is as good a time and place as any to try to dispel the tenacious idea that the so-called "Black Belt" of the South is a region-wide strip of dark soil stretching from the Atlantic to Texas. Many a writer is helping to perpetuate that misconception, although some do acknowledge that the "Black Belt" expression is more descriptive of the Negro distribution than of soil condition. There actually is a belt of black soil in the South, but it is of small consequence insofar as any regional significance is concerned, since it exists primarily in Alabama and Mississippi.

But quite apart from soil characteristics, across the South there does stretch a wide belt in which reside large numbers of Negroes. This particular "Black Belt" traces the generally southward and westward movement of slavery, and reflects the path of the plantation culture from Tidewater Virginia along the Carolinas' seaboard and coastal plain, and thence across Georgia and through Alabama to the Mississippi delta lands, where the strip widens to a breadth of almost four hundred miles along both sides of the Mississippi in the river areas of the four states of Mississippi, Lousiana, Arkansas, and Tennessee. The "Black Belt" continues westward along the Louisiana-Arkansas border as well as into eastern Texas.

In its curving sweep from Chesapeake Bay to the Mississippi, the "Black Belt" averages about two hundred miles in width, extending that far inland from the coast, but widening substantially as the Florida peninsula juts south from Georgia. Throughout most of this strip, Negroes make up anywhere from 25 to 50 per cent of the population. In some areas their numbers drop as low as 16 per cent, and in others they range as high as 60, 70, and 80 per cent. The heaviest concentration of Negroes, as was the highest concentration of slaves, lies in the farmlands of the interior South, excepting, of course, the heavy distribution along the South Carolina coast and (to a lesser extent) those of Georgia, North Carolina, and Virginia. But the heavy incidence of Negroes stops short of the mountains throughout the entire region, and is noticeably lighter along the coast lines of Florida and along the Gulf Coast.

In another—and more sensitive—semantic area, the integrationists, propagandists, and their fellow travelers have borrowed heavily from the trade-talk of the professional educators, sociologists, and psychologists. Some of the words thus obtained seem designed either for camouflage or confusion, for they add little to real comprehension. Take, for example, the term "intergroup relations." In nine cases out of ten, "intergroup" means "interracial," but there seems to be some desire for avoiding use of the word "race" wherever possible. Similarly, it appears more fashionable, from the integrationist point of view, to speak of "human relations" rather than "race relations." Instead of agencies such as the old "Conference on Education and Race Relations," which functioned back in the 1930's with headquarters in Atlanta, there now are "Councils on Human Relations" scattered throughout the South, most of them under the aegis of "The Southern Regional Council."

Of more concern to the Southerner, however, are the "loaded" words which are pointed his way—words which have taken on special connotations at the hands of propagandists. One of these, obviously, is "discrimination," which once meant nothing more than the drawing of distinctions between persons, places, or things. The word actually had, and in the advertising world still has, some prestige value, since persons of "discriminating taste" were those who relied on high standards of value in determining whether or not something or someone was acceptable. That still is a valid meaning of the term, but it has more often been twisted to imply that "discrimination" in itself is evil, especially when distinguishing between persons on the basis of race.

The word "prejudice" is used these days as a shaped charge against the South, for it is brought into play by integrationists in many instances where it actually is not the apt word. The South has no quarrel with the dictionary definition of the word (in *Webster's New Collegiate Dictionary*) —"preconceived judgment or opinion; unreasonable predilection or objection; especially, an opinion or leaning adverse to anything without just grounds or before sufficient knowledge." The South *does* quarrel with the tendency of non-Southerners to credit "prejudice" with being the motivating force behind all racial separation in the region. For one thing, most of the white Southerner's judgment of the Negro is due, not to any preconceived judgment, but to a mature evaluation based on years of first-hand observation and association which is much closer than that between whites and Negroes in the non-segregated North.

But quite apart from the validity of such judgment, the matter of motivation brings into play the additional word "segregation." If "segregation" is meant to convey its literal sense of isolation, of secluding one from others, then it is misused in many of its present-day applications. The word "separation," which draws a relatively fine line in place of the chasm of true segregation, is a better term to describe the state of distinction between whites and blacks in the South. To play with terminology a bit, the better description would term the distinguishing process as "selective separation" rather than "prejudicial segregation."

Herbert Ravenel Sass, the Charleston author whose *Atlantic Monthly* article, "Mixed Schools and Mixed Blood," made an impact on readers in November of 1956, put it this way:

"Not prejudice but preference is the word that truth requires. Between prejudice and preference there is vast difference. Prejudice is preconceived judgment or feeling without sound basis. Preference is a natural reaction to facts and conditions observed of experience. . . ."

An artificial antonym, "desegregation," has emerged within the last few years, unaccompanied by anything approaching a precise meaning. The most general and seemingly most acceptable meaning of "desegregation" is that of a reversal of segregation. Its relationship to the companion word, "integration," is none too clear, but the latter is at least dignified with a dictionary definition. But even the definition, "act or process of making whole or entire," leaves much to be desired in a search for precise meaning in the field of race relations. Consequently, here is yet another word which varies in meaning from person to person and from situation to situation.

One of the most heavily weighted and most consistently used terms of opprobrium used against the South is "white supremacy." Undoubtedly there are many Southerners who actually feel that the white race is superior to the black, on grounds of past achievement, present performance, and future promise, but this attitude is not the essence of the current controversy. The issue of racial segregation as opposed to integration does not depend upon any premise of supremacy of one race over the other. The question deals with preferential association, regardless of superiority or inferiority, and the designation of racial preference as "white supremacy" represents a malicious—and effective—attempt to smear the segregationist. Yet surprisingly, those who delight in dubbing all Southern segregationists "white supremacists" seem never to apply that description to the idol of the North, Abraham Lincoln, who in 1858 said this in debate with Stephen Douglas:

"I will say then that I am not nor ever have been in favor of bringing about in any way the social and political equality of the white and black races—that I am not, nor ever have been, in favor of making voters or jurors of Negroes, nor of qualifying them to hold office, nor to intermarry with white people; and I will say in addition to this that there is a physical difference between the white and black races which, I believe, will forever forbid the two races living together on terms of social and political equality. And inasmuch as they cannot so live, while they do remain together there must be the position of superior and inferior, and I as much as any other man am in favor of having the superior position assigned to the white race."

Even the word "Negro" itself now stands as something of an irritant between whites and blacks, and is used vocally as a word-weapon to express either class-consciousness or contempt, depending upon the user's point of view, intent, and pronunciation. For with the deterioration of racial amity following the Supreme Court's desegregation decision, the word has become more than ever charged with overtones which make it susceptible of manipulation by pronunciation.

Even well-intentioned Southerners have some difficulty in pronouncing the word in the fashion preferred by Negroes —"knee-grow." Regional speech habits are such that, for the phonetically untrained, it is hard to get full registration of the "knee" in the first syllable, and equally hard to bring out the "r" in the second. The pro-integration Southern Regional Council admits, in one of its periodic publications, that the "r" is "always hard for a Southern tongue to manage." As a consequence, Southerners of both races have found it simpler, phonetically, to slide into the use of "nigger" for Negro in the absence of other considerations.

But those other considerations have altered the picture in recent years. Most particularly, the Negro has himself become increasingly sensitive to the "nigger" pronunciation as he has improved his economic, educational, and political status. And although many Negroes still use the term jocularly, familiarly, and sometimes accusingly among themselves, they are more and more resentful of its use by white persons. So sensitive are they on this score that the professional Negro (a growing element in the South—and elsewhere) challenges the use of the pronunciation "nigra" (Deep South) and "nig-grow" (Chesapeake Bay) which decent Southerners employ in a not-altogether-successful attempt to be polite about the matter. The Negro insistence upon "knee-grow" is a bit difficult to understand, for that pronunciation is relatively uncommon in the common speech of both the Southern white and the Southern Negro. A possible explanation comes from one of the nation's top linguists, Southern-born and Southern-reared Dr. Raven I.

McDavid, Jr., who now is engaged in an abridgement of the Mencken series on *The American Language*. Says Dr. Mc-David:

"The Northern pronunciation 'knee-grow' and its variants started as a spelling-pronunciation, in all probability, since there were relatively few Negroes in the North before the 1860's. Because the Negroes had the impression, true or false, that the New Englanders and other Northerners were more sympathetic than others, there would be a natural inclination to adopt the Northern polite pronunciation as being less condescending and patronizing, and to avoid the Southern one."

Dr. McDavid acknowledges that, though he now uses "knee-grow" regularly as a matter of *noblesse oblige,* it still seems unnatural "because it is not in my native dialect." He notes that "the pronunciation 'nigger' is probably oldest and most generally distributed, and it represents a normal phonological development in English. Yet regardless of its frequency, nearly all Americans, of whatever race or region, recognize it as derogatory. In itself—like any other word— it is innocent; but not so innocent are the covert implications of the voice-qualifiers that often attend the use of this word or the associations with a stratified caste system.

"In England, before the recent influx of West Indians, it was a harmless word; now, I gather, it has become derogatory there, too, because the West Indians represent potential economic competition to the English working-class—just as the Southern Negro represents an economic threat to the poor whites, and to demagogs . . . elected by poor white votes."

Most contemporary Southerners feel that the changed attitude of which Dr. McDavid speaks is due more to emotional than to economic factors. The resentment felt by whites against the efforts of Negroes to force racial integration of the schools is reflecting itself in small ways as well as large, and the heightened use of the word 'nigger' by persons who formerly avoided it is but one indication of the changed attitude. It is likewise true that the white Southerner is able to infuse the word "knee-grow" with derogatory sentiment through the deliberately over-meticulous pronunciation which may well become as distasteful to Negroes as the more familiar and earthy form, "nigger."

Although the pronunciation of the word has taken on added significance in these times of renewed racial sensitivity, it long has been a sore spot among Negro leaders. Along with the Negro campaign against the use of the spelling or the pronunciation "nigger" have gone other related campaigns, one seeking general capitalization of Negro; another asking for the use of courtesy titles such as "Mr.," "Mrs.," and "Miss" for Negroes; and a third seeking the elimination of words such as "darkies" from song and story.

The battle for the capitalization of "Negro" seems largely won, although many a white man does not like to see Negro spelled with a capital "N" while white gets only a lower-case "w." Almost won, but not quite, is the fight for courtesy titles. More and more newspapers, in the South as well as in the North, are falling into line in that regard. Many a Southern reader, however, still refuses, consciously or unconsciously, to employ the terms in his own conversation although he has accepted them in the press.

The fight against the use of words such as "darkies" has taken on additional impetus since the Supreme Court's school integration decision, although it cannot be said that the court's ruling had anything to do with that particular issue. H. L. Mencken, in his *Supplement One* to *The American Language,* traces the movement back to 1936, when a Negro newspaper, the Baltimore *Afro-American,* started crusading against the Stephen Foster classic, "My Old Kentucky Home," because it used the words "darky" and "darkies." The crusade, widened to include other songs and stories which use that and similarly "offensive" words, has continued to this day. It has not, however, enjoyed the unanimous approval of all Negroes. The outspoken Negro journalist, George S. Schuyler, who has been as prompt to deflate members of his own race as of others, had this to say after the anti-"darky" campaign was initiated by the *Afro-American*, the NAACP, and similar agencies:

"Will someone who has the gift of logic and intelligence tell me what is the difference between *darkey* and *Negro?* . . . . There can be no more real objection to *darkey* than there can be to *blondie*. It is a far more acceptable term than *wop* or *kike*. As my friend J. A. Rogers [a Negro historian] once profoundly remarked, the difference between *Negro* and *nigger* is the difference between *sir* and *sah*. Granted that the overwhelming majority of Negroes are opposed to the use of those terms, I can see no point in constantly making a wailing protest against their use."

Yet the Negroes have indeed wailed throughout these past years, and with such intensity that publishers of books and of songs, vocalists, and even powerful radio and television networks have capitulated to their demands. Such truckling cost one publisher a contract for songbooks with the State of Georgia in 1955. Alterations of Stephen Foster's words to "My Old Kentucky Home" and to "Old Folks at Home" brought this biting comment from Georgia school officials:

"We are intrigued with the conceit of the modern bard who attempts to teach Stephen Foster the art of folk song writing. . . . The revised versions of his songs, sung for 100 years without resulting in disastrous social consequences, are completely divorced from the plantation scene, the motif that Foster used so effectively that his works are loved throughout the world. . . . Surely these 'liberals' who decry all suggestions of censorship over the literature today will be disturbed to discover the censor directing his attentions to the folk songs of the nation."

Two years later, additional complaints of the alteration of Foster songs came from officials of both Kentucky and Florida, where the two songs cited above are used as state songs, and from numerous other Southerners, including a number of Congressmen. Demands for an investigation of network suppression of the songs came from both Florida and Kentucky Congressmen, and their fellow Southerners rallied to their support. Florida's Gov. LeRoy Collins said, "The ban is so ridiculous I cannot believe the networks are serious." Some of the networks retorted that there was no ban on the songs, but all the major networks except the Mutual Broadcasting System acknowledged that they observed policies which would have the effect of substituting other words for "darkies."

Here, for the record, are statements from network officials who replied to direct inquiries from the writer concerning their policy of altering words:

Mutual Broadcasting System, Inc., July 24, 1957: "We have checked quite thoroughly with our music clearance department here and find no specific policy on our part for substituting words in the lyrics of these songs. It is known, however, that many artists have on their own accord changed some of the phrases. We would have no record of such action if it were done on our network."

American Broadcasting Company, July 23, 1957: "ABC policy is not to accept any program which misrepresents, ridicules or attacks any individual or group on a basis of race, creed, color or national origin."

Columbia Broadcasting System Television, Aug. 2, 1957: "It has always been the policy of CBS Television to change or eliminate words or phrases in songs or program copy that might offend individuals or groups. The implementation of this policy stems from our desire to operate in the public interest and in good taste. This procedure applies to popular as well as traditional songs."

National Broadcasting Company, Inc., July 23, 1957: "The Television Code of the National Association of Radio and Television Broadcasters includes the following observation:

" 'Words (especially slang) derisive of any race, color, creed, nationality or national derivation, except wherein such usage would be for the specific purpose of effective dramatization such as combating prejudice, are forbidden, even when likely to be understood only by part of the audience. From time to time, words which have been acceptable, acquire undesirable meanings, and telecasters should be alert to eliminate such words.'

"Editorial activity in relationship to the songs of Stephen Foster has sporadically been misinterpreted as a banning of these songs. This is not the case. There is a single word change made in Foster's 'Old Folks at Home' which we feel meets the requirements of the code wordings of the above cited and at the same time avoids violation of the spirit of the song itself. Specifically, in the following in the closing chorus of 'Old Folks At Home' the word 'chillun' replaces the original 'darkies.'

> " 'All de world is sad and dreary
> Everywhere I roam
> Oh chillun how my heart grows weary
> Far from the old folks at home.' "

In none of the above letters is there any explanation of wherein the word "darky" derides, ridicules, misrepresents, or attacks the Negro race. On the contrary, its use carries an affectionate and nostalgic connotation which once served as a bond of friendship between all Southerners, white and black. Let the reader who may not be familiar with some of the Foster songs judge of their content and intent through this opening verse of "My Old Kentucky Home":

> "The sun shines bright in the old Kentucky home;
> 'Tis summer, the darkies are gay;
> The corn-top's ripe, and the meadow's in the bloom,
> While the birds make music all the day.
> The young folks roll on the little cabin floor,

All merry, all happy and bright;
By-'n-by hard times comes a-knocking at the door:—
Then my old Kentucky home, good night!
Weep no more, my lady,
O, weep no more today!
We will sing one song for the old Kentucky home,
For the old Kentucky home, far away."

A statement reflecting something of the public appreciation of the Stephen Foster tradition was inserted into the
Congressional Record of July 29, 1957, by Florida's Rep.
Robert L. F. Sikes. What follows was taken from a letter
to Sikes from Earl W. Brown, chairman of the Stephen
Foster Memorial Commission at White Springs, Fla., on the
banks of the Suwanee River:

"As you well know it was by legislative enactment that
the State of Florida adopted 'Way Down Upon the Swanee
River' as the Florida State song; and in a similar manner
'My Old Kentucky Home' was adopted as the State song of
Kentucky. But the importance of Foster as a composer and
the durability of his songs goes far beyond the confines of
the United States, as it is the most universally loved and
used music of the world today, and has been for the past 100
years. These lyrics, as originally composed, were the basis
on which Foster was elected to the hall of fame, the only
composer ever having been accorded this high honor."

But the alteration of musical lyrics has not stopped with
the traditional works such as those by Foster. A revived
popular song, "Mississippi Mud," now carries the substitute word "people" for "darkies" where that latter word appeared in this version, popular some 25 years ago:

"When the sun goes down and the tide goes out,
The darkies gather 'round and they all begin to shout . . ."

How many other songs of this type have been changed is
anyone's guess. It also will be guesswork to determine just
how widespread will be the effect of such censorship. Here
is one example of how the alteration spreads: The 1957 ver-

sion of the Rotary International songbook omits all references to "darkies" both in Foster's songs and in James Bland's "Carry Me Back to Old Virginny."

Songs are not the only objects of this compulsion toward racial censorship. Pressure has been brought to bear, with a distressing degree of success, on publishers to make other changes more acceptable to the color-sensitive National Association for the Advancement of Colored (or should it be "non-white"?) People. The venerable child's classic, "Little Black Sambo," now has become "Little Brave Sambo," in its more modern and race-conscious version. In the old version, it was banned from the schools of Rochester, N. Y., at the request of local NAACP officials. In 1956, it was barred from the public schools of Toronto, Canada, where a delegation of black, excuse me, brave, parents complained that the book was a cause of anguish to all Negroes.

Not infrequently, the NAACP does itself and the Negro race a thorough disservice by seeking to suppress, revise, or otherwise censor literary or musical works which to it seem objectionable. In September of 1957, for example, the New York City Board of Education dropped Mark Twain's *The Adventures of Huckleberry Finn* from its list of approved textbooks. There was some dispute as to whether the action was motivated by a decision that the book was not properly a textbook, or whether its references to "niggers" was offensive to Negroes. Whatever the primary reason for dropping the book, a spokesman for the NAACP made it clear that the Negro organization strongly objected to the "racial slurs" in Twain's works. The fact that Twain's treatment of the Negro was sympathetic and was an effective argument against slavery and racial discrimination seems not to have entered the thinking of the NAACP.

The Christian Science Monitor scored the incident editorially in this wise:

"All of this is of a piece with the pressures to ban from the radio much-loved Negro dialect songs. Some of these, whether evolved from cotton-field chants or written by Stephen Foster, make up a priceless portion of America's none-too-extensive store of folk music.

"Are we to rewrite history, like the Soviets, and deny that the American Negro, however remarkably, has risen from primitive cultures in Africa? Are we to pretend that he always and everywhere has spoken as though he had just stepped out of the University of Chicago or Harvard College?"

The idiocy of the *Huckleberry Finn* incident upset even so pro-integration a newspaper as the *New York Herald Tribune,* which said this editorially: "Anybody who has ever really read *Huck Finn* knows that Jim the Negro comes out far and away the noblest character in the book, far and away superior to any Whites in it. . . . When are our teachers going to be allowed to start teaching and stop being the punching bags of pressure groups?"

Continuation of this censorship trend may soon lead us into the completely neutral world of "Old Afro-American Joe," "Mister Remus," and "Mister Thomas's Cottage." All of which brings to mind a well-appreciated story which has circulated through much of the South during these days of racial tension:

It seems that a Negro spokesman for a local NAACP branch visited the town librarian with the mission of having removed from the library shelves all books containing the word "nigger." After making his purpose known, he listened stolidly while the stunned librarian sought to explain that some of the world's best literature contained occasional unpleasant or derogatory words.

"Why even Shakespeare's works," said the librarian, "contain dozens of references to 'bastards.' Surely you don't think that I should remove all of Shakespeare's works because of that!"

"Well," replied the NAACP spokesman, "I don't know about that. Maybe them bastards just ain't as well organized as us niggers."

On a completely serious note, the American reader has cause to wonder whether in the future he will ever again have opportunity to read such delightful stories featuring Negro dialect as those of Octavus Roy Cohen or Roark Bradford, or whether he can look forward to the re-printing of *Uncle Remus* and the other works of Joel Chandler Harris, or whether movie-goers will henceforth be afforded the wholesome and lovable entertainment provided by such amiable Negro characters as Hattie McDaniel and "Stepin Fetchit." The outlook is bleak.

A similar sober-sided resentment against anything placing Negroes in amusing situations, even though laughter be with them rather than at them, may have prompted Philadelphia City Councilman Raymond Pace Alexander to sponsor a 1954 resolution to bar "blackface caricatures" from the city's annual New Year's Day Mummers Parade. The Associated Press quoted Alexander, a Negro attorney, as saying: "It's an insult and an affront to the intelligence, the standing and the accomplishments of the American Negro as well as a de-grading influence in the life of the community in which the Negro lives."

An echo of the same sort of thinking comes from New Orleans, where the NAACP protested the happy parading of the (Negro) Zulu Aid and Pleasure Club in the annual Mardi Gras celebration. The NAACP's thinly-veiled threat that if the parade were not conducted with more propriety the NAACP would seek its discontinuance cost the affair much of its spontaneity. Prior to the 1956 Mardi Gras, the NAACP field secretary at New Orleans, Clarence Laws, said: "There is a wide feeling that the parade degrades and ridicules the Negro race. It has become a stereotype and an insult to the race, and many Negroes are disgusted with it."

The pallid parade which followed his remarks disgusted

both Negro and white spectators and possibly left a dead-ashes taste in the mouth of King Zulu of 1956, who was reputed to have spent $800 on regal trappings for the occasion. He certainly had little cause to repeat the joyous exclamation of the 1954 Zulu King, Willie Boone, who was quoted far and wide as having commented: "It certainly makes a king feel scrumptious percolating down the boulevard followed by his entire residue."

The 1956 parade was described by James Alexander, grand marshal of the Zulu parade, as the worst he had seen in 40 years of watching. The 1957 parade was virtually a repeat performance, and the suspicion is strong that among New Orleans Negroes, many of whom seem a little scared of the NAACP, there is a fervent wish that that organization would stop interfering with their Mardi Gras fun. One indication of this is the increasing number of "splinter groups" of Negro marching clubs whose members drill, dress, and drink as they please.

In August of 1950, a dancing Negro doll, made in Japan and depicting a Negro figure standing beneath a Lenox Avenue-125th Street sign, was withdrawn from the New York toy market. The Associated Press reported that the jig-dancing doll was removed from store shelves when the NAACP complained that it "served to perpetuate an old stereotyped conception of Negroes which recent developments in race relations have all but banished."

A mural depicting an early-day Charleston port scene, with Negro slaves at work about the South Carolina port, was ordered removed from an army cafeteria in Washington in March of 1954. Maj. Gen. L. K. Hastings, the quartermaster general, ordered the mural cut out because he was convinced that the painting was "a potential powderkeg" which could increase racial tension. A number of Negroes at the installation thought the mural inoffensive, but others complained that it had prompted white workers to make derogatory remarks about Negroes. Then, as would be expected, the District of Columbia unit of the NAACP urged removal of the mural because "the slave picture reflects on race and color of Negroes, thus encouraging anti-Negro sentiment."

At first blush, this business of commercial, literary, and musical censorship seems only the foolish petulance of a hyper-sensitive and inferiority-complexioned racial group which is chagrined over its own characteristic color. On second look, the practice begins to take on a more ominous outlook, something in the nature of the distortions so terrifyingly portrayed in George Orwell's book *Nineteen Eighty-four*.

What frightened Orwell's protagonist could frighten anyone faced with the motto: "Who controls the past controls the future; who controls the present controls the past." His apprehension arose out of this thought:

"If the Party could thrust its hand into the past and say of this or that event, *it never happened*—that, surely, was more terrifying than mere torture or death. . . ."

That fictional state of affairs may be a far cry from what actually is being done today, but the frame of mind which prompted Orwell's "Party" and that which moves the NAACP today are distressingly alike. If the NAACP finds certain words not to its liking in various songs and books today, and if those words are changed through a massive program of coercive collusion, then will not the next step be to change some of the recorded facts and events of history, such as the existence of slavery, which might be offensive to the NAACP?

One of the most glaring examples of deliberate pro-Negro distortions of the truth occurred in the selection of quotations from Thomas Jefferson for inscription within the Jefferson Memorial at Washington, D. C. One such inscription bears these words:

"Nothing is more certainly written in the book of fate than that these people are to be free."

But that is not the entire quotation, and in that abbreviated form it conveys a meaning quite apart from that intended by Jefferson. Here is the full body of the sentence from which the partial excerpt was lifted:

"Nothing is more certainly written in the book of fate than that these people are to be free; nor is it less certain that the two races, equally free, cannot live in the same government."

The extreme self-consciousness of Negroes is reflected by their increasingly apparent irritation at the use of terms which formerly were used by white friends and neighbors with genuine affection. For example, literally millions of white Southerners grew up in the habit of calling elderly Negroes "Uncle" or "Auntie." In very large measure, that habit was an index of an integrated social relationship which seemingly should have been cherished rather than spurned by the Negro, for it is a frequent Southern custom for youngsters to refer to close although unrelated friends of the family as "Uncle" or "Aunt." But the trait, at least insofar as its application to colored folk is concerned, seems distasteful to the modern Negro, perhaps because of recent indoctrination against anything and everything which smacks of the "Uncle Tom" pattern of Negro cooperation with whites.

This story is told of the late Mary McLeod Bethune, the South Carolina-born Negro woman who contributed much to her race's educational uplift (the story comes from an article in the Negro newspaper, the *Chicago Defender*, of May 25, 1957):

"She had a rapierlike wit that could be positively devastating. Once riding a train in the South, a brash conductor came thrugh the car in which she was sitting and said loudly:

" 'All right Auntie, give me your ticket.' Came the sweet and deadly reply, 'And which of my sister's children are you?' "

The "rapierlike" rejoinder may very well serve as an example of color-conscious repartee, but it certainly contributed nothing to amicable relations between the two parties to the incident, nor to good relations between the two races.

A sign of the times in Northern publications is the tendency to portray all white Southerners as speaking with the broadest and most bucolic of Southern accents, while allowing Negro Southerners to express their thoughts in well-worded, well-phrased, and well-rounded bits of Oxonian English. Take the following as just one example:

William Rotch, editor of *The Cabinet,* of Milford, N. H., was one of the New England editors who visited Mississippi in October of 1956 at that state's invitation. Rotch quotes a white newspaper publisher in this fashion:

"Ah never have, and Ah never will, publish the picture of a niggah in mah paper."

Immediately thereafter, Rotch quotes some of Mississippi's Negro citizens, having them say such things as this:

"We want to educate our people to the importance of voting. My father died several years ago at the age of 67. He was a fine father and a fine man, but he never saw a ballot. To me this seems a terrible thing, and I want my children to know a better life."

(No "Ah" for "I" and no "mah" for "my" when the words come from a black man.)

And Southern dialect, which once sparkled so delightfully in the *Saturday Evening Post* stories of Octavus Roy Cohen and others, has returned to that magazine, but this time out of the mouths of white segregationists rather than Negro protagonists. John Bartlow Martin turned the trick in his 1957 series of articles, "The Deep South Says Never." In that thorough-going survey of the Southern scene, Martin manages to handle his quotations in such manner that "all of his Negro sources talk like Oxford dons, while all of the white people talk like Southern white people," to use the apt description voiced by Editor J. J. Kilpatrick, of the Richmond *News Leader*.

All this points up to the existence of a war of words as well as of ideas in the segregation controversy. Thus far, the South has been at a disadvantage in this semantic conflict, for it has relied upon what might be termed "defensive" terminology, couching its case in terms of "constitution government," "local self-determination," "states' rights," and "racial integrity"—all of which denote conservatism and a preservation of the *status quo*. On the other hand, the non-Southern integrationists and the few Southern submissionists have chosen to employ words and phrases best described as "offensive" in every sense of the term.

Out of a well-stocked arsenal of smear-words, these individuals have shot off fine volleys of such word-missiles as "hate," "bias," "prejudice," "unChristian," "undemocratic," and countless others designed to stultify both the persons and the principles of Southerners who stand against race-mixing. The use of these word-weapons may bring a sense of satisfaction and of superiority to those who delight in baiting the South, but they intensify rather than lessen the South's spirit of resistance by so doing. Words can hurt, and all the more so when those whom they wound feel that the hurtful words are unjustified. Southerners, like Scots, have long memories, and what may give a South-baiter a sense of malicious satisfaction today may linger to hamper his cause tomorrow.

4

The Paper Curtain

THE South suffers today, as it has suffered for generations, from an inability to get a fair hearing in the market-place of national public opinion. Perhaps a small measure of blame can be charged against Southerners themselves, for they have failed to aggressively propagandize their side of the racial controversy. In remaining relatively silent through the years, the South has made possible a virtual cornering of non-Southern news media by propagandists who work effectively in tacit agreement that the Southern region and the Southern white man are always to be portrayed in the sorriest light possible.

On the other hand, it is to the credit of Southern newspapers that they have, in notably full degree, given fair and complete coverage to the developments of racial integration and resistance, although most of them have editorially opposed any desegregation—at least on a "forthwith" basis. That has been true despite some serious suggestions from prominent persons that perhaps the press could best help in the Southern fight by "covering up" resistance efforts so as to keep both the Negroes and the North in the dark as to what was afoot in the South.

By contrast, non-Southern newspapers have not accorded the racial question anything like the same degree of objective news coverage. Despite the preachments of their editors against "discrimination," they have been guilty of glaring discrimination in their selection and portrayal of news events, North and South. Many of them have blatantly exploited every splash—or ripple—on the Southern scene with headlines and editorials which would lead their readers to believe that anarchy reigned in the South. At the same time, they have minimized, obscured, or completely ignored instances of racial discord in their own backyards—some under the pious pretext of "serving the public interest." Thus have these editors prostituted their own profession by setting themselves up as judges of what should and what should not be printed, not because of any legitimate newspaper consideration of morality, decency, or avoidance of libel, but simply as a matter of press-determined "public policy."

The day may well come in the metropolitan areas of the North, after some really serious racial outbreak, that the residents of those areas will turn wrathfully to their political leaders, and with even greater indignation to their newspapers, and ask, "Why weren't we told about these conditions?"

But the Northern newspaper editors, and the civic and political leaders with whom they have entered into what amounts to a conspiracy of silence, rationalize their suppression of racial news in this wise: We feel it best for the community that our reports play down incidents of racial discord lest they make the situation worse, and contribute to even more discord. We will report the essential facts, but we will not identify persons or groups by race.

To the Southern newspaperman, that sort of pious deter-

mination of what is good for the community smacks of journalistic dictation and censorship.

Much of the Northern aversion to a factual presentation
of race news on its own doorstep seems to stem from a lack
of journalistic "guts." Northern editors, no less than Northern politicians and federal judges, read the election returns,
and they reason, with logic if not with courage, that the
wiser course is to play along with what seems to be the
general sentiment in their community. Besides which, since
they don't have to live with the trouble they stir up, it is a
great deal safer to lambast the distant whites of the South,
who are in no position to retaliate. To criticize the politically potent Negroes in their own territory might be hazardous. Furthermore, there is the not inconsiderable consideration that much of the ownership and the advertising
support of the Northern press is intimately identified with the
very organizations which are teamed with the NAACP in
its drive against the South. It is a rare editor indeed who
has the fortitude to stand against that tide, and to devote
the same measure of exposure and exploitation to local race
news as to that emanating from the faraway South.

It is a paradox of the times that while Northern editors
complain so bitterly about the white man's tendency to
think of Negroes in stereotyped terms, these same editors
contribute heavily to the perpetuation of the Yankee stereotype of the South. They always have recourse to the stereotyped outpourings of such renegade muck-rakers from the
South as Erskine Caldwell, Tennessee Williams, and many
others of their ilk. These expatriates have long since learned
the secret of fouling and feathering their nest at the same
time by writing the sort of trash which appeals to Northern
publishers and to a depraved reading public.

But whereas the fictioneers may have license to pervert
the truth to their own money-grubbing purposes, the newsman should take no such liberties with the facts. Neverthe-

less, it is no trick at all for a newsman, and even less difficult for radio and television "reporters," to come up with whatever portrayal of a given situation may be most in demand by his bosses, or by his readers-listeners-viewers. Human nature being what it is, and infinitely varied, all shades of opinion and of expression can be gleaned in almost any locality on almost any topic. By shrewd selection, whether consciously or unconsciously done, a "sampling" of public opinion can be made to reflect any preferred point of view. The press accomplishes that purpose by accentuating facts and quotations which, by that accentuation, effectively outweigh the opposition view. Skilfully done—and most of the "foreign correspondents" dispatched from Northern papers into the Southern theater of operations are well-skilled in those techniques—such press reports can convey an impression all the more effective because it is purveyed by indirection in the guise of presenting "both sides" of the picture.

The radio and television oracles apply the same techniques in their approach to pure reporting, to which they add another dimension (in the case of radio) and two more dimensions (in the case of television) by adroit selection of those persons to be heard or seen. It is a rare day indeed when persons of respectability are chosen to bespeak the cause of segregation, although hosts of such persons are readily at hand. Most of the mass media of the North seem to have covertly agreed, as was the case a century ago, to deny the existence of any middle-class leavening of Southern society. They prefer to think of and treat the Southerner in terms of either the brute or the Cavalier, with nothing in between.

Among the magazine folk, there are many who seem to revel in smearing the South and Southerners by adjective and innuendo, rather than by the more open attack of hostile editorial. This subtle device of attack by indirection is among the more insidious campaigns being waged against the South because its virulence frequently is cloaked in clever words and pungent phrases.

Perhaps a better concept of what the South has been up against can be gained from an examination of the policy statement of one of the prime South-baiters in the business, *TIME* magazine:

"The editors recognize that complete neutrality on public questions and important news is probably as undesirable as it is impossible, and are therefore ready to acknowledge certain prejudices which may in varying measure predetermine their opinion on the news."

It is obvious that one object of *TIME*'s more positive "prejudices" is the South's determination to preserve the Southern prejudice against forced racial integration. Here is a bald-faced instance of prejudice versus prejudice, the difference being that the Southern point of view never sees the light of day, at least not in the columns of *TIME*.

All this does not mean that there has not been ample space given to the South and its racial problems over a span of years—it simply means that only one side of the picture has been given. From time to time, in a well-publicized show of magnanimous "fairness," national magazines print articles by prominent "Southerners," most often identified with the region only by residence or ancestry, certainly not by likemindedness. Some of the spokesmen acceptable to Northern publishers are able craftsmen—editors such as Ralph McGill, of Atlanta; Hodding Carter, of Greenville, Miss.; C. A. (Pete) McKnight, of Charlotte, N. C.; Jonathan Daniels, of Raleigh, N. C., and Harry S. Ashmore, late of the Carolinas and later of Little Rock, Ark. These are in the forefront of the Southern "liberals" or "moderates," depending on how you choose to designate "enlightened" newsmen whose views are about three whoops and a holler down the road from the rest of their fellow-Southerners. Their views are well-phrased, sometimes stimulating, and usually adrift somewhere in between apology to the North and reproach to the South.

As "leaders" of liberal Southern thought, they beckon their followers, whose numbers are something less than legion, to come along the road of "reason" and into the meadows of "moderation." Unfortunately for them, many a hard-shelled Southerner has come to equate the word "moderation" with "integration," distinguishing between the two only in the degree of time and torture. Thus it can hardly be recorded that the views of these editors are the views of the South generally, although they do have their supporters and admirers.

But if these editorial writings are not fully representative of Southern thought, they are at least based on a reportorial knowledge of the facts and an editorial awareness of their implications. The same cannot be said for the "scribbling women" who prate of the joys of race-mixing with such fervor that they seem to have persuaded themselves that integration is the one way to happiness. Whereas the "liberal" editors might enjoy a measure of grudging respect from Southerners who recognize their merit while opposing their views, the Lillian Smiths and Sarah Patton Boyles are generally despised for their pious preachments that *Now Is The Time* (for integration) and "The South Will Love Integration."

Yet these are the sort of people who are singled out for quotation, for special articles, for public appearances by non-Southerners who want or who SAY they want someone to speak for the South. Inevitably, hosts of uninformed Northerners, Easterners, and Westerners get the completely erroneous impression that these are voices not only *from* but *of* the South. The deception leads to an even greater misconception—the conclusion that there are only a handful of segregationists in the South, and that those few must be poor benighted illiterates whose consuming passion is lynching "niggers."

The fact that literally millions of intelligent, informed, articulate, and perfectly sincere Southerners favor racial segregation is never brought home to non-Southern audiences. The conclusion is inescapable that this censorship is arranged by premeditation, for in the very fall of fortune there should arise *some* opportunities for the true Southern side to be heard.

Thomas R. Waring, editor of *The News and Courier*, of Charleston, S. C., described the situation forcibly in a 1955 article in *The Masthead*, quarterly publication of the National Conference of Editorial Writers.

"A paper curtain," Waring wrote, "shuts out the Southern side of race relations from the rest of the country. . . . Not since 'Uncle Tom's Cabin' became a best-seller in 1851 . . . has there been so powerful a blast of propaganda as to becloud the issues with emotions. This time it is not only a book—though books, movies, plays and other media are used—but chiefly a deluge of daily and weekly gazettes with an anti-Southern slant that is molding public opinion. . . .

"So far, the national press supports those who would force mingling of white and Negro people. At pamphleteering the press is being fairly successful. At reporting the news it no longer sticks by journalistic principles it once held with pride. . . . How can Americans hope to understand what happens inside a foreign country when our largest and most powerful journals present no more than a lop-sided version of a big segment of our country?"

It could properly be added that those very individuals who most bitterly attack white Southerners for their alleged prejudice against the Negroes are themselves guilty of an anti-Southern prejudice which colors both their thinking and their writing. This sectional bias against the South sometimes is based on the individual's tendency to side with the underdog in any controversy (which in the particular problem aligns him, he thinks, with the Negro is sympathy). The bias might also stem, as Professor John Dollard, of

Yale, points out in his study of *Caste and Class in a Southern Town,* from "an abolitionist tradition which has soaked into our frame of social perception." But whatever the source, the end result is an unwillingness to accept the testimony of white Southerners at true value, and a proclivity to seize upon incidents and attitudes which show whites in the worst and Negroes in the best light possible under a given set of circumstances.

Unfortunately, there are very few observers, researchers, or writers who have the perception and the sense of personal fairness which brought this admission from Professor Dollard:

". . . I had the typical sectional bias to be expected of a northerner and I thereupon set out to isolate and discount it. For one thing, I began to pay serious attention to what Southern white people told me about the interracial situation, and although I did not always agree with them, I always learned from them. The persistence of an unacknowledged and unresisted sectional bias might have barred me from much indispensable information. . . ."

In contrast with that recognition of and attempt to compensate for sectional bias, most of the writers who have poured into the South in race-writing assignments have neither admitted nor allowed for their prejudices. They have listened, with varying degrees of politeness, to the explanations and protestations of their white Southern informants, and have discounted what they heard. A considerable number, to quote Dollard again, "have left a bad taste, sometimes repaying with ill-humored misrepresentations the courtesy of their Southern hosts."

The truth of this has been brought home forcibly to Southern journalists, who have in recent years undergone the unusual experience of serving as interviewees instead of interviewers. The Northern correspondents who "invaded" the South to make first-hand reports on the segregation situation frequently made the local newspaper their first point of call, there to "pick the brains" of fellow-journalists who had been living with the situation for years. Almost invariably—until Southern patience began to wear thin under the constant friction of misrepresentation, omission, and distortion of the reports which appeared as a result of such interviews—the Northerners were accorded every courtesy, given every assistance, and frequently entertained as highly-regarded guests in Southern homes. In all fairness, it must be acknowledged that a handful of the wayfaring strangers from Northern publications did make an honest effort to appraise the situation factually, and to report in similar vein. But these were in the minority, and the greater number simply gave added justification to the observation made a half-century earlier by Thomas Nelson Page in his study, *The Negro; The Southerner's Problem:*

"No statement of any Southern white person, however pure in life, lofty in morals, high-minded in principle he might be, was accepted. His experience, his position, his character, counted for nothing. He was assumed to be so designing or so prejudiced that his counsel was valueless. . . ."

Much of that attitude lingers today among non-Southern writers who consider that only they, as outsiders, can give an objective portrayal of the Southern scene as it is—little realizing, or little caring, that the word pictures they paint reflect anti-Southern bias. Sometimes the prejudice shows through clearly in patent efforts to discredit, embarrass, or humiliate the Southern whites, while glorifying the Negro in spirit if not in person. Other times, the bias shows through the self-assumed perception of the non-Southerner, as evidenced by one of the New England journalists who visited Mississippi in October of 1956 at the invitation of that state:

"What we remembered most vividly are the eyes of the

colored men we met in an office near the hotel where our
party was being entertained. . . ."

Then, too, there was the writer on that same trip who,
manifestly disappointed at the lack of complaints of Negroes themselves over segregation, opined that they (the
Negroes) had been "brain-washed" by the Southern whites.

But despite such infrequent reactions as these, the net result of the Mississippi tour was all to the good. It brought
into the South respectable journalists who never before had
been confronted with the racial problem at first hand, and it
gave them some insight into the complexity and ramifica-
tions of the problem regardless of where their sympathies
might lie—either before or after the visit. In the course of
their eight-day stay in Mississippi, the New Englanders had
ample opportunity to talk with Southern whites and with
Southern Negroes, in private as well as in public, and to
form their own unguided opinions. They became aware of
the determination of the whites to resist integration, of the
aspirations of the Negroes to better their own prospects and
those of their children, of the discord and of the accord
characterizing white-black relationships in various spheres
of action, and of the genuine efforts to improve school and
other facilities for both races. Reactions and conclusions
were as varied as would be expected from members of such
an individualistic group, but even so short a stay as eight
days could not help giving them a sounder basis for their
future writings on the subject.

One of the most gratifying remarks (from the Southern
viewpoint) came from J. Clark Samuel, of *The Foxboro*
(Mass.) *Reporter:*

"It would be hypocritical and foolhardy for any writer
who has spent but a few days there [in the Deep South] to
presume to tell these people how they ought to run their
affairs and how to change their ways overnight."

Unfortunately, that sort of advice has been little heeded

in the rush of writers, photographers, and "researchers" into the bounty land of the South. Some journalists of dignity and dedication did come along to observe, to listen, to learn, and to write factually of the situation. They were outnumbered, however, by packs of journalistic jackals who slithered into every nook and cranny where they might snatch a bit of racial offal to carry back to their Northern lair, there to yelp over it in print while they worried their sorry spoil to the bone.

These were the lads of the smart-aleck brigade, bright boys from the big cities, "foreign correspondents," as it were, in the war zone of the South. And where they could not find conflict, they sought to make it. Where there was peace, it had to be "a troubled peace." Where Negroes professed accord with racial separation, such accord patently had come from "brain-washing." Where whites presented a solid front for segregation, there was necessarily "fear to speak out." In all places, in all things, the white man was the villain of the piece.

If the crusading correspondent ran out of reportorial adjectives with which to color his dispatches, he always could turn to the stock cast of characters which fill the "literary" works of those apostate Southerners who have found profit in despoiling their own heritage. But one Southerner who has made his mark without wallowing over-much in such garbage is Robert C. Ruark, a North Carolinian who paid his respects in January of 1957 to the "realistic" writers who achieved notoriety through serving up an adulterated potion of "po' white trash." Ruark wrote:

"One of these days . . . I am going to write a book about the South which is not littered with clay-eaters, lint-headed mill hands, idiots, itinerant preachers, juvenile delinquents, morons, slatterns, cripples, freaks, and other characters who don't wash, live off sardines and soft drinks, hang around bus stations, and breed merrily within the family. . . .

"It is possible to grow up in the South without a

full chorus of nymphomaniacs, drunkards, Negro-lynchers, randy preachers, camp meetings, hookworm, albinos, dirty hermits, old mad women, and idiot relatives to form your early impressions. But the literary output of the last 25 years wouldn't have it so . . ."

How sardonic it is to read in *Life* magazine, of March 5, 1956, this lament from Novelist William Faulkner:

"The rest of the United States knows next to nothing about the South. The present idea and picture which they hold of a people decadent and even obsolete through inbreeding and illiteracy—the inbreeding a result of the illiteracy and the isolation—as to be a kind of species of juvenile delinquents with a folklore of blood and violence, yet who, like juvenile delinquents, can be controlled by firmness once they are brought to believe that the police mean business, is as baseless and illusory as that one a generation ago of (oh yes, we subscribed to it too) columned porticos and magnolias. The rest of the United States assumes that this condition in the South is so simple and so uncomplex that it can be changed tomorrow by the simple will of the national majority backed by legal edict."

What says Faulkner to the irresistible charge that he has been one of the foremost contributors to that mistaken impression of the South which he now warns the North against accepting?

Southerners, despite their reputation as firebrands, have been remarkably placid in submitting to the unrelenting stream of abuse, vilification, ridicule, and scorn poured over them in the press, in literature, on the stage, over radio and television, and in motion pictures. Meanwhile, other identifiable groups of persons have been so prompt and so vociferous in registering protests against even a semblance of disrespect that we have now reached the point where the Southern white man is the handiest villain to have around. To cast a Negro, an Italian, a Mexican, an Oriental, or any

of a dozen other recognizable types as villains is sure to pro-
voke the wrath of whatever group the individual might typ-
ify, or to incur the displeasure of some "do-good" organization which champions the rights and sensibilities of the
"down-trodden" all over the world. So, with nobody speaking up for the Southerner, he becomes the perfect foil and
is habitually if inaccurately depicted as a slovenly, hard-
drinking, half-demented individual with a "nigger-hating"
compulsion.

In the field of news reporting, the anti-Southern bias not
only is damaging to the present by distorting the true state
of affairs, but is of incalculable harm to the future historian
who seeks to document what actually took place in these
troubled years of the mid-twentieth century. For an aside
on that little-regarded aspect of the situation, note these
words of the late Claude G. Bowers, distinguished American historian:

"In research for *The Tragic Era* I scoured the newspapers and was shocked to find that even the Associated
Press was sending out the most atrocious lies about the
South. Some gin drunk Negro raped or killed a small child
and he was lynched, and the AP reported he was lynched
because of his idolatry of Lincoln. It is not that bad now
[July of 1957] in the press, but I noticed this week that a
colored boy in Chicago was slugged to unconsciousness by
four white boys, but the story was on a back page in small
type. Had the incident happened in the South it would
have been played up under flaming headlines on the first
page."

The sanctimonious South-baiting editors, who wear blind-
ers on their telescopes to keep from seeing anything nearby
while gazing south, got their come-uppance from one young
Alabama editor who returned their fire with devastating effect. Grover C. Hall, Jr., editor of *The Montgomery Advertiser*, got fed up with playing host to throngs of visiting

journalists who descended upon his city during the well-publicized Negro boycott of city buses, during the Autherine Lucy incident at the University of Alabama, and at any other time they felt like "exposing" racial disharmony in the Deep South. Without attempting to cover up anything in Montgomery, in Alabama, or in the South, Hall sought to interest his visitors in reporting on racial friction in the North and West. Failing in that, he resolved to have the job done, at least in some measure, by the *Montgomery Advertiser* itself. What he and members of his staff learned, mostly by way of long-distance telephone calls, was eye-opening stuff, much of it well-hidden from the light of day insofar as the press itself was concerned.

From March through July of 1956, the *Advertiser* ran a series of pungent editorials and penetrating news stories under the general title, "Publish It Not in the Streets of Askelon." As the series progressed, the land of Askelon had changed from the reference in II Samuel to a vast area of the American North and West, where newspapers played false with themselves and with their readers by suppressing or ignoring the facts at hand concerning race relations.

Among the interesting facets of the *Advertiser* series was the revelation that Northern newspapers, for all their piety about racial integration, have not yet seen fit to integrate the pictures of Negro brides and brides-to-be among those of the white social strata who do make the society page. Those findings were tendered to the Associated Press for the possible use of that wire service, but were rejected. The rejection prompted an editorial lament of "The Paper Curtain Around the South" in the *Macon* (Ga.) *News,* which had this to say:

"Having by enterprise found all this out, Hall, editor of the *Advertiser,* offered the story to the Associated Press. The Montgomery AP Bureau chief questioned the wisdom of filing the story. The Atlanta bureau took a quick look and decided it was not of interest to the public, so the story of

Northern racial discrimination was not relayed to other papers for publication."

When the AP's Atlanta Bureau was asked to comment on the *Macon News* editorial, Bureau Chief Lew Hawkins replied:

"This article was concerned mainly with Grover Hall's claim that Northern newspapers do not carry pictures of Negro brides. We considered it, in Montgomery, Atlanta and New York, from the standpoint of our basic question in all such matters—'Is it news?' We concluded it was not."

Nevertheless, the *Montgomery Advertiser* series did win notice in a few periodicals, notably the *U. S. News and World Report,* and succeeded in jarring a few smug editors loose from their myopic moorings. There was some favorable response in the non-South as well as in the South, along with confirmation of Grover Hall's thesis that "race disharmony follows wherever the Negro settles in significant numbers."

The series brought to light the existence of a number of Northern communities which are much more tightly segregated than anything to be found in the South. It documented the determined and successful stand of the Michigan city of Dearborn against ANY Negro infiltration among its 130,000 residents—and this in the state of that most "liberal" of liberals, Gov. G. Mennen Williams, fair-haired boy of labor and of its soul-mate, the NAACP. The *Advertiser* quoted Dearborn's volatile Mayor, Orville Hubbard, on the subject:

"I am for complete segregation, one million per cent, on all levels. I believe in economic equality [for Negroes] but social equality is a horse of a different color. If a man works —I don't care what color he is—he ought to be paid. But I'm against any of this social dream stuff. . . . The politicians have made the race question a football. It's hot up here, but we've taken an open stand in our community. Detroit hasn't done it; they're in a hell of a mess."

But Dearborn is just one city among a number which frown on Negroes to such an extent that none are welcomed as residents. Wyandotte and Owosso are among several Michigan communities which retain their exclusively white character. In Illinois there are Pekin, Washington, and Morton in virtually the same status, the *Advertiser* found. In Ohio, there are Fairborn and Medway.

But finding those segregated communities, most of which are in areas where Negroes are nearby in substantial numbers, was not too surprising. Nor was it really significant that the existence of such communities seldom received any newspaper attention and indeed was almost unknown to newspaper editors in the same region. What was significant, disturbing, and distressing to Southern newsmen who take seriously their journalistic obligation to print the news fairly and squarely was the obvious double standard employed by the Northern press generally in reporting racial friction. In the words of an *Advertiser* staffer, Tom Johnson:

"There is one ironic, almost ludicrous, flaw in the northern press coverage of racial news. Put simply, it is this: If it is Southern racial disturbance, splash it across the front pages with lurid headlines. If it is a disturbance in the paper's own town, play it down."

The *Advertiser* did not stop with that observation, however. It backed it up by citation after citation of Northern racial incidents which received so little emphasis in the Northern press as to be almost unnoticeable. To give but one example, the *Detroit Times*, constant preceptor of the South and exploiter of Southern racial incidents, gave this sort of treatment, on page 16, to a Detroit "incident" in which a mob of several hundred persons stoned the house of a couple thought to be Negro:

"It took more than 50 policemen to disperse a crowd of 300 who staged a demonstration last night against a couple who moved into a northwest neighborhood Sunday.

"Stones were thrown through two windows in a home . . . but no one was injured."

A third paragraph told of a policeman's injury en route to the scene; and that was the whole story. Nowhere was there a mention of the word "Negro," no inkling was given to the racial complexion of the riot, and little attention was paid to the affair at all. Yet the *Detroit Times* had gone all out in its display of the racial disturbances in Alabama.

And the *Detroit News,* which had dispatched a special correspondent all the way to Mississippi for the Emmett Till trial, stuck this Detroit riot away on page 60.

The same sort of perverted journalism was recorded in the *Advertiser*'s series for many another Northern metropolis with respect to other racial outbreaks, yet it was virtually impossible to find editors who would admit their malfeasance in office. Nor would they acknowledge the existence of any "understanding" which constrained them to play down news of local racial strife. Tom Johnson got close to that sort of an agreement when he reported the existence of a "code of ethics" purportedly agreed to by press, radio, and television in order to give "temperate, moderate" treatment to race news in Chicago.

More light on that situation is shed by an Associated Press dispatch out of Chicago under date of July 27, 1955. It follows:

"CHICAGO, ILL. (AP)—Nine major Chicago radio and television stations have agreed upon a common program for handling news of racial disturbances in the event of such an outbreak.

"News directors of stations involved in the agreement say the program is designed to minimize the danger of increasing such disturbances by radio and television broadcasts. The agreement covers the handling of newscasts on race tension, gang fights and similar situations which could grow into major mob violence.

"Also a party to the agreement is the City News Bureau

of Chicago which furnishes local news to Chicago newspapers, radio and television stations.

"In the event of a disturbance the radio-TV editors have agreed to use extreme caution in describing the trouble. Use of the word 'riot' is to be avoided unless the trouble becomes a major conflict. Use of other language that might possibly lead to a renewal of a disorder already quelled also is to be avoided."

In September of 1957, as this book was in preparation, the City News Bureau of Chicago was asked by letter whether such an agreement was still in effect, and what it actually contained. No reply was ever received.

But evidence that some such attitude, if not in the form of a written agreement, prevails in Chicago was reflected in the press' treatment of the racial violence which erupted in Chicago's Calumet Park area during the closing days of July, 1957. Before the fighting between whites and Negroes was brought under control over a period of several days, scores of persons were hurt and hundreds of Chicago policemen were assigned to the area. Yet little inkling that anything of really serious proportions had taken place filtered through the heavily censored pages of the big Chicago and New York metropolitan dailies. There was, it is true, considerable agitation in the *Daily Defender*, Chicago's Negro tabloid, and the screaming headlines in that paper told the tale in these bold streamers, carried over several days:

"HOODLUMS ROUT PICNIC, 30 HURT"; "RIOT FUGITIVE TELLS TERROR"; "SUSPEND COPS LAX ON RIOTERS"; "934 COPS KEEP RIOT AREA CALM."

But for a report on what the big dailies did, read these excerpts from editorials which appeared in two South Carolina newspapers, whose editors maintain an understandable vigilance to see what play is given race news in the North. Said *The News and Courier*, of Charleston, on Aug. 1, 1957:

"It is too bad no seismograph records the range of press

hypocrisy in the North. The handling of the Chicago race riots would have registered severe shocks in some big cities.

"Editions of *The New York Herald Tribune* for Monday and Tuesday received in Charleston contained not a line about a serious racial clash in the country's second largest city.

"*The New York Times* on Monday printed an Associated Press dispatch seven inches long on page 10. *The Times*, with unrivaled facilities of its own for gathering news all over the world, did not even see fit to print the full AP account. Tuesday's issue of *The Times* sent to Charleston contained no story at all on further disorders occurring in Chicago on Monday.

"The handling of the local story by *The Chicago Daily News* also is interesting. It was printed on page 3 under a headline saying 'Man Fined $50 in Race Flareup.' *The Daily News* devoted its entire back page to pictures of earthquake damage in Mexico City. No pictures showed the race riots in the city where *The Daily News* is published. The riots were called 'racial disturbances' throughout."

"Does any reader wonder how these newspapers would have displayed 'racial disturbances' had they occurred in South Carolina, Mississippi, or elsewhere this side of the Paper Curtain? Race riots aren't news in the North."

Let us break in at this point to comment on the typical inference that Northern racial troubles have been "heightened by the waves of both white and Negro migration that have swept northward in recent years." Obviously, race troubles stem from the presence of Negroes in large numbers and just as obvious is the fact that the nation's supply of Negroes comes, in large measure, from the South. But the inference that the movement of Southern whites in the Chicago area is somehow responsible for racial friction is misleading, perhaps deliberately so. It completely overlooks the fact that those elements which are most determined to resist Negro encoachment into their residential communities are not made up of Southerners, but of Italians, Poles, and other national groups which have no connection with the South whatever.

An irrefutable illustration of this contention is the South Deering Improvement Association, which was formed about 1927 and which has recently waged a constant campaign to keep Negroes out of this Chicago community. In the words of its 1956 president, Louis P. Dennocenzo, the neighborhood is composed of "Yugoslavs, Irish, Polish, Italian, Mexican, Hungarian, and maybe some Lithuanians."

Further evidence of the complexion of the neighborhood and of the Improvement Association is reflected in the militant *South Deering Bulletin* which bears the slogan "White People Must Control Their Own Communities." The August 1, 1957, issue lists the following as comprising the committee in charge of advertisements for the bulletin: Tony Mancini, John Nawojski, Mario Di Cicco, Emil Di Giacomo, and Perry Scalsetti.

Since these national groups are themselves potent and vocal in Chicago and other Northern areas, the metropolitan press carefully refrains from charging them with being responsible for racial friction. Instead, by direct accusation or indirect inference, there always is the implication that the troubles somehow stem from the South. The Chicago papers are not the only offenders in this respect, as witness this crack in an editorial from the "liberal" *Milwaukee Journal:*

"Negroes, mostly rural Negroes from the South unaccustomed to Northern ways or city life, have been arriving in Chicago at a rate of around 2,500 a month for years. . . . They have pushed rapidly into old white slum areas, where the emotional boiling point is low. And they have competed for jobs and housing with thousands of newly arrived hillbillies and poor whites, many of whom have come North with all the worst of the Southern racial prejudices, with a taste for strong liquor and quick tempers."

Here again is the pontifical Northern editor seeking to blame the far-away South for race troubles in Chicago. Contrast that sort of sly but slanted writing with this factual report from the *U. S. News and World Report,* which sought to learn the why and wherefore of the Calumet Park and similar racial disturbances:

"Greatest impact of the Negroes is upon persons of Polish and Irish descent, many of them workers in the stockyards and steel mills. They live in the path of the Negro expansion, which is mainly toward the South and West."

The chiding from Southern editors in 1956 and 1957 caused some of the Northern press to begin showing signs of touchiness over assertions that they were failing to give the people the full truth. Some Northern papers actually began reporting fairly, or nearly so, on disturbances in their own backyards, but most of them met Southern criticism with pious statements of good intentions and public policy.

When *The New York Times* was asked whether it had a policy against making racial identification in crime news, this answer came back from Robert E. Garst, assistant managing editor:

"It is not true that *The Times* habitually omits all reference to race in crime news. When a suspect in a crime is being sought, we do specify race as a method of possible identification and arrest of the criminal. However, it is our practice never to designate any person by his race, unless it is pertinent to the story and, in general, reflects credit on his race. The fact that a man might be a Negro does not seem to us to play any part in a situation where he may also be a criminal, but if a Negro becomes a college president, for example, we do feel that that reflects credit on him and on his race."

The Southerner finds it regrettable that the good grey *Times* cannot be as charitable to the Southern white as to the northern Negro. Yet somehow, *The Times* finds it expedient and not at all disturbing to its peace of mind to give prominence to any incident involving racial friction in the South, even though the identical set of circumstances in New York City would not merit so much as a paragraph of *The Times'* valuable space.

Amusingly, *The Times'* split personality on the race question carries over in its editorial columns as well as in the news pages. After years of excoriating the South for its failure to embrace the Supreme Court's race-mixing dictum with unrestrained fervor, *The New York Times* shied off from a city ordinance which bars racial discrimination in New York apartment houses. When the ordinance was at issue in the spring and summer of 1957, here, in part, is what *The Times* had to say editorially:

"We do not think that the people of New York have been adequately prepared for the passage of this bill and we fear that the consequences of its adoption in such circumstances would be a stopping of large-scale construction and a drastic depreciation of property values."

Is it amiss to ask *The Times* if it thinks the South is prepared to accept school integration, or would that be suggesting that *The Times* maintains a double-standard editorially as well as reportorially?

Looking backward in time, the current lament of Northern editors over Southern refusal to accept the Supreme Court's mandate seems ridiculous in view of the torrent of censure loosed against the Court by the press and the politicians of the North when the Supreme Court handed down its famous decision in the Dred Scott case. When the Court declared abridgements of slave-holding rights to be unconstitutional, many a Northern newspaper gave vent to editorial expressions which make some of the current expressions from the South seem pallid by comparison.

For a relatively mild expression of Northern resentment against the Court, take this excerpt from an editorial of the *Daily Republican*, Springfield, Mass., of March, 1857:

"The history of judicial decisions in this country contains nothing so important as this. It establishes a new order of things, revolutionising law, overturning precedents, outraging the sentiments of the civilized world, and setting at nought all the opinions and actions of our fathers."

5

The Alien Voices

THE Southerner, concerned with the necessity of working out his own problems in his own fashion, nowhere has sought to impose his will or his customs upon other sections of the country. His quarrel has been, and is, with the central government's continual encroachment into affairs best handled on the state and local level, and with the propensity of other regions to stimulate the government to such encroachment, usually at the expense of the South. At no time has the Southerner denied the right of the Northerner, the Eastener, and the Westerner to integrate their schools and their society to whatever degree thought desirable. Yet out of all those regions have come bitter denunciations of the South for its failure to subscribe to viewpoints preached, if not practiced, in those non-Southern regions.

From Massachusetts, for example, has come this vitriolic statement by the State Democratic Party as part of its 1956 platform: "We express our deep concern and manifest indignation of any effort, by any group, anywhere in the land,

whereby the Constitution, as interpreted by the Supreme
Court, is flaunted [sic] for the base reason of maintaining a
decadent way of life which from its inception was alien to
the American ideal." Such excoriation comes with singular
bad grace from a state which was in substantial measure
responsible through its slave-traders for creating the South's
Negro problem; which fathered the anti-administration
Hartford Convention of 1814-1815; and which even earlier
had heard one of its own U.S. Senators (Timothy Picker-
ing) propose that the New England states secede from the
Union and form a "Northern Confederacy."

And from the Democratic Party of the State of Michigan,
land of race riots and labor strife, has come by way of party
platform a document labeled "The Michigan Declaration."
It quotes the words of Gov. G. Mennen (Soapy) Williams:
"We stand unrelentingly for the principles that the Constitution must be the law of the land, everywhere in the land;
that no part of the Nation may be permitted to say it is not
the law for them; that the President may not ignore enforcement, nor Congress support evasion."

Southerners were amused in the summer of 1957 to note
the general hubbub which broke out in the otherwise well-
ordered city of Levittown, a planned community of some
60,000 residents in Bucks County, Pennsylvania. The cause
of the demonstrations was the entry into the massive housing development of one, mind you, *one* Negro family. And
note that this occurred in the non-segregated state of Pennsylvania, north of the Mason-Dixon line, north of the "nation's showcase" of Washington, and far from the storied
land of intolerance and bigotry—the South.

But if Levittown were in the South, between 10,000 and
25,000 of its people would be Negroes, depending upon the
area of the South in which it might have been located. And
if there were that many Negroes in the city, they probably
would be living on the same streets as whites in many in-

stances, in the same block in other instances, or perhaps side by side in other instances.

And even if Levittown were located anywhere else in the country, and subject to the national rather than the Southern ratio of Negroes to whites, then the city would have at least 6,000 Negroes. But the Levittown unpleasantness arose out of the presence of *four* Negroes: an electrical technician, his wife, and their two children. Mass meetings were held, demonstrations were conducted in front of the house into which the Negro family moved, stones were thrown at the residence and at the state troopers who were dispatched to the scene, and, in general, there was a fair measure of pandemonium.

And from California, fabled land of sunshine and anti-Asiatic hysteria, has come this resolution (following a number of whereases) from the state legislature:

"Resolved by the Assembly of the State of California, That it memorializes the executive branch and Congress of the United States to take the necessary action to support the recent decisions of the Supreme Court on civil rights, by the utilization of available agencies and facilities to maintain peace and order, protect the rights of citizens, and enforce the laws of our land."

Is it fair to point out that the State of California never ratified the 14th amendment which precipitated most of the current racial dispute? And is it fair to speculate whether the California legislature would react in the same manner if the state had more than 4,750,000 Negroes, as would be the case if California's Negro ratio were the same as Mississippi's? Or, perhaps more pointedly, remembering days of World War II, what would be California's attitude if the state had 4,750,000 Japanese instead of the 85,000 whose presence aroused such frantic discrimination in the early 1940's? If either of those conditions prevailed, could California Congressman Leroy Johnson say then what he pro-

claimed in the House of Representatives on March 15, 1956:
"In California we have no segregation problem"? As a matter of fact, could he accurately make such a statement today?

The same line of questioning might apply to the State of
Illinois, where the legislature (as will be seen below) took
the Southern states to task for having adopted interposition
resolutions. If Illinois had South Carolina's proportion of
Negroes, the resulting 3,135,000 black residents of the state
might find an attitude somewhat different from that evoked
by the approximately 700,000 who now reside in the state.
But in the absence of the greater number, and in the presence of the minority group political pressures, the Illinois
General Assembly in March of 1957 piously adopted what
could be called an "anti-interposition" resolution:

"Whereas the United States Supreme Court and various
Federal courts have been subjected to severe criticism as a
result of the decisions and decrees in the school-segregation
and related cases which declare that segregation and discrimination because of race, color, religion, or national origin in public schools and facilities violate the principles of
the Constitution of the United States; [here follow six more
whereases]

"Be it therefore . . . Resolved, That segregation and discrimination because of race, color, religion, or national origin in public schools and facilities is prohibited by the
Constitution of the United States, and no State has the right
to maintain at its own expense racially separate public
schools or facilities; and . . . [more of same]."

Formal denunciations of the South such as these official
statements are pallid expressions in contrast with some of
the invective heaped upon the South by individual spokesmen in high places of government. Here is a sample of the
language used by the latter-day Abolitionists to whip up
public sentiment against the South—language worthy of
that master of anti-Southern abuse, Thad Stevens, and

similarly having the advantage of being spewed forth in the halls of Congress. On Tuesday, February 7, 1956, there came forth (and were recorded in the *Congressional Record*) these words from the Honorable Irwin D. Davidson, then representing New York's 20th Congressional District:

"A small mob of cowardly hooligans, blinded by ignorance and hate, inflamed by liquor and bigoted venom, have caused all this, and have destroyed all that we have worked so assiduously to accomplish. The objective of this foul rabble's hatred is a single defenseless girl named Autherine Lucy, 26 years old. She happens to be a Negress. When she attempted to attend classes at the University of Alabama, the mob collected and greeted her with stones, mud balls, and eggs as fetid as the breath used by these erstwhile men, turned to beasts, in their vituperative catcalls."

Such words disclose the refusal of the integrationists to admit that there is any measure of sincerity, of conviction, or of kindliness among segregationists who genuinely favor racial separation as a pattern for peaceful and equitable living by persons of different races who share the same time and space of history.

Equally typical of the muddled thinking which characterizes the integrationist proponents of centralized government is a statement addressed in 1956 to Congressman Hugh J. Addonizio by New Jersey members of a "Leadership Conference on Civil Rights." The statement extols the Bill of Rights of the Federal Constitution and adds these observations:

"Not for 80 years has the Congress of the United States passed any civil rights legislation. Fortunately, our Federal system of government has not allowed this failure on the part of the national legislature to deprive all citizens of the benefits of wise and humanitarian legislative practices. Many States of the Union have found it necessary to pass civil rights legislation.

"We, in New Jersey, can be rightfully proud of the leadership which our State government has provided in this essential field . . .

"It is unfortunate, however, that citizens of New Jersey, traveling in other parts of the country, do not have the benefit of similar legislation. We, the undersigned organizations, therefore take this opportunity on this, the 164th anniversary of the adoption of the Bill of Rights, to urge our New Jersey Representatives to exert every effort to see to it that Congress passes such laws which will guarantee to the citizens of New Jersey the same kind of protection in all parts of the Nation as we have in our own State."

Listed as signers of the statement were the following organizations: Americans for Democratic Action; American Jewish Committee; American Veterans Committee; B'nai B'rith; Ethical Society of Essex County; International Ladies Garment Workers Union; Jewish Labor Committee; Jewish War Veterans, Department of New Jersey; National Council of Jewish Women, New Jersey region; National Council of Negro Women; National Frontiers Club; New Jersey CIO Council; National Association for the Advancement of Colored People.

It is ironic that the imposing array of organizations, a veritable "who's who" of South-baiters, should make their pitch for federal enactment of civil rights legislation in the name of the Bill of Rights. For such organizations, the Bill of Rights stops with the Eighth Amendment and completely discountenances any emphasis on the Ninth and Tenth, which together emphasize the rights and powers retained by the States and the peoples thereof.

The South finds no quarrel with New Jersey's enactment of anti-discrimination legislation, and it applauds the reference to "our Federal system of Government" which makes it possible for the several states to enact such legislation as they see fit. But under the same line of logic, and under the self-same federal system of government, the right of New

Jersey to enact civil rights legislation must be accompanied by the right of South Carolina, or any other state, *not* to enact such legislation if the people of that state do not want it. What the New Jerseyites want is to place the image of their state upon all of the United States, through Federal enactment of laws desired by the people of New Jersey.

The Southerner who is interested in documenting the identity of those organizations and individuals who constitute the greatest challenge to continued racial separation in education, employment, and other areas can readily do so by wading through some of the various printed reports of hearings conducted by Congressional committees on "civil rights" legislation. There, in chapter and verse, is the recorded testimony of persons who bring constant pressure to bear on the Congress to enact federal legislation designed to invade the rights of the states, usurp the prerogatives of the employers of the nation, and sweep away all barriers which separate whites from Negroes.

Next to the National Association for the Advancement of Colored People, officials of organized labor (notably the AFL-CIO and its affiliated unions) stand first and foremost among bodies which champion integration on all fronts, not just that of employment. They belabor the Congress itself; the South generally and Southern states separately; the President (when he seems not to be moving fast enough to suit them); and anyone and anything else which seems to stand in the way of integration. "White dominion," says the CIO, "is dead or dying everywhere in the world, not only in Africa, but also here in the United States." And despite the fact that the South represents the least-organized area of the nation and therefore the Number One goal for organization, there has been no mincing of words on the part of national labor leaders who favor the elimination of racial segregation.

CIO President Walter P. Reuther, May 17, 1954, immediately following announcement of the Supreme Court's desegregation decision: "The unanimous decision of the Supreme Court outlawing racial segregation in the schools is a heartwarming reaffirmation of the American democratic principles that are inherent in the 14th Amendment to the Constitution. . . . The CIO is proud to have played a role as a 'friend of the court' in the school segregation cases and in many of the earlier civil rights cases that built the legal groundwork for today's decision by the Supreme Court."

CIO Secretary-Treasurer James B. Carey, May 17, 1954: "This decision represents the official recognition of our Government that the separate but equal doctrine is inconsistent with the fundamental equalitarianism of the American way of life. . . . The CIO is dedicated to the protection of our democratic system of government and the civil rights and liberties of all Americans . . ."

Tennessee State CIO Council, June 17-19, 1955: "Be it resolved, That the 16th annual state convention go on record as favoring action designed to bring about the fulfillment of the Supreme Court's decision on integration. . . ."

Texas State CIO Council, September, 1955 (in adopting the report of its Human Rights Committee): "We are aware of the recent rise of the so-called Citizens Councils in the state of Texas. We recognize them for the blackmail outfits they are and for the denial of human rights and resistance to government by law upon which they thrive. . . ."

David J. McDonald, president of the United Steelworkers of America, March 15, 1956: "We must wipe out the Mason-Dixon line in American culture."

If there still be need for establishing the premise that the NAACP and the AFL-CIO are soul-mates on the question of racial integration, these few references might remove any lingering doubts:

The NAACP's national office distributed a press release under date of May 13, 1954, telling of a $75,000 grant presented to the NAACP Legal Defense and Educational Fund by the Philip Murray Memorial Foundation. The news release included these statements:

"The grant, the largest ever made by a foundation to advance the program of the NAACP, was presented by CIO President Walter Reuther to NAACP President Arthur B. Spingarn here [New York] on May 12 before a distinguished gathering at the Carnegie Endowment Building. . . ."

The list of other organizations which stand as proponents of enforced racial integration and therefore as opponents of the South is long, obvious, and ominous. It includes the following, enumerated with a characteristic statement from the organization policy:

The Anti-Defamation League of B'nai B'rith: "It is our feeling that our American system can tolerate no restrictions upon the individual which depend upon irrelevant factors such as his race, his color, his religion, or the social position to which he is born."

American Jewish Congress: "To sum up . . . we should have a comprehensive bill, and the three most important components in that comprehensive bill are FEPC, a Fair Employment Practices Commission, a Civil Rights Division [in the Department of Justice] and a Commission on Civil Rights."

Americans for Democratic Action: "We . . . support legislation and administrative action on the Federal, State, and local level: . . . To eliminate segregation and other forms of discrimination in housing, education, employment, transportation, recreation, government supported financing, the National Guard and other areas of life. . . . To broaden the coverage of existing civil rights laws. . . . To remove the poll tax and other disfranchising practices [etc.]."

American Council on Human Rights (a cooperative program supported by five collegiate sororities and fraternities —Alpha Kappa Alpha Sorority, Delta Sigma Theta Sorority,

Kappa Alpha Psi Fraternity, Sigma Gamma Rho Sorority, and Zeta Phi Beta Sorority, representing a membership of about 70,000 students): "Our organization is dedicated to the task of seeking the extension of fundamental human and civil rights to all who live in the United States and to secure equality of treatment and opportunity for all without discrimination and segregation because of race, religion, or national origin. . . ."

But enough. These samplings of pious anti-Southern, anti-states' rights expressions can be repeated *ad nauseam*. Practically every "liberal" organization in the country (including some officially tainted with the subversive label) felt impelled to pass resolutions condemning the Southern attitude toward segregation and suggesting that the federal government "do something about it." It is noteworthy that none of these organizations, so much concerned with preserving the "American way of life," has any kinship with American history or is rooted in the American constitutional tradition. On the other hand, such organizations as the Daughters of the American Revolution, the Sons of the American Revolution, the Colonial Dames, and others, have refrained from joining in the chorus of the South-haters. Indeed, they are among the friends of the South, and defenders of an American way of life that is grounded in history and bitter experience, rather than in sociology and delusions of the welfare state.

6

Scribes and Pharisees

THE South traditionally has been adjudged a
stronghold of religion—an area where both whites and Negroes take their churchly responsibilities seriously. From
scoffers of the H. L. Mencken stripe have come belittling
remarks which characterize the South as "the Bible Belt,"
but Southerners have not resented the appellation for the
simple reason that they find no offense in being accused of
addiction to the Word of God. Yet all of a sudden, the
Word seems to have changed, but by secular rather than
divine decree. A way of life based on racial separation and
subscribed to by ministers and laymen alike for generations
in the South, and for centuries elsewhere, now is labeled
"unChristian" by clergymen whose powers of divination
seem to have blossomed forth simultaneously with the Supreme Court's delivery of Chief Justice Warren's sermon
from the bench. On May 16, 1954, the Southerner was following a pattern of living which met the tests of constitu-
tionality and presumably of Christian conduct. On May 17,

with the Warren pronouncement, that pattern was pronounced unconstitutional and unChristian, as the Court drafted its own revised standard version of both the Constitution and, seemingly, the Bible.

The alacrity with which church spokesmen jumped aboard the Supreme Court's bandwagon bespoke volumes. It disclosed race-mixing sentiments which, for the most part, had been bottled up within the bosoms of many a would-be social gospeleer who heretofore had found it advisable to keep his own counsel.

It must be admitted, however, that there already had been expressed a measure of integrationist sentiment by non-Southern clergymen who were sufficiently removed in point of space and knowledge to speak freely, if ignorantly, on the matter of Southern race relations. It must be admitted also that an occasional Southern preacher, schooled in the modern ministry of the social gospel and imbued with the necessity of re-working the world into a pattern of indiscriminate brotherhood, was eager to establish himself as an enlightened liberal amongst benighted conservatives.

As early as 1946, the organization which subsequently became the National Council of Churches of Christ in the U.S.A., issued this statement:

"The Federal Council of the Churches of Christ in America hereby renounces the pattern of segregation in race relations as unnecessary and undesirable and a violation of the Gospel of love and human brotherhood. Having taken this action, the Federal Council requests its constituent communions to do likewise. As proof of their sincerity in this renunciation they will work for a non-segregated Church and a non-segregated society."

And work for non-segregation it did, proceeding to draw inspiration and guidance from the upper crust of clerical big-wigs rather than from the membership on the congregational level, most of whom were ignorant of what was going on in the titled hierarchy which controls not only the Council but many of its constituent denominations.

Furthermore, there were church leaders who were distressed over the inadequacy of education opportunity for Negroes in parts of the South, and others who felt a certain moral although hardly an acute discomfiture because of racial segregation within their own denominations. But by and large, despite such fulsome and distorted statements as those emanating from the Council of Churches, most clergymen, North and South, continued to preach the word of God and leave the secular business of public school education to public officials on the sound theory that church and state should be kept distinct from one another.

All that changed with the Supreme Court decision outlawing segregation. The Court's pronouncement seemed to invite a deluge of endorsements from churchmen, churchwomen, and church groups. Some Southern men and women were among those who rushed to touch the hem of the Supreme Court garments, but the vast majority of Southerners, of high rank and low, maintained a conviction that the issue of public school education is not a function of the church and is not properly a subject of religious concern.

The question remains, therefore, why did the matter become so intimately and so immediately involved in church affairs? One answer, perhaps, lies in the possibility that a confused sense of guilt may have motivated many of the preachers and their more pious lay brothers and sisters who began seeking to outdo the Supreme Court itself in seeking a racial amalgam in the public schools as well as in the churches.

It is a matter of record, in both past and present history, that there have been numerous instances of injustice, of oppression, of bitterness, and even of violence under the Southern system of racial segregation. Because these things were most frequent in the South, and because here the lines of racial demarcation have been clear and visible, the sensitive-souled preachers, both ordained and unordained, have fallen victim to their own mistaken judgment that the evils are the result of segregation. But as a matter of additional record, although less obvious, there is the undeniable fact that similar instances of racial friction and Negro oppression have occurred in those parts of the country where there is no pattern of formal segregation. Unfortunate though it may be, the real truth of the matter is that racial discord accompanies the Negro, whether in a segregated or an integrated role, just so long as he is present in any substantial numbers.

The distressing aspect of the situation, insofar as the South is concerned, is that the concentration of Negroes in this region has brought about a concentration of attention from the do-gooders who do not comprehend the fact that the South's peculiar problem with respect to Negroes is one of numbers as well as of nature.

There also is the suspicion, though by way of surmise, that the problem of public school integration is so replete with all the raw material of sociological experimentation that proponents of the social gospel have not been able to resist the temptation to dump it into their test-tubes of research. Here is an issue which lends itself handily to pious preachments over the welfare of little children, the brotherhood of man, and the blessings of democracy. Consequently, what was once an area of learning now has become an arena for social conflict and ferment. It is not enough to provide youngsters of all races with adequate schools, competent instruction, and ample opportunity to develop their educational capacities; there must be added the overburden of a pseudo-religion which holds that the will of God is inoperative among persons who, for reasons of peace of community and pride of identity, prefer the company of their own kind.

The dreadful thing about the do-gooders' approach is that they are quite willing to risk the health, happiness, and harmony of countless individuals in a vast sociological experiment which has nowhere been tested by force. In the non-Southern regions of the United States, where natural preferences tend to maintain actual if not legal segregation, the races still are separated by custom and conduct, so that there is no real integration. In South and Central America, where there has voluntarily been true integration, the results have produced a racial conglomeration of mixed breeds which is abhorrent to the vast majority of white Americans, certainly to those of the South.

Yet the American integrationists have succeeded to an astounding degree in gaining church support for their effort to break down racial separation in all walks of life. The average Southerner is well aware of the fact that numerous church "leaders," including those of the two denominations most numerous in the South (the Baptists and the Methodists), have spoken out against segregation; but few Southerners realize the extent to which virtually ALL denominations have aligned themselves with the integrationists. Whether such alignments and professions of church policy actually reflect the will of the rank and file of church membership is highly questionable, but as long as such expressions go unchallenged they will gather momentum sufficient to overwhelm those who belatedly would make their voices heard. It is high time that the church laity should call for an opportunity to make its own voice heard in the open forum of free debate.

Here are a few of the clerical professions made public by church groups which saw fit to specifically endorse the Supreme Court's decision:

United Church Women of 15 Southern states, meeting in Atlanta, Ga., on June 21, 1954—"We accept with humility the Supreme Court decision as supporting the broad Christian principle of the dignity and worth of human personality and affording the opportunity of translating into reality Christian and democratic ideals. . . ."

Southern Baptist Convention, May 28, 1954—"We recognize the fact that this Supreme Court decision is in harmony with the constitutional guarantee of equal freedom to all citizens, and with the Christian principles of equal justice and love for all men. . . .

Catholic Interracial Council—May 18, 1954—"This is a logical step in the expansion and perfection of American democracy. . . . We are confident that throughout the country thoughtful citizens will support with appropriate efforts this historic re-affirmation of the principle of the equality of men before the law."

Congregational Christian—June 30, 1954—"Whereas the Supreme Court of the United States has declared segregation in tax-supported accommodations and services, including public schools, to be contrary to the Constitution, Be it Resolved that we call upon all Americans to undertake timely and tolerant implementation of the Supreme Court decision. . . ."

Reformed Church in America—Extracted from a statement adopted by the General Synod of Reformed Church in America: "We believe that the recent Supreme Court decision on the ordered, gradual desegregation of the public schools of our land represents an effective legal expression of Christian attitudes and convictions at the present time . . ."

Synagogue Council of America—"The Synagogue Council of America greets with deep satisfaction the historic decision of the Supreme Court of the United States ending segregation in the public schools of America. . . ."

The Protestant Episcopal Church, at its General Convention of 1955, adopted a resolution commending: "To all the clergy and people of this Church that they accept and support this ruling of the Supreme Court, and, that by opening channels of Christian conference and communication between the races concerned in each diocese and Community, they anticipate constructively the local implementation of this ruling as the law of the land. . . ."

Perhaps the most discouraging aspect of the situation is the willingness of church leaders to have integration brought about by force of law. Even the Baptists, ordinarily staunch champions of separation of church and state, have recorded themselves in favor of state action in fields which are bound to have an impact upon church activity, such as fair employment practices laws.

But despite assertions in favor of compulsory integration, the church fathers have not been able to force-feed their flocks with integration, and a massive wall of resistance has arisen within the framework of many of the churches themselves. Despite the preachments of national church groups and of titular leaders in all denominations, the rank and file of Southern church-goers still refuse to be led by the hand into the paths of integration, and seem increasingly willing to make that opposition known both within and without the church.

A significant evidence of this refusal to accept clerical dictation with respect to integration has come from the Roman Catholic Church, normally regarded as being most responsive to directions from the higher levels of Catholic authority. Writing in the March 8, 1956, issue of *The Reporter*, Louisa Dalcher tells of the segregation controversy in the New Orleans setting. Her article, entitled "A Time of Worry in 'The City Care Forgot,'" quotes these paragraphs from a letter written to the Rev. Edward B. Bunn, president of Georgetown University, by Emile A. Wagner, Jr., a Catholic member of the Orleans Parish School Board:

". . . We Catholics are confronted with a dilemma in conscience. From my knowledge of the personal convictions of the clergy in this area, both Jesuits and otherwise, and it is fairly extensive, I would say that many, if not more than half, are convinced the question of integration has no moral significance. . . .

"With such a division among the clergy, I believe it most unfair for one segment to arrogate to itself all righteousness and to declare that those who do not conform in their opinion have strayed from Catholic doctrine. . . ."

A year later, The Association of Catholic Laymen (headed by Mr. Wagner) addressed a formal letter to Pope Pius XII in Rome, asking that he stop racial integration in the church. Said the letter in part, as reported by the Associated Press from New Orleans:

"For over two years now conscientious and sincere Catholics in the archdiocese of New Orleans have been confronted with the strange new doctrine, propounded by our archbishop, his excellency, Joseph Francis Rummel, that the segregation of the white and Negro races is 'morally wrong and sinful.'

"Indeed, this concept is both new and strange, for even the clergy and church itself have participated and are participating in the perpetuation of this type of segregation by, among other things, sanctioning the establishment and maintenance of separate churches and schools.

"Despite the fact that no competent attempt has been made to offer a conclusive proof to establish the validity of the principle nor to demonstrate a bishop's authority to define a matter of morals, Catholics have been admonished that they are bound in conscience under pain of possible serious sin to accept it. . . ."

Within the Protestant denominations which make up the vast bulk of Southern churches, there is a quiet revolution brewing among hosts of Southern church-goers who are becoming increasingly fed up with the integrationist preachments of the various denominational hierarchies. One thing which has thus far prevented any large scale revolt from the established churches is the fact that the denominational attitudes have been manifested in words rather than deeds.

Yet even so, the continued admonitions of high church officials and the continued adoption of pro-integration statements by church councils and the like are driving countless Southern church members closer and closer to the point of open rebellion against the leadership of their denominations.

Another deterrent to overt breaks within the several denominations has been the fact that most individual congregations have ignored, repudiated, or denounced the integrationist proclivities of their parent organizations. But even within the ranks of the multitudinous Southern Baptists, resentment is taking the form of open discussion of the possibility of withdrawing from the Southern Baptist Convention. For example, several Baptist denominations of South Carolina took firm positions in the summer of 1957 against high-level Baptist leanings toward integration, including in their resolutions of protest such significant statements as these, taken from a resolution adopted September 1, 1957, at the regular church conference of the First Baptist Church of Sumter:

"Whereas, the members of the First Baptist Church of Sumter, South Carolina, hold no prejudice in their hearts against the Negro. We love the Negro and would fight for him to defend his rights but we are opposed to amalgamation of the races, to which integration inevitably leads, Therefore,

"Be It Resolved, That the members of the First Baptist Church of Sumter, South Carolina, hereby express unalterable opposition to the expressions of approval given by the Southern Baptist Convention to the opinion of the Supreme Court of the United States, in which segregation in public schools was held unconstitutional; and . . .

"Be It Further Resolved, That it is the sense of this Church that if such practices are continued by the Southern Baptist Convention, it will be for the best interest of the Baptist Churches of the real Southern States to withdraw from the so-called Southern Baptist Convention and organize an association of Churches that share the view herein expressed . . ."

Baptist reaction against the integrationist trend is not confined to South Carolina, however. In October of 1957, the 23-church Trenton Baptist Association of Louisiana formally requested that the Southern Baptist Convention rid itself of the Christian Life Commission. Two months previously, the weekly paper of the Louisiana Baptist Convention, *The Baptist Message,* had criticized the Christian Life Commission for favoring racial integration in public schools and in churches.

Within the next most numerous Southern church, the Methodist, similar expressions of segregationist sentiment have come by resolution and otherwise from a great many congregations which oppose the integrationist professions of certain Methodist bishops and influential agencies within the church. But, lacking the congregational autonomy of Baptist churches, many a Methodist church finds itself in the unhappy position of being hog-tied to a denomination which continues, at least at the upper level, to preach a brand of race relationship unacceptable to the mass of the Methodist rank and file in the South.

There is little doubt that the reaction among the Methodists would be even more acute if they were all aware of the wording of the 1956 edition of the Methodist *Discipline* concerning "The Methodist Church and Race." Paragraph 2026 of the *Discipline,* which is the church's statement of policy, binding in matters of church law and heavily influential in matters of individual belief, now reads in part as follows:

"The teaching of our Lord is that all men are brothers. The Master permits no discrimination because of race, color, or national origin.

"The position of The Methodist Church, long held and frequently declared, is an amplification of our Lord's teaching. 'To discriminate against a person solely upon the basis of his race is both unfair and unChristian. Every child of God is entitled to that place in society which he has won by his industry and his character. . . . To deny him that position of honor because of the accident of his birth is neither honest democracy nor good religion.' (The Episcopal Address, 1952 and 1956). . . .

"The decisions of the Supreme Court of the United States relative to segregation make necessary far-reaching and often difficult community readjustments throughout the nation. We call upon our people to effect these adjustments in all good faith, with brotherliness and patience. . . ."

Of all denominations which have followings in the South, the one which has remained most steadfast in its defense of racial segregation is the Southern Methodist Church. This denomination, which stemmed doctrinally and spiritually from the old Methodist Episcopal Church, South, refused to follow that organization into merger with the Northern Methodist Church "on the grounds of the alarming infidelity and apostasy found therein." Despite the loss of all property and the name "Methodist Episcopal Church," a number of staunch Southern Methodists agreed in January of 1939 to perpetuate their own conception of Methodism in the South and laid the groundwork for what became the Southern Methodist Church.

Among other features which distinguish this peculiarly Southern denomination from other Methodist groups is its adherence not only in practice but in principle to the policy of racial segregation. The statement of doctrinal belief of the Southern Methodist Church contains this paragraph treating "Of Segregation":

"We believe that the holy writ teaches the separation of peoples, at least, to the extent of the three basic races, namely: Caucasian, Mongoloid, and Negroid. Many instances of separations of peoples is found in the Bible and probably the greatest instance of all is the tower of Babel. God has set the boundaries, and woe be unto man if he attempts to cross these boundaries. At the same time, we believe, that all races are entitled to equal opportunities in all fields."

And it is worth noting that the Church of Jesus Christ of Latter-Day Saints has taken no official position on the matter of racial segregation, although there is no color restriction as to membership in the Mormon Church.

At least one Conference of Advent Christian Churches (that of South Carolina) has recorded itself in favor of racial separation. In October of 1957, the South Carolina conference adopted a resolution stating:

"We believe that God's word teaches us that people of this earth have been divided and separated for reasons known only to him, and because we are geographically situated so that love of our many colored neighbors makes it [separation] necessary to the welfare of both white and colored races, be it resolved that we go on record as favoring the segregation of the two races in public life—further that we use every means in our power to promote the welfare and happiness of our Negro fellowman—further that equal but separate facilities be provided for the colored race."

Some Southern clergymen have learned the hard way just how determined their congregations are to maintain the racial integrity of their churches. These last few years of racial controversy have brought about the displacement of a number of clergymen whose pastoral views favoring integration were too much at variance with those of their congregations. Sometimes, such ministers eased out of situations which showed signs of becoming intolerable because of differing viewpoints. In other cases, outraged congregations simply effected the out-of-hand removal of ministers whose views proved too radical for the peace of mind of the church membership. Not yet have enraged mobs literally driven pastors from their pulpits, as was done occasionally in the days leading up to the War Between the States.

Distressing as all this is, and may become, it is simply another reflection of the adherence of Southern communities to the way of life which has become traditional and typical. Furthermore, it is quite likely that continued agitation from the pulpit for integration will bring about still more rifts within church ranks, and possibly contribute to sizable shifts of church affiliation, or perhaps the establishment of new and independent churches or church groups. Most white Southerners are unwilling to concede that the only Heaven-bound vehicle requires forcible intermingling of passengers, and they are willing to risk arriving at the same destination by other means. They will agree that in the eyes of God all men are equally good, or bad, and that racial distinctions neither enhance nor lessen an individual's standing in the Kingdom of God, but they will NOT agree that ethic brotherhood requires ethnic fraternizing.

Southerners are suffering, as have hosts of unhappy victims before now, from the persecutions of those whose besetting weakness is idealism compounded with ignorance. These well-intentioned but poorly-informed saviors of the South may have a role to play in the grand scheme of things —the point is debatable—but when their actions run ahead of their understanding, the results are deplorable. The integrationists of the present, like the abolitionists of the past, are so convinced of their own rectitude that they are heedless of the fact that they interfere with the accomplishment of their own goals.

In their blind fervor, they fail to recognize the fact that even if integration WERE a desirable goal, which few Southerners are prepared to admit, it can hardly be achieved with the tactics now being applied in the conflict.

Americans generally, and Southerners particularly, are little inclined to accept dictation from others, least of all from others who live elsewhere and who have at best only a superficial knowledge of the situation they seek to "improve." Inevitably, pressures build up back-pressures, and the net result is stalemate, controversy, and bitterness. The proof of that lies in the obvious and measurable deterioration in race relations in the South since the Supreme Court sought in 1954 to order a cultural change which was not acceptable to the people most directly affected.

An insight into this facet of American nature was provided, quite without reference to any racial considerations, by then Secretary of Defense Charles E. Wilson when he addressed the graduating class of the National War College on June 11, 1957:

"Historically, we Americans do not believe in dictators or in people who sit in ivory towers and try to tell everybody what to do. You cannot force people, especially in our country, to come into agreement where there is no agreement. Fortunately, under our form of government nobody attempts such a thing very often."

The Secretary veered from truth somewhat in that last sentence, for the very administration of which he was a part was at that very moment seeking to do precisely what he said could not be done; that is, to force people to come into agreement where there was no agreement.

But even more to the point, philosophically, are these words from the noted theologian, Dr. Reinhold Niebuhr:

"The tragedies in human history, the cruelties, the fanaticisms have not been caused by the criminals . . . but by idealists who did not understand the strange mixture of self-interest and ideals which are compounded in all human motives, by reformers who fail to understand the necessities of personal reformation . . . by the wise who do not know the limits of their own wisdom, and by the religious who do not know that 'in God's sight no man living is justified.'"

In applying that general thought specifically to the integration problem, Dr. Niebuhr says:

"We must beware of the self-righteous fanaticism of idealists who do not know the complexity of the problem with which they are dealing . . . The integration of schools should come very gradually and . . . northern idealists haven't a notion of what the disparity of culture means. Since the South was making so much progress I was sorry about the Court decision, though, I think, the Court once challenged, could not render any other decision."

The self-righteousness, the smugness, the supercilious attitude by which the Northerner indicates that he knows better what is good for the South than do those who live there —these are the things which infuriate Southerners and determine them all the more against yielding to outside pressures or propaganda. When these preachments come from the clergy, as they do with almost nauseating frequency, the Southerner feels a strain on his religion as well as on his temper.

Some of that resentment shows through in a July 11, 1957, speech by Judge Walter B. Jones, president of the Alabama Bible Society and of the Jones Law School before the Baptist Laymen of Alabama:

"According to the base standards of these self-righteous critics, a person may love justice, do mercy, walk humbly before his God, and follow the teachings of the Master; and yet, because the beacon light God set in his bosom, all the teachings of history, all the experiences of mankind, will not permit him to believe in integration, he is denounced as un-Christian by people who would lead their race, and their nation, to destruction."

The mistake made by so many clerical advocates of integration is equating integration with good, and segregation with evil. Nowhere is that error more clearly illuminated and exposed than in Dr. E. Earle Ellis' article, "Segregation and the Kingdom of God," which appeared in the March 18, 1957, issue of *Christianity Today*. The Florida-born scholar, assistant professor of Bible and Religion at Aurora College, Aurora, Illinois, writes:

"Segregation does not necessitate bad race relations, nor does integration guarantee good ones. On the contrary, the very opposite often appears to be true. . . . Southerners often wonder whether integrationists are as interested in good race relations as in forcing a particular kind of race relations. The unfortunate fact is that ardent Christian integrationists, however conscientious, are one cause of the worsening race relations in the South today. Their moral superiority complex, their caricature of the segregationist as an unChristian bigot and their pious confession of the sins of people in other sections of the country have not been wholly edifying. . . ."

One of the relatively few Episcopal ministers to stand four-square against integration of the races raises his own warning against the trend toward socialism which is caught up with the race-mixing preachments. Here are the words of the Rev. Henry E. Egger, rector of St. Peter's Episcopal Church, Charlotte, N. C., on the morning of September 15, 1957:

"The decision of the Supreme Court of the United States to mix our white and Negro students in the schools is infinitely more prompted by socialistically inspired thinking than it is by any legal justification. Unadulterated socialism is behind this social leveling, and, if we do not have the courage or the energy to stop it, we will lose what freedom we have left."

The Rev. Mr. Egger sees the distinct threat of racial amalgamation in school integration:

". . . our spiritual affinity, or likeness, or attraction does not call for enforced physical proximity and is in no way dependent upon it. Every hue and cry to the contrary, I say that enforced physical proximity or closeness of the races does promote interbreeding. . . ."

One encouraging development within the realm of Southern church affairs has been the formulation of a statement of policy on race relations by the Board of Directors of the Southern Presbyterian *Journal*. Meeting at Weaversville, N. C., in August of 1957, the directors of the semi-official organ of the Presbyterian Church, U.S. (Southern) adopted this statement:

"We are convinced that the matter of enforced integration is largely politically motivated and is being used by politicians for partisan advantages. Out of this unfortunate context, fraught with political implications, this problem has been thrust upon us in the churches. . . .

"We deplore the fostering of social contact in the name of Christianity where such contacts are unnatural and forced. Therefore, we affirm that voluntary segregation in the churches, schools and other social relationships is for the highest interest of the races, and is not unChristian."

But in sharp contrast with that statement has been the welter of religious and pseudo-religious "literature" which has sought to correlate integration with morality. In much of this outpouring, the ugly word "hate" has crept deeply into the presentations.

Indeed it has not only crept in, it has been shoved into the discussion deliberately by those who seek to weaken the position of the segregationists. It is one of the smear words used to discredit those who genuinely and sincerely favor racial integrity over racial conglomeration. Yet it is an unfair word, a prejudicial word, and it is so used by the propagandists and, unfortunately, by many clergymen who see in the race question an opportunity to preach brotherly love and to scorn hatred.

There are those white persons, undoubtedly, who do hate Negroes, just as there inevitably are those Negroes who hate whites. But the rival factors of love and hate do not properly enter into the debate over racial separation, especially as it concerns public schooling. Not only is it possible, but it is proven, that persons can exercise preferences, that they can even discriminate, to use another word which the propagandists have lowered to the level of a smear term, without evoking any sentiments akin to hatred.

In the normal course of events, individuals constantly exercise preferences among people as among things. In a free society, persons who share the same background, the same standards of values, the same attitudes, and the same experiences will gravitate together. Harvard men can band themselves together without hating Yale men. Baptists can join hands in mutual enterprise without hating Methodists. Youngsters may go their collective way without hating their elders. And most assuredly white people can prefer each other's company without hating persons who do not happen to be white.

There is an artificiality, a deliberate warping of the situation, in allegations that racial preference necessarily is based on racial hatred. There is the suspicion, too, that a tinge of artificiality might attach to the professions of love which spew forth from the lips of those who continually preach of the brotherhood of man. It is one thing to berate others for a lack of love; it is something else again to practice that love unreservedly and unashamedly. Yet there is room enough and plenty for those who thus love the Negro to render him a real service.

The Negro needs stimulation, and encouragement, and motivation to improve his lot, to raise his standards, to better his performance in the realms of family, society, and community. While the average white man, busy in his own self-betterment, is relatively content to let the Negro develop at the Negro's own pace, it might well be that the articulate Negrophiles among the white integrationists could find soul-rewarding gain through plunging into the ranks of the Negroes to help spur them onward to better things. The task is formidable and the road would be hard, but to those who feel the call, energy turned in that direction might profit them, and the nation, more than does their sideline coaching to more reluctant Southerners.

To their credit, it must be admitted that a few ministers, a few educators, and a few laymen have undertaken to move into the darker circles of Negro society—there to work among the people they love. Whether their accomplishments will prove worth the effort and the sacrifice—to them and to their children who thereby become pawns of sociological experimentation—is something that only time will tell. But at least they show the courage of their convictions.

Gaining additional adherents to that sort of sacrificial undertaking might prove difficult, however, for it is a truism that more people are willing to give lip service than labor to a cause, especially one which runs counter to accepted community practices throughout most of the nation. Even the propagandists themselves concede that point, as witness this unhappy expression from Isaac Toubin, Executive Director of the American Jewish Congress:

"Unfortunately, our indignation at segregation and other forms of racial discrimination is frequently in direct proportion to the remoteness of the evil. As the problem approaches us our indignation recedes. Many of us are horrified at *apartheid* in South Africa, incensed at segregation in the South, but cautious and circumspect when confronted by patterns of segregation in housing, employment or education when they occur in our own communities."

It seems not to have occurred to the members of the American Jewish Congress, who have an elaborate program for bringing about racial commingling at all levels, that they might properly lead the way by organizing a massive foray of Jews into the ranks of Negroes and Puerto Ricans in New York, thereby giving life and spirit to their professed belief in the desirability of all-out integration.

Apropos of this point, it is incomprehensible to the average Southerner why Jews, who have so carefully nurtured their own culture for centuries and who today still maintain rigid barriers against non-Jews in many phases of their cultural life, should be so determined to break down the Southern culture pattern of racial segregation. Yet there is no more insistent and clamorous foe of segregation than the

American Jewish Congress, which takes gleeful delight in
pointing out that two of the six sociological studies upon
which the Supreme Court based its desegregation decision
were conducted under the auspices of the Jewish Congress.

Here is a revealing statement from a propaganda piece
published by the American Jewish Congress under the title,
Children, Together:

"School officials and the community need to recognize
the intrinsic value and importance of providing each child
with an opportunity to become part of a heterogeneous
student body—one that contains different economic levels
and cultural backgrounds—racial, religious, social, and ethnic. For a child cannot learn his mores, social drives and
values—his basic culture—from books. . . . It is the purpose of education in a democracy to provide a child with
the opportunity to associate freely with children of diverse
backgrounds and to permit him goals and aspirations not
limited to those provided by his own socio-cultural environment. This cannot be achieved within the framework of
segregated education . . ."

There, in sum, is the startling thought that children
should not be permitted to be educated in their natural environment, but must be subjected to one made artificially
polyglot. Contrast that view, now, with this observation of
William C. Fels, Associate Provost of Columbia University:

"University faculty members set high educational standards for their children, as you would expect. The problem
for them has not been caused by the students being Negroes
or Puerto Ricans but BY THE SOCIO-ECONOMIC COM-
POSITION OF THE GROUP AND WHAT THIS MEANS
IN PRACTICAL TERMS FOR THE EDUCATIONAL
PROCESS" [capitals mine].

Obviously, "socio-economic composition" of a school
group means nothing to the American Jewish Congress. Nor
does the Congress look kindly toward any arrangement
which permits parents to have a voice in deciding where

their children shall attend school, unless that voice echo the integrationist cry of the AJC.

The authors of the propaganda pamphlet, *Children Together*, designed primarily as "a manual for study groups on integration in public education," seem particularly indignant over the "gerrymandering" device whereby school lines are drawn so as to exclude non-white pupils from certain schools. "This tactic," they cry out, "is clearly illegal and can be remedied in the courts."

Yet, with that blindness which affects so many "liberals" when they are asked to see an opposing point of view, these purveyors of the AJC creed turn right around, three pages later, and call for reverse gerrymandering to achieve the goal of integration:

"Rezoning calls for official redrawing of school district lines in order to achieve a more heterogeneous student group in particular schools—breaking the segregated pattern and eliminating gerrymandered school districts. . . . School boards should avoid selecting school sites that are located in racially homogeneous areas. In selecting school sites an effort should be made to locate new schools in 'fringe areas,' that is, areas that have a mixed racial composition or are within easy reach of several racial or ethnic groups . . ."

Whether the North will be submissive enough to swallow that dose at the hands of the American Jewish Congress is something that only the North can answer. The Southern answer to that line of reasoning is a resounding "No," for now, and for as long into the future as present-day Southerners can see. And in their refusal even to consider such a proposal, Southerners have good legal grounds, stemming from federal courts as a direct consequence of the Supreme Court's desegregation decision itself.

What is proposed by the American Jewish Congress, and what is being done by the New York City School Board in its program of forced integration, actually is a discrimination against children on account of race, since the plan involves moving whites, blacks, and others as pawns in a vast sociological experiment. It is significant, although apparently not to many New Yorkers, to note what the federal district courts most intimately involved in the Supreme Court school cases have had to say on that general subject since the 1954 decision. Mark these works of the three-judge court which carried through on the Kansas case (Brown v. Board of Education of Topeka) in October of 1955:

"Desegregation does not mean that there must be intermingling of the races in all school districts. It means only that they may not be prevented from intermingling or going to school together because of race or color. If it is a fact . . . that the district is inhabited entirely by colored students, no violation of any constitutional right results because they are compelled to attend the school in the district in which they live. . . ."

Another strong case in point, at least insofar as the federal court language is concerned, is provided by the South Carolina (Clarendon County) case. When that case came back before a three-judge court in July of 1955, this is what the late Senior Circuit Judge John J. Parker said for the court:

"It is important that we point out exactly what the Supreme Court has decided and what it has not decided in this case. It has not decided that the federal courts are to take over or regulate the public schools of the states. It has not decided that the states must mix persons of different races in the schools or must require them to attend schools or must deprive them of the right of choosing the schools they attend.

"What it has decided, and all that it has decided, is that a state may not deny any person on account of race the right to attend any school that it maintains. . . ."

Another Hebrew organization which actively works for integration is the American Jewish Committee, described by one of its officers as larger and older than the American

Jewish Congress, but like it, devoted to the purpose "of reducing anti-Semitism and increasing intergroup cooperation." In reply to a question asking why the Jewish Committee is concerned with the matter of race relations concerning public schools in the South, this response was forthcoming from the Committee's New York headquarters:

"The answer is that the American Jewish Committee recognizes the interrelatedness of minority group problems, in that a successful threat or challenge to the civil rights of any minority group ultimately affects other groups as well."

But lest it be assumed that organizations such as the American Jewish Congress, the American Jewish Committee, B'nai B'rith and its Anti-Defamation League speak for all Jews in America, it is noteworthy that many a Jewish Southerner stands firmly for continued racial segregation in the public schools and just as firmly opposes the interference from national Jewish organizations purporting to speak for Jews generally. One evidence of that split within the ranks of American Jewry is a little publication called *A Jewish View on Segregation*, written by a Jewish member of a Mississippi Citizen's Council and published by the state's Association of Citizens' Councils. In it the author points out several facts well-known to Southerners, if not to Northerners:

Numerous Southern Jews are members of Citizens' Councils.

A Jewish attorney, William Gerber, of Memphis, played a leading role in the Congressional investigation of the impact of racial integration upon the public schools of Washington, D. C.

The Citizens' Councils are not anti-Semitic.

Apropos Gerber, it is revealing to note these extracts from a letter he wrote in February of 1957 to Henry Edward Schultz, national chairman of the Anti-Defamation League of B'nai B'rith:

"My appointment was wholly unsolicited. It was made

after I had acquainted the members of the subcommittee
with the fact that I was born in Russia, that I was a Jew, that
I was a past president of the local B'nai B'rith lodge, and
that after admonishing some of the members of the subcommittee that my sympathies would naturally lean toward
minority groups . . .

"Why the Anti-Defamation League should have become
so saturated with its importance in this highly controversial
matter is beyond the comprehension of thousands of American Jews who have not been consulted or given an opportunity to express their views on the merits of this policy. A
small group of so-called leaders in the order, who are bi-
ased in favor of integration, are attempting to speak and act
for thousands who do not support your views and resent
reading in the press your partisan criticisms on a matter that
does not come within the purview or functions of the league.

"The NAACP was created for the purpose of advancing
the causes and protecting the interests of the American Negro. The Anti-Defamation League of B'nai B'rith was created for the purpose of preventing the defamation of Jews.
If you will let the NAACP take care of the Negroes and con-
fine the best efforts of the Anti-Defamation League along
the lines for which it was created, we will all be much better off."

Statements such as Gerber's reflect the demonstrable fact
that Jews have met with more tolerance, more acceptance,
and have become better assimilated in the South than in any
other part of the nation. The proof of that is spread throughout Southern history, and has been evidenced by the selection of Jews for major political roles by non-Jews who gave
them their confidence and their support. The list is long,
and includes distinguished judges, Congressmen and Senators.

The fact that ALL Jews do not subscribe to their views is
well-known to the leaders of the American Jewish Congress
and may be responsible for the patronizing and belittling

attitude they take to their dissident brethren. Listen to these condescending words from Shad Polier, AJC vice president and chairman of its Commission on Law and Social Action, as he speaks in 1957 to an NAACP convention in Detroit:

"The organized Jewish community of today is united against racial segregation. Not a single responsible Jewish organization defends that institution and virtually all have spoken out against it. . . . In all this, I am talking of the *organized, vocal* part of the Jewish community. . . .

"A few, very few, Southern Jewish communities not only have embraced the program of silence for themselves but have sought to impose it on their Northern brethren. Falling into the trap of viewing non-Southern Americans as 'outsiders,' they have demanded of the American Jewish Congress and all other national organizations 'an immediate cessation of any overt action . . . on behalf of the Negro.' Since I am here [at the NAACP convention], it is not necessary for me to say that the American Jewish Congress has rejected this demand."

Unfortunately, there is the danger that the proliferation of semi-religious propanda directed toward integration may result in a by-product of Southern hostility against some of the agencies which prepare and disseminate such preachments. Sociologists such as Dr. Robin M. Williams, of Cornell University, have suggested that feelings aroused against the Negro might spill over into other fields. The Associated Press story of January, 1957, which carried that warning, made reference to Catholics and Jews as possible recipients of prejudice arising out of what Dr. Williams calls "whipped up" feelings.

A more valid warning might be aimed at Jewish, Catholic and other religious groups which themselves invite retaliatory prejudice by their own criticism and condemnation of the South. The matter is not so much one of anti-Negro feeling "spilling over" into other fields as a matter of Catholic, Jewish, and other organized groups engendering prejudice

against themselves. If they would leave the South alone,
Southerners would be only too happy to leave them alone
or, better still, to continue holding out to them the hand of
fellowship which has brought them more intimately into the
fold of native culture than has been true in any other part
of the country.

7

Latter-Day Abolitionists

THE integrationists have succeeded, through their long years of persistent and persuasive propaganda, in dragging the school segregation question into the realm of morality. In doing so, they may have achieved a major purpose and a major advantage, but they have simultaneously laid the basis for opposition which, by invoking morality on *its* side, becomes all the more resistant to change.

So long as social problems grow out of disputed facts, or even out of contrary opinions, there is hope of reconciliation or compromise. The application of good sense and good will, coupled with a studious examination of the facts of the matter, frequently can resolve differences and result in what the Quakers call, with apt phrase, "the sense of the meeting."

But once a controversy becomes enmeshed in opposing *moral* values, the likelihood of an amicable solution fades away into nothingness. For one thing, advocates on each side then promptly discard all thoughts of compromise, saying fervently, albeit sometimes fatuously, that "right is on our side." Today's integrationists, like yesterday's abolitionists, proceed on the adamant assumption so virulently stated by the anti-slavery, anti-Southern, anti-segregationist Charles Sumner: "There is no other side." When such dogmatic morality enters the picture, reason flies out the window.

In this fight over the issue of racial segregation, the cause of "morality" so piously advanced by the integrationists falls flat because there is no sense of "immorality" on the part of the segregationists. Despite the refusal of the NAACP and its colleagues to recognize or acknowledge the fact, there is a widespread and honest conviction among hosts of white Southerners that racial separation is a positive good for BOTH races, at least at this stage of the cultural development of the two. There are, of course, countless Southerners who do not foresee any time when racial intermingling will be desirable or inevitable, but even those who do admit that possibility are for the most part sincerely opposed to integration at present.

Being of that mind, they feel no sense of wrong-doing in seeking to preserve a social structure they genuinely feel to be right, proper, and desirable. Consequently, these Southerners are not being influenced by the efforts of their integrationist preceptors to shame them into another way of life. Instead of giving rise to any sense of contrition and correction, all this moralizing by the integrationists simply antagonizes Southerners who are satisfied that their course of conduct is the correct one in this time and in this place.

A statistical bolstering of this argument comes from the National Opinion Research Center, which published some findings on "Attitudes Toward Desegregation" in the *Scientific American* of December, 1956. The article, by Herbert H. Hyman and Paul B. Sheatsley, tends to discount the existence (at least in the minds of most Americans) of any "moral dilemma" between segregation practices and the traditional American concept of "fairness" and "equality." According to Hyman and Sheatsley, "a majority of the U.S.

people have not considered Negroes to be mistreated.

"To the question, 'Do you think most Negroes in the U.S. are being treated fairly or unfairly?' about two-thirds of the respondents have consistently answered, 'Fairly.' Southerners have been even more prone than Northerners to say that Negroes are treated fairly. . . . It would be difficult to prove the point, but certainly a study of the comments people make in answering the question reveals little soul-searching, hesitation or feeling of guilt. . . . What these findings suggest is that the appeal to the American creed of fair play as an argument for integration is not a widely effective argument."

The findings of the National Opinion Research Center in this respect are at considerable variance with the hypothesis posed in Dr. Gunnar Myrdal's voluminous work, *An American Dilemma*, wherein he postulates in the very title of his book that there is a continuing, uneasy, and guilt-ridden conflict between what he calls "the American creed" and racial segregation. The difference may well lie in the fact that the NORC set about finding out what people actually think, whereas the pro-integration sociologists who aided Myrdal influenced his writings, consciously or unconsciously, by reporting on how they thought people SHOULD think.

The NORC report, based on the findings of more than 200 resident interviewers located in a "master sample" cross-section of American cities and counties, also embodied data somewhat at variance with the claims of propagandists who advance the argument that only the South opposes integration.

"In the U.S. as a whole," the article states, "60 per cent of the whites interviewed favored integration on public transportation facilities, 51 per cent did not object to living near Negroes, but only a minority of 48 per cent supported school integration . . . Perhaps the most striking result here is the fact that among the three aspects of integration, the North is the least tolerant toward residential proximity, while the South is more tolerant toward this than toward desegregation in schools or transportation."

This Northern opposition to white-Negro proximity in housing brings to mind this Negro analysis, quoted by Bem Price in his Associated Press survey of Southern sentiment in September of 1954:

"Up North they don't care how high you get, just so you don't get too close. Down South they don't care how close you get as long as you don't get too high."

But to revert to the NORC opinion report, it reflected a moderating attitude toward racial associations over the period from 1942, when the questions first were put to interviewees, and 1956, which provided the basis for the latest conclusions. But even the gradual change coupled with the accomplished fact of school desegregation in some hitherto segregated schools had not brought about acceptance of integration by even a majority of the residents of the affected communities. Where integration in schools had been achieved by 1956, 69 per cent of the white people still opposed desegregation. Thus, adds the report, "It is clear that those authorities who have integrated schools in the South have not had a majority mandate from the people. Rather, these leaders seem to have utilized their constituents' relative tolerance to push on ahead of public opinion."

The article also noted that young people, of both the North and the South, indicate a greater willingness than their elders to accept integration. That is not a surprising finding in itself, for youngsters are ever inclined to be more liberal in outlook than older folk. Southerners who have observed that phenomenon over a period of years likewise have observed that as young people mature, marry, and become parents that their attitudes become increasingly conservative in general, and far less integrationist in particular.

Most adult Southerners feel a sense of positive obligation in resisting integration, although the feeling seldom hits print and never gets across to the public outside the South.

Resistance, albeit lawful resistance, becomes a duty of those white (and black) Southerners who sincerely feel that integration is wrong—morally and materially. It should be obvious to all by now that there are millions of Southerners to whom indiscriminate racial mixing is not only distasteful, but actually improper, offensive, and hurtful to the integrity of dignity of the two races. To deny these persons the right to follow their own consciences in the matter of race relations is to stigmatize their sincere beliefs and force them into a mode of conduct shaped by persons with other and opposing views.

But if the non-Southerner will acknowledge the validity of these firmly-held convictions and admit of the right of Southerners to hold views at variance with his own, then in all fairness he should acknowledge the right of the Southerner to exert his every legal effort to preserve the standards and customs which to him are worth preserving.

The non-Southerner also would do well to realize that man's spirit of resistance may be strengthened rather than crushed by oppression, whether real or fancied. There is a measure of perversity in all men (those of the South have their full share) which makes them say, "We will not," when someone commands, "You must."

If proof be needed of that trait of human nature, it is readily and amply supplied by the reaction of the South to the pressures applied by the Abolitionists in the months forerunning the War Between the States. Robert S. Henry felt that when he wrote these lines in *The Story of the Confederacy:*

"One of the tragedies of the War Between the States while it lasted and for many years afterward (perhaps even to this day) was that neither side could realize or appreciate for what the other was fighting. To many of the North, the war of the South was a wicked and causeless rebellion undertaken to keep black men and women in slavery; to the like-minded in the South, the war of the North was a design of conquest and subjugation, hypocritically masked as a crusade for freedom. In this poisonous atmosphere of distrust, in this clamor of the vocal extremists, there was scarcely chance for the men of moderation to be heard, and less for them to be heeded."

That last sentence of Henry's could have been written only yesterday, and in fact IS being written in almost the same language by some writers of the moment, both North and South. But moderation, by very definition, is a less powerful force than extremity. When two opposing pressures are brought together, whatever lies in between gives way unless it is strong enough to withstand BOTH pressures.

The only hope for a resurgence of moderation in the segregation fight lies in a lessening of the anti-Southern pressure which provoked the pro-Southern reaction. Thereafter could come middle-ground talks, aimed NOT necessarily at integration (which is the only subject most "moderates" wish to discuss) but at determining what course will best serve the people and meet the needs of the individual communities of the South. Otherwise, the issues tend to resolve themselves into conflicts which take on the absolute qualities of black versus white.

Anything that pits the Southern white against the Southern Negro simply because of color does a disservice to both. If there be any peaceable adjustment of the complex problem of race relations, it must be bi-lateral. Somehow, somewhere, and sometime, there must be a meeting of the minds for the formulation of a pattern of peace, progress, and prosperity for both races. Such a pattern can hardly be expected to emerge from an atmosphere laden with racial animosity. Yet such animosity is bound to spread and deepen with every arbitrary act based solely on racial considerations.

If the integration issue is forced to the point of an ultimate setting of white man against black man on a basis of color alone, then the consequences will indeed be fearful.

Yet just that sort of an eventuality is embodied in the constant drive of the NAACP and the rest of the "Do-gooders Alliance" toward integration by force.

Already the intensity of the controversy has driven most of the "moderates" from the field of public debate. If the fight gets hotter, then inevitably sides will have to be taken on a basis of color alone, and that means black versus white in every sphere of Southern life. It will mean that nothing will exist between the two opposing camps save a no man's land into which individuals venture at considerable risk.

One of the South's "liberals" who has publicly expressed his opposition to compulsory segregation warns of the consequences of compulsory integration. Speaking for his like-minded moderates, William Faulkner wrote in *LIFE* magazine on March 5, 1956:

"But if we . . . are compelled by the simple threat of being trampled if we don't get out of the way, to vacate that middle where we could have worked to help the Negro improve his condition—compelled to move for the reason that no middle any longer exists—we will have to make a new choice. And this time the underdog will not be the Negro, since he, the Negro, will now be a segment of the topdog, and so the underdog will be that white embattled minority who are our blood and kin. . . ."

Such a complete severance of relations between whites and blacks already has been hinted at in a mid-summer 1957 statement of the Lieutenant Governor of Alabama, Guy Hardwick:

"All white men will, of necessity, be drawn together by common bonds of resistance. And I predict they will refuse to employ, feed, clothe, or otherwise aid or assist Negroes if the latter insist in disrupting and upsetting our way of life in Alabama."

What Lt. Gov. Hardwick forecasts will be hard on white Southerners, and harder on black Southerners. It would mean the loss of millions of dollars in business by white firms, and the loss of even more millions of dollars in wages by Negroes. It would mean a drastic alteration in the pattern of agriculture all over the South, at the expense and to the occasional ruin of the white farmer, but to the exclusion and to the certain ruin of the Negro farm laborer, tenant, or sharecropper. It would mean a tragic set-back to the entire region in every conceivable way; but even that realization might not suffice to head it off if white Southerners are goaded beyond their limits of tolerance.

The News and Courier, of Charleston, S. C., gives this unhappy estimate of such a situation (July 23, 1957):

"If and when a showdown is forced on the South, the whites will prove themselves richer, stronger, smarter and more numerous than the Negroes. They are also on home ground. It would be difficult to drive them out of their positions even with the bayonets that President Eisenhower assures the public he has no intention of using. To tear up the South for the sake of empty promises of 'equality' would be more ruinous to the Negroes than to the whites."

Integration, to the non-Southerner, is a matter of hypothesis, perhaps caught up with the stuff of "brotherhood" and "democracy" as spuriously applied to the issue. Integration will not affect HIS way of life one whit; it will not compel HIS children to enter a strange and strained school world where cross-currents—cultural, moral, and intellectual—will create such discord as to nullify the learning process; it will not evoke in HIM the perpetual concern over the possibility of physical strife flaring up within or without the classroom, or within the community itself. No, to the non-Southerner, all this is academic—an interesting sociological experiment bedecked with the outward trappings of altruism but internally loaded with explosive potentialities.

Yet this non-Southerner is all too willing to acclaim the Supreme Court for its determination to reorder the life of a quarter of the nation; to applaud the President for dispatching combat-hardened troops into the South to enforce integration; and to sustain self-serving politicians who use the issue as a vote-getting device.

All this makes for an unwholesome rejection of the American belief that government derives its just powers from the consent of the governed. The arbitrary action of nine men who comprised the Supreme Court of the United States in May of 1954 not only swept aside the legal precedents of generations, but in effect established a new form of school government in a large area of the nation, without in any wise seeking the consent of the people most affected by that major alteration in the governmental structure.

There is something essentially repellent to the American sense of fair play in this manifestation of federal authority. As reported time and again by observers on those scenes where integration has actually been achieved, the general public even in those areas remains opposed to that pattern of racial admixture and would much prefer separation of the races in the public schools. Yet the will of the people counts for nothing. Significantly, the federal authorities have not even sought an expression of the will of the people on a national level to determine whether they support the action of the federal judiciary.

The time may come when the federal government will have to decide precisely how ruthless it is willing to be in compelling Southerners to accept race-mixing on terms unacceptable to the South. It must decide whether it is willing to impose a major injustice upon the entire South in order to correct whatever minor injustice may conceivably be involved in requiring Negro students to study among their own kind, if self-association in fact be an injustice. If in reaching that decision, the government places the preferences of Negroes above the rights of whites, a crisis in the exercise of governmental authority inevitably will arise. There are hosts of Southerners who will submit to nothing short of pure, unadulterated force if the issue is pressed to the ultimate. The depth of their feeling on the subject of integration is as great as that which motivated the Roman Catholic Bishops of the United States in their November 16, 1957, statement with respect to obscenity in literature and motion pictures, wherein they argued for "the right of parents to bring up their children in an atmosphere reasonably free from defilement, the right of children to be protected from grave and insidious moral danger, the right of all not to be assailed at every turn by a display of indecency."

It may be ferociously denied that there is any analogy between integration and obscenity, but in the minds of a myriad Southerners, the one is to be resisted as fiercely as the other. That is a frame of mind which the non-Southerner, and the federal government, may as well accept as existing, even if it may be incomprehensible to those who have never lived among masses of black folk.

All too frequently, non-Southerners make the grievous error of assuming that attitudes which they do not hold, or cannot understand, are consequently of little or no importance. Faulty reasoning of this sort has contributed greatly to the worsening of North-South relationships in the matter of civil rights and race relations. Northerners, and to a lesser degree Westerners, develop their attitudes and impressions concerning race relations in an atmosphere decidedly different from that which prevails in the Southern states. Having neither experience in nor knowledge of the Southern situation, they look at the Southerner's problem as though it were in a non-Southern frame of reference. As a consequence, they come up with assumptions and presumptions which— to their mind—would solve the problem, but which have little connection with the realities of the situation actually confronting the Southerner.

Here again is an instance of the integrationist's unwillingness to deal forthrightly with the facts of life, an unwillingness stemming from a misplaced sense of self-righteousness and a mistaken notion of omniscience. The trait, however, is not peculiar to the integrationist of the 20th Century, but characterized his Abolitionist forebears and other do-gooders throughout history who have sought to impose their sense of values upon others.

One of the most telling analyses of this type of damaging self-delusion came more than a half-century ago from the late Professor Edward Augustus Freeman, an English historian of note. Writing of "Race and Language," Professor Freeman said:

". . . nothing can be more shallow, nothing more foolish, nothing more purely sentimental, than the talk of those who think that they can simply laugh down or shriek down any doctrine or sentiment which they themselves do not understand. . . . Men who sit at their ease and think that all wisdom is confined to themselves and their own clique may think themselves vastly superior to the great emotions which stir our times, as they would doubtless have thought themselves vastly superior to the emotions which stirred the first Saracens or the first Crusaders. But the emotions are there all the same, and they do the work all the same. The most highly educated man in the most highly educated society cannot sneer them out of being."

On the contrary, such sneering generally intensifies the emotions and solidifies resistance. Southerners are not to be cowed into abject surrender of convictions so tenaciously held and so long embedded in their personal and regional consciousness. Nevertheless, they are constantly harassed by latter-day Abolitionists who have it within their power, and seemingly within their purpose, to drive a barbed wedge between the South and the rest of the nation—a wedge which will be much harder to dislodge than to insert.

It is that war of words which threatens to alienate the South from the non-South, precisely as was done in the years leading up to the War Between the States. In retrospect, with what can now be a relatively dispassionate appraisal of what was said by persons in authority, not the

frantic and somewhat lunatic fringe, it seems as strange as it
was distressing that the North and the South came to blows.
If there could have been a "cooling-off" period, if the radi-
cals of the North and the firebrands of the South could have
been removed from the scene, it is quite possible that armed
conflict could have been avoided.

Again today, there is little inclination on the part of the
self-professed saviors of the Negro to understand the rami-
fications of a problem which they know only at a distance.
Nor is there any manifest desire to see that problem as anything other than a moral mission worthy of a Twentieth
Century Crusade—spearheaded by the federal government.

Today, the South would welcome and respond to the platform of a party (either party) which would say, as did the
Republicans in 1861:

"The maintenance inviolate of the rights of the States,
and especially the right of each State to order and control
its own domestic institutions according to its own judgment
exclusively, is essential to that balance of power on which
the perfection and endurance of our political fabric depend."

Instead, what do the Southerners of today get? From
BOTH national political parties, from all three branches of
the central government, and from self-appointed preceptors
in other areas of government, the South gets constant pressure, and incessant vituperation, to yield the few remaining
vestiges of state sovereignty, and to submit to the omniscience of a federal authority which grows by feeding on its
own parts, all under the spurious label of progressive liberalism.

Indeed, this is the age of phony liberalism, and those bel-
licose "do-gooders" who masquerade under the name of
"liberals" are nothing more than dictatorial martinets whose
tolerance extends only to those who think as they do. Loud
in their protestations against suppression of speech in their
favor, they are just as articulate in their own efforts to deny
or denounce the exercise of that same right by those who

may be on the other side. Their concern lies not so much in establishing a climate of free expression, but in exploiting a situation in which they can promenade as saviors of the oppressed. Significantly, they frequently seem relatively unconcerned over working out a passable solution to a pressing problem, apparently preferring to aggravate the situation so that they can continue to play their self-created messianic roles to the hilt.

For a superb expression of true liberalism, turn back the pages of Congressional history to the days of the late Sen. William E. Borah, one of the nation's really great liberals of all time. Amidst a Congressional effort to pillory the South with a so-called "anti-lynching" bill, Sen. Borah had this to say:

"Notwithstanding anything that has been said or that may be said to the contrary, this is a sectional measure. It is an attempt upon the part of the States practically free from the race problem to sit in harsh judgment upon their sister States where the problem is always heavy and sometimes acute. It is proposed to condemn these States and the people in them because it is claimed that they have failed properly to meet and adjust this most difficult of all problems. . . .

"We know now what those [Reconstruction] measures in those days did. They retarded and frustrated the coming together of the people of the different States. They gave us the Solid South. . . .

"It is not in the interest of national unity to stir old embers, to arouse old fears, to lacerate old wounds, to again, after all these years, brand the Southern people as incapable or unwilling to deal with the question of human life. . . . Nations are not held together merely by constitutions and laws. . . .

"I reject the pending measure as fundamentally not in the interest of the white people of the South, not in the interest of the black people of the South, not in the interest of eliminating crime. . . .

"Mr. President, we are dealing with the race problem. We need not blind our eyes to that fact. And the race problem is a problem which does not readily yield to legislative solution, to the rigid demands of the law. . . . Only the patient process of education, the uplifting power of religion, the tolerant, noble-minded men and women who give their thoughts to the cause can remove or mollify such injustices or such harshnesses. . . ."

Those sentiments of Sen. Borah evoked this expression from a newspaperman whose father was a Union soldier during the War Between the States and whose own writing career spanned many years of editorial work on papers and magazines from Connecticut to Oklahoma. Harking back to Borah's statements, Richard Lloyd Jones, publisher of the *Tulsa Tribune*, had this to say:

"Contrast this broad-minded reasoning and understanding pronouncement of Borah with the rabble-rousing, anti-Southern rumblings of those who do not comprehend and cannot contribute to the problem's solution.

"The South makes no move to direct the conduct of the North. Our regional problems are best solved in the regions where they are born. Leave the South alone."

In many respects, the refusal of the North to leave the South alone has had a harmful effect upon the very individuals about whom the Northerners profess most concern—that is, the Southern Negro.

For more than a century, the Southern Negro has been the recipient of harsh treatment directed not so much at him as at those for whom he has become something of a symbol. The white Southerner, frustrated by his geographical inability to strike back at the despised Abolitionists of yesteryear and the equally despised integrationists of today, often has vented some of his spleen on the hapless Negro who happened to be available in the time and place of Southern reaction. This sublimated form of retaliation is hardly laudable, but is nonetheless understandable and natural.

More of it can be expected in the future if Northern integrationists, with or without political backing, continue to
pillory the white South in the guise of helping the black
South.

Meanwhile, the harried Southern Negro, who may or may
not agree with the fulminations made in his behalf, stands
to lose more than he gains. In most of the South, he is now
possessed of all the purely legal rights which are coming his
way, and continued agitation from the North can add little
to his political status, and may subtract a bit by making it
more difficult for him to move through whatever governmental processes may be involved in the exercise of his
political rights. On the other hand, and this has become
quite apparent in the last few years, the Negro becomes—
willingly or unwillingly—the object of the white Southerner's resentment. Basically, the white Southerner has little
quarrel with his Negro neighbor, and frankly despises the
Northern propagandists—including the Supreme Court of
the United States—with far greater intensity than is ever
directed toward the Negro. Yet because the propagandists
and the political persecutors are so far removed from the
Southern scene, there is a natural if somewhat irrational
tendency to deal out vicarious vengeance by striking back
at the only accessible element of the oppressor; to wit, the
Negro.

This striking back does not mean physical violence (although that too sometimes arises) so much as it entails the
more subtle forms of retaliation. When the Northern integrationist extols the virtues of the Negro, based perhaps on
his limited contact with cultured Negroes, the white Southerner promptly begins a public enumeration of the Negro's
vices. When the Northerner prates of "civil rights" the white
Southerner puts increased stress on the principles of "states'
rights." When the Northerner preaches the "brotherhood
of man," the Southerner calls for "freedom of association"
and proceeds to sever longstanding ties which formerly

linked him amicably with his Negro fellow-Southerners.

The net result is that the Northern action brings about almost the reverse reaction from that intended. Instead of bringing Southern whites and Negroes closer together, it drives them farther apart since, in the eyes of the white Southerner, the Negro is identified with those forces which seek to pillory and persecute the South.

The heart of the problem lies in the achievement of community acceptance of whatever pattern of race relations seems best for that community. Where there is acceptance of integration, there can be race-mixing with no one the worse save for the few bitter-enders who must then find some personal way out of a situation which meets with the approval of the community in general.

But where there is NOT community acceptance, no amount of pressure—federal, religious, or otherwise—will bring about a satisfactory situation. The matter of race relations is too close a thing, too personal, too intimate, ever to be disposed of by proclamation or by pressure. It involves the person-to-person relationship grown giant-sized. It embodies the dealings of one personality with another multiplied a million-fold, and it is not a thing to be handled by impersonal formula or governmental edict, although both these things can sometimes smooth away artificial barriers which exist vestigially rather than reasonably.

In the years preceding the Supreme Court decision of 1954, and in a diminishing degree since then, Southern communities were making notable progress in the expansion not only of racial amity but of bi-racial achievement. The granting of equal salaries for teachers was one of the major developments along that line, and is now so well established throughout the region that the exceptions to that rule make the news.

Numerous Southern communities have Negro firemen and policemen, and Negroes long have held postal jobs in many parts of the South. More and more hospitals are according full staff privileges to Negro physicians, and, until the disruption of the Supreme Court decision, there had been an increasing degree of interracial consultation and planning on matters affecting community projects in education, recreation, housing, employment, and other matters throughout the South.

Negro lawyers are in many communities members of local bar associations, just as Negro doctors and dentists are members of professional associations in those fields.

The pressures which built up following the desegregation decision, however, tended in large measure to "freeze" things as they were, and indeed in many cases to undo the good that had been accomplished by slow, patient work over the years. In many a Southern community today, it is well-nigh impossible to arrange an interracial meeting, no matter how laudable the object, without risking an upsurge of bitter accusation and indictment. White persons who formerly were willing and anxious to lend a helping hand in private and in public to their Negro neighbors, now remain aloof, not only because of the tense atmosphere but because of doubt as to the true intent of the Negroes they formerly befriended.

There have been little things, too, which reflect the temper of the people, and perhaps these are even more important in the long run than the bigger outbreaks as being evidential of the disruption in race relations.

Florida's Gov. LeRoy Collins had this to say in March of 1956:

"For as long as I can remember, the Florida A.&M. [Negro] University choir on Sunday afternoons has held vesper services open to the general public. Many white citizens have over the years attended these concerts with great admiration for the excellence of these Negro voices singing the spirituals of their race. But this has almost completely stopped, I am advised. The singing still goes on each Sunday, and it is as good as it has ever been, but there are no longer white listeners. Fear of being labeled integrationists has intimidated them into staying away. . . .

"A Tallahassee television station received a barrage of angry protests recently because a group of Negro singers participated in a program all by themselves.

"These things don't make good sense but they are happening nevertheless. They are just a few of the danger signs. They signal not just a halt in the advancement of good race relations, but actually a decided move backward. They show the insidious results when our people are pulled by one side or the other into the fighting pit of the extremists. . . ."

A Southern editor, highly respected in all parts of the nation, and the 1957 president of the American Society of Newspaper Editors, is Virginius Dabney, editor of the Richmond *Times-Dispatch*. Writing in the *U. S. News and World Report* of March 15, 1957, he said:

"The tragic fact today in the South is that hardly any liaison remains between the white leadership and the Negro leadership. Not only so, but, until a few years ago, Negroes were being elected regularly to city councils and school boards in several Southern States, and it was the most natural thing in the world for white and colored leaders to sit down together for discussion of their mutual problems.

"These things are no longer true. The two races have been driven apart by the rancorous arguments over segregation, with the result that hardly any of the avenues of communication exist in most areas. . . ."

And from the Northern press came an appraisal of the change noted in Tuscaloosa, Alabama, home of the University of Alabama and scene of the riotous demonstrations which prevented the admission of the Negro applicant, Autherine Lucy. This is taken from *The New York Times Magazine* of Feb. 26, 1956, under the by-line of Wayne Phillips:

". . . the educated Southerner and the transplanted Northerner have worked cautiously and diligently in years past toward harmonious relations between the races, breathing life into Christian platitude about brotherhood and respect for man. Much of this was done through the Interracial Committee of the town's Religious Council, a small but potent group of Negro and white leaders organized eleven years ago. . . .

"But the moderate approach was rapidly losing ground [after the Lucy incident]. There was little the newly formed Council could do save issue an appeal for peace and moderation. Public programs which would have brought Negroes and whites together were called off rather than attract attention. Those who favored a gradual approach to integration feared to say anything on that subject. Public officials who had privately assisted the work of the Interracial Committee could no longer afford to be identified with it in any way. Liberal union officials dared not be accused of anything radical on the race issue. The bridge that had so painstakingly been built between the races was all but destroyed."

A tragic by-product of these revived tensions and of the coercive actions which produced them has been the violence of word and deed stirred up among those Southerners who habitually live on the edge of brutality. The South, no less than other regions of the nation, has its share aplenty of individuals who think with their fists in the absence of anything else to think with. There remains more than enough of the "po' white trash" in the South to cause trouble even in times of relative tranquility. These unfortunate and frequently antisocial individuals normally can be kept in line by the forces of law and order, coupled with the pressure of public disapproval—except perhaps when inflamed by liquor, by fleeting passion, or by occasional mob psychology. To the credit of the South generally, these "low-down fellows" (as they were aptly termed in Reconstruction Days) had been losing in both numbers and effectiveness in recent years.

But now, under the emotion-charged atmosphere which has stemmed from Negro and Northern pressures, North and South, these malefactors grow more numerous and more dar-

ing. They detect, or think they detect, an attitude more tolerant of their violence, at least insofar as that violence is directed against the forces which threaten the broad social
order of Southern whites. Consequently, they become bolder
and bolder, not realizing or little caring that they compound
the difficulties of their homeland. Indicative of this has been
the resurgence of the KKK in divers places and under various
names.

All this places an unconscionable burden upon decent
white Southerners who seek to preserve the social order
through peaceable, although adamant, resistance to arbitrary
and unreasonable changes imposed from afar. Engaged as
they are in a cold war of nerves, of propaganda, and of litigation with their Northern persecutors, respectable Southerners
find their efforts repeatedly frustrated and their good work
often nullified by ill-considered actions of stupidity and vi-
ciousness on the part of a mis-guided minority.

And let it be recorded here that the much-maligned Citizens Councils' of the South, save for a tiny handful of maver-
ick organizations masquerading under the same name, have
been a notable influence in suppressing and preventing violence—rather than contributing to it. The caliber of both the
leadership and the membership of the Citizens' Councils has
been such as to deter organized and unorganized violence in
innumerable communities throughout the Deep South. Were
such organizations not in existence, there would by now have
been countless instances in which irresponsible groups or
individuals would have taken illegal measures of their own
devising for striking back at integrationists, white or black, or
at black folk for the simple reason that they happened to be
Negroes. Those who condemn the Citizens' Council movement do so out of an abundant ignorance of the composition
and purpose of the Councils, and out of an abysmal failure to
realize the stark terror which would have reigned in many
areas had there been no such restraining and respectable
force about which segregationists could rally.

8

The Dark Multitude

THE sheer weight of Negro numbers has posed one of the chief obstacles to any mutually satisfactory solution of the race problem in the United States, not so much because of the national ratio of one Negro in ten Americans, but because of the far heavier regional concentration of Negroes in the South. There is the feeling on the part of many Southerners that if Negroes were distributed throughout the nation in the one-in-ten ratio, the race problem would fade away into nothingness. That somewhat sanguine hope is one of the factors which leads most Southerners to favor any program, organized or unorganized, which shifts Negroes from the South to other areas. Along with that feeling, however, is one less altruistic in nature: the desire to have non-Southerners "share the burden."

Out of this all-pervasive Southern wish for a re-distribution of the Negro population have come numerous proposals for a re-shuffling of the Negroes on a nationwide basis. With almost predictable regularity, suggestions are made for the relocation of the South's Negroes into areas where there are now only a few blacks. Some of the recommendations call for governmental sponsorship on the federal, state, or local level; some urge private or corporate initiative for such projects; and some, less publicized and less acceptable to the body of national public opinion, entail the use of economic, social, and political pressures to help persuade Southern Negroes to move elsewhere.

These plans for redistributing Negroes within the United States are recurrent rather than new, but still more venerable are the proposals that Negroes be moved out of the United States entirely and into other lands. That sort of a suggestion began to make its appearance almost from the time that Negroes first were brought into the American colonies. As early as 1773, two ministers of Rhode Island, the Revs. Samuel Hopkins and Ezra Stiles, sought to raise funds for colonizing free Negroes from America on the west coast of Africa.

One of the earliest and most prominent proponents of Negro colonization was Thomas Jefferson, who suggested such a project to the Virginia legislature in 1777 and who subsequently carried the idea before the national government and urged its adoption throughout the remainder of his life. Here is a sample of Jefferson's views on the desirability of separating the race physically:

"Nothing is more certainly written in the book of fate than that these [Negro] people are to be free; nor is it less certain that the two races, equally free, cannot live in the same government. Nature, habit, opinion have drawn indelible lines of distinction between them. It is still in our power to direct the process of emancipation and deportation, peaceably, and in such slow degree, as that the evil will wear off insensibly, and their place be . . . filled up by free white laborers."

Two other notable Americans subscribed to the separatist view in statements a few years after Jefferson's time.

Said Henry Clay in 1829: "If we were to invoke the greatest blessing on the earth, which Heaven, in its mercy, could bestow on the nation, it would be the separation of the two most numerous races of its population, and their comfortable establishment in distinct and different countries."

And this is the view of Daniel Webster: "If any gentleman from the South shall propose a scheme to be carried on by this government upon a large scale, in the transportation of the colored people to any country or any place in the world, I shall be quite disposed to incur almost any degree of expense to accomplish that object."

It remained, however, for private enterprise and philanthropy to make any genuine effort toward colonization of those Negroes willing to be transplanted from America to other lands. The American Colonization Society (formally, The American Society for Colonizing the Free People of Color of the United States) achieved some degree of success in establishing a Negro settlement on the west coast of Africa in that region which came to be known as Liberia. A noteworthy aspect of this endeavor was that its backing came in substantial measure from Southerners, men such as the Georgia slave-holder named Tubman, who freed his thirty slaves and turned them over to the Society with a $10,000 gift.

The Liberian enterprise met with only limited success, and at no time did it attract the enthusiastic support of any large proportion of either Negroes or Abolitionists. The former, even when free, evinced little inclination to leave the United States, and the latter were much more concerned with the immediate freeing of Southern slaves than with the welfare of those Negroes who already had been freed.

The colonization plan continued to crop up in official circles, however, and found strong support from President Abraham Lincoln, if not from Congress. In August of 1862, Lincoln addressed these remarks to a delegation of Negroes who called upon him at the White House to discuss the idea of colonization:

"And why should the people of your race be colonized?

Why should you leave this country? This is perhaps the first question for proper consideration. You and we are different races. We have between us broader differences than exist between almost any other two races. Whether it is right or wrong I need not discuss; but this physical difference is a great disadvantage to us both as I think. Your race suffer greatly, many of them by living among us, while ours suffer from your presence. In a word we suffer on account of each side. If this be admitted, it affords a reason at least why we should be separated. . . ."

Congress appropriated $600,000 for experimentation with Lincoln's plan, but nothing significant came of it. An interesting aspect of the scheme was the prompt and vigorous opposition it aroused from Central American countries when it became known that they were being considered as possible sites for the colonization of American Negroes. The U. S. Minister to Nicaragua, A. B. Dickinson, described that antipathy in no uncertain terms in a communication of September 12, 1862, to Secretary of State William H. Seward.

But neither Lincoln's colonization plans nor any of the numerous others which followed awakened any substantial interest among the Negroes themselves. Since their forcible transplanting from Africa to America, they have shown a decided reluctance to return to their original homes, or to any other location outside of the United States. Negroes have ever been a gregarious race, given more to local meanderings within the framework of familiar settings than to any hazardous ventures into strange and challenging territory, even though such ventures conceivably might take them out of the aura of racial segregation to which they attribute their social blight.

The idea of shifting the Negro population gained a new contemporary impetus toward the end of 1948, when the Birmingham newspaper columnist, John Temple Graves, began promoting the plan in his widely-distributed column. Graves credited a Birmingham attorney, Joseph P. Mudd, with reviving the plan with a proposal involving a voluntary, Congressionally-sponsored program, to extend over a ten-year period. During that period, the federal government would provide transportation and aid in securing housing for Negroes willing to move from the South into other areas. Non-Southern states would be challenged to prove the sincerity of their anti-Southern strictures by agreeing to receive a pro rata share of Negroes and to help them find employment.

The population shift actually was proposed in the Congress in January of 1949 by Sen. Richard B. Russell, of Georgia. Linking the proposal with an attack on President Truman's "civil rights" proposals, the Georgia senator sponsored a bill calling upon the federal government to finance the transfer of 1,500,000 Negro families into Northern or Western states, with their place being taken by non-Southern whites moved into Dixie as replacements. An initial appropriation of $500,-000,000 was asked to get the program started, with $1 billion earmarked for continuation over the program through each of four successive years.

Apparently, not too many people took the Russell proposal seriously. The late Walter White, then executive secretary of the National Association for the Advancement of Colored People, termed it "purely a gesture."

And here is the reaction of the liberal Democratic U. S. Senator Hubert H. Humphrey, of Minnesota, writing at the invitation and in the column of John Temple Graves:

"Helping Negroes to move from the South is not the issue. It is only an attempt to whitewash any future actions by saying that Negroes can move if they want to anyhow. While the proposal provides voluntary assistance, the practical results will hardly be voluntary. The scheme, in fact, was borrowed from the Hitler-Stalin school of shifting populations one doesn't want around. I am indeed shocked that such a proposal has been introduced into the Congress of the United States. . . ."

The Washington columnist Ray Tucker, developing Sen. Russell's plan for a Volunteer Racial Relocation Commission, reported in February of 1949 that something along this line was contemplated under the Russell plan:

Negroes to move *from* these Southern states in these numbers: Alabama—700,000; Arkansas—287,000; Florida—324,-000; Georgia—772,000; Louisiana—600,000; Maryland—20,-000; Mississippi—850,000; North Carolina—620,000; South Carolina—624,000; Tennessee—217,000; Texas—282,000; Virginia—393,000.

Negroes to move *into* these non-Southern states in these numbers: California—566,000; Colorado—100,000; Connecticut—137,000; Illinois—402,000; Indiana—220,000; Iowa —237,000; Massachusetts—375,000; Michigan—317,000; Minnesota—269,000; Missouri—134,000; Nebraska—117,000; New Jersey—189,000; New York—776,000; Ohio—351,000; Pennsylvania—519,000; Washington—160,000; Wisconsin—301,000.

In March of 1949, former Gov. Sam Jones, of Louisiana, made a straightforward presentation to the nation in behalf of a federally-sponsored but voluntary dispersion of Southern Negroes. Writing in *Life,* Jones offered a plan which he described as "a rational adaptation of Northern ideas as they have been presented for two decades." The non-Southern view of the race problem, he said, conceives the solution to be a responsibility of the federal government rather than something to be worked out by the states on their own terms and in their own territory.

If the problem is really a national one, Jones wrote, then it is entitled to federal aid in its solution.

"The solution . . . is the shifting of the Negro population so that it will constitute an equal portion or percentage of the population in every region, state and locality—or as nearly so as is reasonably possible. Senator Richard Russell of Georgia has recently proposed that the U.S. government finance a program to stimulate the migration of 1,500,000 Negro families from the South to other parts of the U.S. . . .

"But the Russell plan must be further implemented. And here we borrow from another idea, popular among those who sponsor civil rights legislation and fight for a solution of the Negro problem. I refer to the Fair Employment Practices Commission. The objective of the FEPC is to eliminate discrimination in employment and thus protect minority groups, such as the Negroes. I do not believe in the FEPC, but a modification of that idea can accomplish the same objective. The plan is simple: let Congress pass a law requiring every employer of ten or more people engaged in interstate commerce to set aside ten per cent of all jobs for qualified Negro applicants who seek the same and make it a crime for any employer to refuse such employment. This would apply, of course, throughout the U.S. . . ."

As might have been expected, the Jones proposal met with little response from the Northern champions of integration, civil rights, and FEPC legislation. Their concern is not a matter of offering genuine help for the Negro or solution for the problem. They wish to harry the South, to belabor it from afar for political purposes, and to superimpose upon it a Northern "solution" which not only would agitate it all the more, but—of vastly greater importance to non-Southerners —would keep the problem off their hypocritical hands.

The year 1957 brought another revival of the resettlement idea, this one going so far as actually to involve the incorporation (in Georgia) of the American Resettlement Foundation, Inc. The non-profit enterprise was chartered to "assist the underprivileged persons of the United States to obtain adequate housing facilities . . . so that such persons will have an opportunity to better their way of life and standard of living." Freely translated, that means that Negro families from Georgia would be transported North and established in hitherto white neighborhoods. Funds were solicited for the organization in the closing months of 1957, but the movement drew opposition from much of the Southern press as well as from some of the region's staunchest segregationists, who feared it might boomerang.

If we accept, merely for the sake of argument, the Supreme Court's hypothesis that Negro children cannot fully develop personality or be properly educated except in the company of white children, then a logical extension of that premise discloses how preposterous it is to seek an intelligent application of that unintelligent doctrine. The fact of the matter is that there simply are not enough white folks in the South to meet the Negroes' alleged need for white company.

What does the Supreme Court consider to be an acceptable ratio of white children to black children, or vice versa? The Court nowhere handed down any formula as a guide, but merely directed that the Southern schools be re-ordered so as to avoid generating any "feeling of inferiority as to their status in the community" on the part of Negro children.

It might be logical to assume that the Supreme Court was thinking in terms of national averages when it said "separate educational facilities are inherently unequal." Since the nation-wide ratio of Negroes to whites is approximately one in ten, then let's try that formula for size on a Southern state—say, South Carolina.

A major obstacle to the application of that formula to South Carolina immediately arises because the state has roughly forty per cent Negroes in its total population instead of the ten per cent which characterizes the nation as a whole. Negroes could not possibly achieve the advantages inherent in exposure to a ninety per cent white population unless some drastic action be taken, either importing more whites, or exporting some of the state's surplus blacks.

The state conceivably, and with all propriety, could call on its Northern neighbors to supplement their denunciations with deeds, and could ask that enough surplus whites (those in excess of ninety per cent of the population) be sent into South Carolina so that the proper ratio could be attained. It might be that some of the nation's leading figures in executive, judicial, and legislative posts would take advantage of the opportunity to have their own presently-segregated children enjoy the fruits of integration by journeying to South Carolina.

On the other hand, the state might work toward the transplanting of excess South Carolina Negroes (there were about 693,000 over and above the ten per cent quota on the basis of the 1950 census) into non-Southern states which fall below their Negro quotas. The possibilities here are wide and varied, but as an example, South Carolina could send about 529,000 Negroes into the State of California, where they might be welcomed by Chief Justice Warren and Vice President Nixon as harbingers of the happier days which would come with an increase of California's Negro population to the ten per cent national average.

That would still leave South Carolina with a surplus of some 164,000 Negroes, but they could be absorbed easily by the State of Minnesota (home of Sen. Hubert Humphrey). Minnesota, incidentally, needs 281,000 more Negroes to bring its colored percentage up from less than one-and-a-half per cent to the average ten per cent ratio. Minnesotans would have to recruit Negroes from additional Southern states in addition to drawing on South Carolina.

Meanwhile, back in South Carolina, the public school administrators might then find their way out of the dilemma which now confronts them. Consider their present plight for a moment:

If they integrate on the basis of current population distribution, they will put twenty-seven white children into a class with three Negro children in the schools of upstate Pickens county. At the same time, they could put only three white children with twenty-seven Negro students in the Summerton District schools of Clarendon county.

Obviously, the same results in personality development could not be obtained, since the Clarendon Negro children would benefit by exposure to only three white children, while those Negroes in Pickens schools would receive a nine-fold benefit, being in company with twenty-seven whites.

Of course, it would be difficult to re-distribute the white and Negro youngsters so that all would profit by the same degree of exposure to each other, but by that time, perhaps the New York City experiment in racial re-shuffling will have produced some effective recipe for boiling all schoolrooms down to a common stew.

Some difficulty might arise if scattered whites and Negroes sought to insist on some imagined right to select their own place of residence and school of attendance, but the Supreme Court certainly would tolerate no assertion of any such fancied privilege as that of choosing one's associates. But while awaiting the Court-directed millenium, do Southerners begin to export Negroes or import whites in order to conform to the national standard?

On a less artificial note, the continuing shift of American population holds promise of easing the South's racial problem, and converting the whole matter of race relations from a regional to a national level. The biggest single factor in this redistribution process is the out-migration of Negroes from the South into other regions. There's a catch-phrase in the South these days which sums up the flux of America neatly in these words:

"Cotton's moving west, cattle are moving east, Yankees are coming South, and Negroes are heading North."

The Negro move to the North is nothing new, however, for that trend began back in the days following World War I. With a few lapses, it has continued ever since, and was accelerated following World War II. In the years preceding the War Between the States, more than ninety per cent of the nation's Negroes lived in the South. In 1900, the South still had 85.2 per cent of the nation's Negroes, but by 1950 that figure had fallen to 62.5 per cent.

Today, the Negro tide continues to flow North—and West —with an accompanying lowering of the incidence of Negroes in the South and a raising of that incidence elsewhere in the nation. In the half-century between 1900 and 1950, while the Negro population of the South was increasing twenty-five per cent, it was increasing at a national rate of seventy per cent, and at the phenomenal rate of 332 per cent in the non-Southern states. During that same period, the white population of the South increased at a rate higher than that of either the nation as a whole or of the non-Southern states as a group. Obviously, a continuation of this trend will spread Negroes throughout the United States rather than having them concentrated in the South as they have been in generations past.

However, the exodus of Negroes from the South has not resulted in anything like an even spread over the rest of the country. Negroes are becoming more and more addicted to urban life; and as they leave the South, they generally head for the larger metropolitan areas of the North and West.

There is evidence that a substantial proportion of the Negroes who migrate to Northern cities already have undergone some measure of urban living in the South. It would appear, therefore, that there is a two-phase movement of rural Negroes to the North—first into a Southern city, and thence to Chicago, New York, or elsewhere.

A measure of the flow into the North is reflected in a 1957 publication from the University of Chicago Press, *The Negro Population of Chicago,* by Otis Dudley Duncan and Beverly Duncan. In their objective study of "residential succession" (the supplanting of one group of residents by another group —in this case, whites by Negroes) the authors evolved such enlightening data as this:

"In brief, Chicago's Negro population in 1950 was sixteen times as large as in 1900 and four-and-a-half times as large as in 1920. With around a half-million inhabitants, the Negro community of Chicago is a metropolis in itself, exceeding in size all but eighteen of the cities of the United States. Of all the cities in the United States—and, probably, in the world— only New York, with three-quarters of a million, has a larger Negro population than Chicago. One out of every thirty Negroes in the United States lives in Chicago."

On the broader picture, without regard to point of destination, Negroes have been moving out of the South since 1940 at a rate of about one per cent of the total Negro population per year. The heavy migration of Negroes during the 1940-1950 decade brought the percentage of Negroes living outside the South up to 37.5, in contrast with the 14.8 per cent figure of 1900.

A continuation of that trend, as pointed out by Drs. John M. Maclachlan and Joe S. Floyd in the University of Florida Press study, *This Changing South*, would result in an almost even distribution of Negro population between the South and the non-South by 1960. That would still leave a higher incidence of Negroes in thirteen states of the South as compared with the thirty-five states of the non-South, but it nevertheless would give other parts of the country an opportunity to cope with what heretofore has been essentially a Southern problem.

But even within the South itself, the Negro population is shifting appreciably—away from the farms and into the cities. Basing their assumption on a continuation of trends which have proved reasonably constant over the last few decades, Drs. Maclachlan and Floyd suggest that in the near future "half of the Negro population of the [Southern] region will be living in cities, nearly a third in rural-nonfarm areas and only a little over 20 per cent on farms."

One factor which undergirds that suggestion is the increased mechanization of Southern agriculture. There is evidence that this mechanization did not in fact drive away farm labor so much as it did replace the labor which left of its own accord. As Negro tenant farmers, share-croppers, and hired hands flocked to the cities during and after World War II for the cash rewards of industrial employment, they left a void which land-owners filled, with varying degrees of success, by crop diversification and mechanization. The new agricultural scheme of things, therefore, makes no provision for the return of Negroes to the farms if they find tough going in the cities, as they did during the depression of the early 1930's. That "barrier," as it is termed in *This Changing South,* is likely to take on added significance when and if Negroes should seek, for one reason or another, to reverse the direction of their migration.

There are no indications, however, that the trend toward the cities will be reversed, either within the South or within the nation. The projection of this Negro urbanization in itself carries significance, for it likely will produce an ever-increasing ratio of Negroes to whites in the larger cities of the South and the non-South. The phenomenal surge of white city-dwellers into suburban residential areas, described in some localities as a "mass exodus," is substantially lowering the proportion of whites living within the municipal limits of most cities. At the same time, the continued influx of Negroes into those cities is using up all available housing, including much of that vacated by the departing white residents. The combined trends of white suburbanization and Negro urbanization is likely to work a drastic change in the complexion of Southern urban life, as it already is doing in other parts of the nation.

Thus, while standing to lose a continuing stream of Negroes to the North and West, the South nevertheless faces new and complex problems if it is to handle the re-arrangement of Negroes (residentially, economically, geographically, educationally, and politically) within the region itself.

Inevitably, the question of race relations will inject itself into the adjustment of these many problems. The matter of school segregation already is an issue, and it is only a matter of time before residential segregation will become acute in numerous areas of the South. Chicago's experience in this regard is meaningful, for it reflects the development of a situation *outside* the South and in an area where racial segregation is presumably dead or dying. The inaccuracy of that presumption, however, is borne out by the facts assembled by the Duncans in their study of Chicago and in their flat statement:

"In fact, on the basis of any indexes proposed to measure the degree of residential segregation of Negro population, Chicago ranks high, if not the highest, among United States cities."

What has happened in Chicago is spelled out in general terms by the Duncans in a paragraph applicable to residential succession in any metropolitan area:

"Specifically, racial succession takes place when one racial category of the population replaces another as residents of an area. Succession occurs over time, and it is convenient to think of it as a process involving a sequence of stages. Referring to the replacement of white by Negro population in a specified area, succession begins with the *penetration* by Negroes of an area hitherto inhabited exclusively by whites. When the number and proportion of Negroes becomes significantly great, *invasion* has occurred. Further increases in Negro population, accompanied by decreases in the white population, amount to a *consolidation* of the area for Negro residence. Consolidation is completed when the area has become exclusively Negro, or virtually so. A final stage, *piling up*, is recognized if, after complete occupation of an area by Negroes, the Negro population continues to increase, entailing an increase in gross and net population density."

The extent to which that "piling up" has occurred in Chicago is evident from the fact that in some such areas the population density had risen to 54,000 persons per square mile by 1950.

Southerners need to concern themselves with the possibility of this sort of development in the South, and to ask what will happen when the rural nature of the South changes; when the region more nearly approximates the rest of the nation in terms of city-country population distribution? That change is already under way in the South, for Southern cities are growing at a pace far surpassing that of cities elsewhere, indeed, twice that of the national average, while the South's rural population is falling.

These changes, however, cannot be evaluated in terms of numbers alone, for despite their growth, Southern cities retain characteristics which set them apart from urban areas elsewhere, especially those of the North and East. In the first place, virtually every Southern city has grown through what might be termed a process of municipal osmosis, wherein the inhabitants of the hinterland surrounding the city flowed into and became a part of the central body. In doing so, they brought with them rural values and attitudes, perhaps more bucolic but not far removed from those already held by Southern city-dwellers, many of whom are themselves removed by only a generation or so from the habitat of the latecomers.

Contrast this osmosis with the process of transfusion which nurtured many a Northern city. Many urban areas which had grown slowly into cities found themselves flooded with streams of non-American immigrants. These new-comers brought with them ideas and attitudes, habits and customs, and even languages, which were foreign to the peoples among whom they set up residence. This Northern pattern of urbanization had a lasting impact upon the way of life of persons living in those heavily-populated centers. Here is an assessment of that impact by Maclachlan and Floyd:

"Under the cultural and technological conditions of a generation or more ago, the urban concentration of population worked against the functioning, or even the very existence, of the informal institutions which are the basic elements of society. The family, under those circumstances, was reduced to the parent-child unit. The neighborhood and the community existed, if at all, in attenuated forms. The rule of custom and the force of community status were weakened greatly by the anonymity of the individual, lost as he was in the nameless and faceless crowd. The immense variety of cultural backgrounds reflected in the largely migrant population led to such a confusion of social values and philosophies that no one code of living could govern the behavior of the whole, so that arbitrary and artificial controls perforce had to take their places."

There, in a single paragraph, is the substance of the cultural distinction between Northern and Southern urban centers. In Southern cities, despite their growing size, the common heritage of the vast majority of urban dwellers contributed to a preservation of "the rule of custom and the force of community status," as Drs. Maclachlan and Floyd express it. That Southern characteristic is being further preserved by the new pattern of urbanization, wherein metropolitan areas are growing *outside* the boundaries of the central city through an accelerated move to the suburbs. Turn again to the words of *This Changing South:*

"For the South, 30 years ago an overwhelmingly rural region, the new metropolitan trend has especial meaning. It seems to be likely that a considerable proportion of the region's people may make the transition more or less directly from the older agrarian way of living to the new metropolitan way, without passing through the phase of centripetal urbanization which other parts of the nation have experienced, and which still impedes their making the same transition. That the urban trend has come to the Southern states later than elsewhere in the country, then, may turn out to their greatest single economic and sociological advantage."

Applying this Maclachlan-Floyd thesis to the Southern tradition of segregation, it naturally follows that such tenacious beliefs will continue to characterize urban as well as rural thinking, at least for some time to come. The growth of self-contained (both culturally and economically) suburban communities will foster a pattern of residential segregation which will effectively lessen the likelihood of school integration. The suburbanites, therefore, may tend toward complacency or indifference on that particular score after a period of isolation from any immediate threat, but the latent resistance to racial mixing will linger indefinitely, nourished not only by memories of other and earlier circumstances, but by the periodic attacks against residential segregation which can logically be anticipated.

Furthermore, if the aggressive race-mixing policies now being pushed by the NAACP and its fellow-travelers in Northern residential areas are duplicated in metropolitan regions of the South, there will be no chance for complacency to develop, even among persons somewhat removed from face-to-face contact with Negroes.

If the issue were not pushed unduly, and if cordial race relations were carefully cultivated by whites and blacks alike, then a higher degree of racial coordination, if not actual integration, might be achieved in big Southern cities than in town and country. A number of factors already are contributing to this likelihood in places like Miami, Atlanta, Charlotte, and a few other cities. For one thing, the urbanized isolation which goes with life in a big city removes much of the day-to-day contact between the races which exists in smaller places. Along with this is the liberality of thought, another wording for "We won't bother you if you won't bother us," which characterizes life in the big city, and which is attributable at least in part to a lessening of family and community pressures for conformity of conduct.

9

White Man—Black Man

THE Southern Negro is faced with the necessity of proving to himself as well as to the region and the nation that he no longer is "a white man's burden." The fact that he already has done so in remarkable degree is at once a credit to his race (or at least to individuals within the race) and a denial of the oft-repeated lament that a Negro cannot arise above his surroundings. The falsity of the latter charge is evidenced on every hand by Negroes who have attained positions of prominence throughout the South, the nation, and the world. They have achieved much in the fields of education, of sport, of art and literature, of music, and others too numerous to mention. Their very eminence testifies to ability which has manifested itself in unmistakable terms—sometimes with white assistance, sometimes despite white opposition, but more frequently in the face of white neutrality or indifference.

In the final analysis, the burden of performance rests upon the individual, and his prospects for success vary in direct ratio to his ability, his ambition, his industry, and his determination to overcome obstacles. Admittedly, the obstacles confronting Negroes—past and present—are formidable and frequently require a greater compensatory effort than would be true for whites. Yet in recent years, that picture was changing, and increasing numbers of Negroes were finding their paths made smoother simply by virtue of the fact that they were Negroes, and were seeking to better themselves. But even before the evolving of that frame of mind on the part of many whites, it was possible for the exceptional Negro to attain exceptional prominence.

Mary McLeod Bethune, who came out of improverished beginnings on a South Carolina farm as the 15th of 17 children born to former slaves, was herself proof of that contention. She fought long, hard and successfully to improve the lot of her race, and she did so in notable degree. Part of her struggle was based on this thought concerning Negroes:

"We all want the same things. We all intend to get them. We've all been hurt and the hurt affects us in different ways. Hurts are sometimes very useful and serve us better than we sometimes realize. They have drawn us together. They have drawn friends to us. They have made us organization minded. They have solidified us and our organizations with the organizations of others on an intelligently aggressive front."

Yet for all of her organizational work, and her continuing drive to improve the standing of the Negro in the United States, Mary McLeod Bethune did not cry out for racial amalgamation. Said she not long before her death on May 18, 1955:

"If our country is torn with controversy over the expansion of social responsibility, over the acceptance of civil rights, it is because a new and more powerful democracy is being born to serve more greatly the people of all races, of this country, and of the world. The one world toward which we are rapidly moving will not, I think, be a world of one race, or a world of one thought, but a world of mutual understanding, respect, and tolerance based on knowledge of ourselves and knowledge of our neighbors."

The remarkable aspect of that statement is its similiarity, in principle, to the formula often cited in this book—the 1896 formula of the Supreme Court for race relations: "natural affinities, a mutual appreciation of each other's merits, and a voluntary consent of individuals."

The prominence of Negroes in their chosen fields gives the lie to allegations that they are forever and eternally relegated to what they like to call "second-class citizenship." Their way has been hard, and still is, but it was becoming easier by the day up until the time that all three branches of the federal government began applying force to the problem of race relations.

But, despite the achievements made by Negroes individually and collectively, there remains too large a measure of truth in the contention that, as a race, they still constitute something of a white man's burden in the South. The Negro in many instances has been content to be a burden, rather than to shoulder the responsibility of lifting his own weight up the socio-economic ladder. The long continuation of this attitude does no credit to either race, since it reflects a tolerance at complete odds with progress. Perhaps tolerance is not the right word, for the situation has evolved out of a marked indolence on the part of a large proportion of the Negroes and a notable indifference on the part of most whites.

Look, first of all, at the plight in which both races found themselves after the Confederate War. On one hand, here were white Southerners, decimated in manpower, stripped of material goods and political rights, victimized by hordes of greedy vultures, and possessed only of the spirit of self-preservation and the determination not to submit to a continuation of black rule.

On the other hand, there were the hosts of freed slaves,

shorn of obligation to former owners and puffed up with promises of a new life, yet without either the knowledge or the capacity to create that new life for themselves. Accustomed as they were to white domination, and utterly without the means for independent survival in a chaotic economy, they soon found their dreams of glory dissipated in the cold light of Reconstruction's aftermath.

Out of this situation came many new adjustments, not least of which was the much-maligned sharecropper system which provided the 20th Century do-gooders with such bountiful anti-Southern propaganda. Yet the system itself was the salvation of both whites and Negroes in many parts of the South, where the whites had only their despoiled lands and where the Negroes had only their labor. It was inevitable that the lands and the hands be brought together, if either white man or black man were to survive.

It also was inevitable that the white land-owner, with his advantages of education, of experience, and of identity with the controlling forces of society, would rise rapidly back into a position of complete ascendancy over the Negro. There were instances aplenty where economic slavery supplanted custodial slavery, without in any real sense improving the status of the former slaves.

But even so, a new opportunity was there for the able Negro with initiative and determination to make for himself a place hitherto denied all but a scarce handful of his race. To their everlasting credit, a number of Negroes did establish themselves as men of substance in their communities. And in the years between then and now, Negroes with those same characteristics have created and occupied positions of self-respect and influence in the fields of business, commerce, education, religion, and the professions, as well as in agriculture. The fact that they did so in the South is a testimonial not only to their courage and capacity, but to the encouragement and assistance given in countless instances by well-wishing white friends.

But what of the vast number of Negroes who have languished in that marginal land of economic indigence, intellectual inertia, and moral laxity? To ascribe their over-long continuance in that state of arrested development to the oppression of white Southerners is to condemn unjustly the white man and to overrate the black man. For even with all the obstacles of tradition and repression which faced them, energetic Negroes still found opportunity to improve their positions far beyond the limits at which most of their race stopped.

It is here that we enter the sociological battleground of racial capacities. And it is precisely here that the white Southerner who has grown up among Negroes begins to scoff at the protestations of sociologists and psychologists who preach the doctrine of equal capacity of whites and Negroes. Without exposing himself to the crossfires of opposing social scientists in that field (where the egalitarians, for the moment, are the most vocal and insistent), the Southern white layman nevertheless raises a premise based on generations of collective on-the-scene observation of the ways of the Negro. The premise is this: That the average Negro (reference here is to the black common denominator, not to the exceptional individual) will find a stopping place of relative contentment far short of anything which will suffice for the average white man. Whether that has anything to do with natural abilities, or whether it be good or bad in the grand perspective is something that mere man cannot say— but he can say with conviction that it is a characteristic which at once impedes the black race's development and confounds the white race's understanding.

In between the industrious and genuinely appreciated Negro worker at the one extreme, and the utterly shiftless drone at the other, there are legions of Negroes who work passably well at their jobs—but only up to a point, at which they stop short. Offer a white man more pay for more work, or harder work, or longer hours, and he generally will take it. Make the same offer to a Southern Negro, and he will find some way of avoiding the extra effort, particularly if the rewards offered are beyond those to which he has geared his way of life. The Negro has his virtues, but too seldom do they include foresight, thrift, and perseverance—those factors by which the white man builds a better life for himself. In saying that, I do a disservice to many a worthy Negro, yet corroboration of the blanket indictment can be found everywhere in the South. Even today, there is still a measure of truth in the evaluation of the Negro given by Ulrich B. Phillips in his definitive work, *American Negro Slavery:*

"Impulsive and inconstant, sociable and amorous, voluble, dilatory, and negligent, but robust, amiable, obedient and contented, they have been the world's premium slaves."

But any application of that description to the Southern Negro of the present must be modified to lessen the stress on amiability, obedience and contentment. The mid-century agitation of the race question, coupled with the desegregation preachments of writers, politicians, and judges, have stirred a sullenness among large segments of the Negro populace, lessening interracial friendliness, engendering suspicion, and prompting discontent. Characteristically, however, the Negro's dissatisfaction has seldom stirred him to any "Operation Bootstrap," whereby he might lift himself to higher levels through his own efforts. On the contrary, the implanted dissatisfaction has taken the form of demands that he be given a place of parity in all things, whether or not he has earned it.

Out of this has grown one of the really difficult problems of the race question—a problem which has been worsened rather than eased by the tactics of Negro spokesmen. Many of the Negro leaders who currently clamor for integration have by their own endeavors achieved positions of relative parity with their white contemporaries in terms of education, financial well-being, and civic accomplishment. But because their acceptance into white society has been so slow and so gradual, they have turned impatiently to the federal courts in an effort to force open the doors. As Alan Paton says in his *Collier's* article of October, 1954: "The cry of the Negro is no longer 'Let my people go'; it is 'Let my people in.'" But the cry is to let all the people in, and that is the specter which haunts the Southerner—not the prospect of voluntarily associating with black men of the same relative standing.

There is reason for such apprehension, going back to the nature of the Negro as reflected in the record of his daily life. Here again, it is meaningless to tell a white Southerner that a Negro has the same hopes and capabilities of the white man, for even a cursory glance at any meter of morality shows that the two races are separated into opposing camps. When the white Southerner sees that illegitimacy among Negroes can run as high as one third of total Negro births; when he notes that the incidence of venereal disease is seven or more times as high among Negroes as among whites; when he notes the commonality of sexual relations among Negroes of all ages, whether married or unmarried— then it is small wonder that the white Southerner shuns such society. And, even more insistently, he refuses to accept any commingling of his children with the black children who have been raised in such an amoral culture. Here again, I do hurt to the number of self-respecting Negroes who seek for themselves and their children the same measures of decency that whites seek. And yet when the issues and the pressures boil up categorically as race versus race, then actions and reactions necessarily take on group characteristics.

Apropos this is the perhaps natural inclination of non-Southern writers and reformers to ascribe to all Negroes the characteristics of the few (frequently well-educated and cultured) Negroes with whom they have come in contact. Furthermore, there is the generally unconscious habit of individuals to attribute to other persons the same motives, drives, demands, and values which actuate themselves. Thus, there results a tendency to attribute to Negroes generally the same incentives which drive middle-class white persons toward goals of social conformity, sexual propriety, and community acceptance. Along with that goes the directly related tendency, as Dollard puts it, to "postulate on their behalf an unhappiness which they [Negroes] do not feel in their lot."

There is a story illustrative of the point: The white man boss who professes wonderment at the capacity of his Negro employe to raise so much unmitigated hell every week-end hears this explanation: "Boss, if you could be a nigger for jes' one Satiddy night, you'd never want to be a white man ag'in!" That story portrays the "earthiness" of the Negro character, the preference for living in the flesh rather than in the mind. The mass of Southern Negroes, regardless of what their future potential may be, are today concerned with the creature comforts of life to the relative exclusion of mental and moral considerations. There is a vestigial and almost childlike love of pageantry, of finery, and of frills and furbelows on the part of the average Southern Negro. His automobile, which entails time payments frequently in excess of home rental payments, is marked by shiny accessories, fox-tails, and other unnecessary but gaudy appurtenances. His home may be without inside plumbing, but if electricity is available he will have a television set. He may sleep three or four in a bed, but chances are that the bed will be covered with a colorful chenille bedspread. And, in a reflection of up-to-date living, he frequently will have a rose-colored or other tinted telephone set, while his wealthier white neighbor remains content with an equally serviceable black set.

Estimates will vary as to just what proportion of the total Negro population can be thus described, but it is substantial. And whatever number it may embrace, it includes hosts of Negroes whose interests and activities lie between the diligent self-improvement of the capable and ambitious black men and the trouble-making incitements of race-conscious agitators.

The obvious fact that hosts of Southern Negroes are relatively content in their present circumstances, or would be relatively content with a reasonable improvement of their lot, constitutes a constant irritant to the militant integrationists of the NAACP and its allied organizations. Since the NAACP, like most organizations of its type, feeds upon dissatisfaction, evidence of contentment are anathema to it. Consequently, there is a constant stirring-up of Negroes with agitation designed to make them unhappy with their lot. And where there is no unhappiness to start with, then unhappiness must be engendered.

The false premises which lead to the "every man a king" concept are employed to stimulate ambition, to generate resentment against others more fortunately situated, and to turn that resentment into a feeling of oppression, whether there be any real basis for such or not. Given enough of this treatment, almost anyone will respond. We have then, in such cases, a situation in which the NAACP is seeking to create a demand for its product—integration—even in the absence of a natural demand. And, just as in the commercial world, advertising is called upon to turn the trick. The brand of living which many Southern Negroes have used throughout the years is assailed as inadequate and unsatisfactory, and the promise of a far superior product, the NAACP brand of racial integration, is held out as the desirable commodity to be sought after. Along with that is purveyed the doctrine that the goal can be attained by agitation rather than by achievement, and herein lies one of the major fallacies of the entire NAACP approach.

There is now, as there was after the Confederate War, a determination that the Negro should not be left free to follow his natural inclinations in adjusting to his environment, but that he must, perforce, be aroused, told of a better destiny, rendered unhappy with his lot, inflamed with desires beyond likelihood of attainment, and prodded into incessant struggle against his surroundings. As a consequence, the constant whining that Negroes are down-trodden, oppressed and discriminated against has inevitably given rise to the feeling that they are, in fact, victimized. This in turn stimulates resentment and a desire to reverse the present balance of things in the South. Negroes who, because of ignorance, incapacity, or sheer inertia, cannot reasonably expect the assumed roles of prominence in their communities now are increasingly demanding of recognition to which they would not be entitled regardless of skin-color. With all this has come a surliness, a false haughtiness, and a rudeness which worsens rather than improves the situation.

And out of this combination of circumstances, augmented by the wilful and gratuitous interference of Northern propagandists and politicians, has come a noticeable lowering in the level of happiness which, for whatever it might have been worth as a desirable intangible, was once a hallmark of the Southerner, white or black.

Yet even as I write these things, I lay myself open to the charge that I set myself as a judge of what Negroes think and why they act as they do. All that can factually be reported is that Negroes act and react in a given way under a given set of conditions. The "why" of their actions is something they alone can disclose. There is always doubt that their own disclosures mirror their real thoughts, since so much of their habitual response to interrogation by whites comes forth in whatever terms seem to them to be most acceptable to their white questioners.

The white man who says he understands the Negro is either a liar or a fool. For all the apparent simplicity of the Negro, he is a complex psychological being, so long beset by adversity and animosity that he has built up a defense mechanism which is difficult for the white man to penetrate.

The Negro is able to dissemble with remarkable effectiveness, to pretend whatever degree of ignorance seems necessary to protect himself and his fellows, and to conceal his inner emotions. Out of this has grown an unwillingness of the white man to place full reliance on anything he is told by the black man. One Southern business man, long known as a friend of the Negro and himself a trustee of a Negro college, summed up his own disillusionment in these words: "You never know what's in the heart of a Negro." Another white South Carolinian, long outspoken in favor of accepting the Supreme Court's integration decision, couched the same sentiment in different words when he addressed the S. C. Council on Human Relations on March 27, 1957. Said James McBride Dabbs:

". . . the Negro is becoming to the white man an unknown quantity—he really has always been an unknown quantity—with a will of his own, with an intention only to be guessed at."

The white man's inability to comprehend, to predict, or to rely upon the Negro's thought processes is a part of the Southern whites' refusal to accept Negroes into their fellowship, or to permit Negro children to mingle with white children in the public schools. Bluntly and basically, the refusal is a vote of "no confidence" in the Negro.

There is a strong element of pathos in the Negro's never-ending quest for admission into white society, and with it is a note of irony that those who come closest to meeting the standards of conduct set by the white man are still excluded from the company of those whites. That particular situation does little credit to the whites who deride Negroes for low standards of health, morality, and social conduct, yet who grant no recognition to those Negroes who do rise above the level of their fellows. Admittedly, the attainment of high personal standards will not automatically break down the Southern opposition to integration, but it would contribute greatly to the establishment of better and broader areas of cooperation and contact between the races.

The problem is not new, and the solution will not be early. A quarter-century before the War Between the States, the perceptive French writer, Alexis de Tocqueville, phrased it in these words:

"The Negro makes a thousand fruitless efforts to insinuate himself among men who repulse him; he conforms to the taste of his oppressors, adopts their opinions, and hopes by imitating them to form a part of their community. Having been told from infancy that his race is naturally inferior to that of the whites, he assents to the proposition and is ashamed of his own nature . . .

"Whoever has inhabited the United States must have perceived that in those parts of the Union in which the Negroes are no longer slaves they have in no wise drawn nearer to the whites. On the contrary, the prejudices of race appear to be stronger in the states that have abolished slavery than in those where it still exists; and nowhere is it so intolerant as in those states where servitude has never been known."

The situation of 1840 is a far cry from that of 1957, yet there is much truth even today in what de Tocqueville wrote. The prejudices of race are not sectional, yet they have been charged against the South as the exclusive property of the Southern white man.

Jerome Dowd, whose 20-year study of the Negro culminated in a 1926 publication, *The Negro in American Life*, has this to say on the subject of racial attitudes:

". . . the feeling of aversion to the social intermingling of two races never arises unless the races exist together in large enough masses to awaken frequent suggestion of consciousness of kind, and intermarriage. In case of such massing together, the feeling of repulsion unconsciously and instinctively arises. For illustration, the white people of California feel a social repulsion to the Japanese but none toward the Negroes, who are not there in sufficient numbers to awaken the feeling; while the white people of the Southern states feel a social aversion toward the Negro, but none toward the Japanese, whom they rarely see. . . . Northern people of the United States who have taken residence in the South spontaneously acquire the same antipathy to the Negro as the native whites. . . ."

Southerners have the feeling that there is an equivalent of a "Gresham's Law" in the world of society as well as in the world of finance. And if bad currency tends to drive out the good in the one field, then bad habits are just as apt to drive out the good in the field of social conduct. Perhaps even more basically, there is the additional fear that impure blood will supplant the pure over a period of time, leading to an inevitable and ultimate corruption of all.

White Southerners have learned at first hand that the two races are widely separated—as groups—not only by law and custom but by conduct, and therein lies much of the basis for the more formal separation. Whatever may be the future of the Negro race, however gratifying its accomplishments may have been since the first slaves were introduced unwillingly to these shores, and however distressing its present outlook may seem, the bald fact remains that present codes of conduct of the two groups are so vastly different as to warrant segregation as a protective device if for no other reason.

The hopes and aspirations of the Negro may be high while the circumstances under which he lives may be low, but this situation does not alter the factual findings which go far toward explaining why white persons, as a category, are unwilling to accept social contact for themselves or educational contact for their children with Negro persons, as another category. These statistical studies which follow are not cited with any intention of demeaning the Negro race, but rather as one vindication of the white Southerner's refusal to accept integration.

Look first at this revealing paragraph in an article prepared for the summer, 1949, issue of *The Journal of Negro Education* by Louis I. Dublin, a vice president and statistician for the Metropolitan Life Insurance Company:

"No comparison of the mortality rates of the two races would be complete without mention of the extraordinary roles played by homicide and syphilis. These two causes are still responsible for far too many deaths among Negroes. The homicide rate among male Negroes in 1946 was 11 times than that for white males. Although a much less frequent cause of death among women, homicide was responsible for 8 times as many deaths among colored females as among white females. The reporting of deaths due to syphilis is notoriously incomplete; yet the rate for this cause among colored men in 1946 was 4½ times the rate for white males, while among females, the ratio of colored to white mortality was over 6 to 1."

To those who attribute the Negro's high rate of illegitimacy and low standard of sexual conduct to social and economic conditions prevailing in the South, the disclosure in mid-1957 of an official report of juvenile pregnancies in the Washington, D. C., schools came as a shock. The report may also have caused some increased concern among white parents who were prepared to enter their children in the integrated schools of the District of Columbia.

It is worth noting that the report in question relates only to pregnancies among students in the JUNIOR high schools of the district. It was prepared by Dr. John R. Pate, director of the District's Bureau of Disease Control and was re-printed in part by the *U. S. News and World Report* of July 12, 1957. The following excerpts were taken from that source and are part of the text of the actual report, with emphasis added in this reproduction:

"During the current (1956-'57) school year there had been an alarming increase in the number of pregnant girls in the seventh, eighth and ninth grades of the junior high schools of the city of Washington coming to the Southwest Health Center to have completed and properly signed physicians' certificates of pupils' inability to attend school. The problem has been increasing over the last two to three years, more than was noted in several years prior to 1954. The fact is that, during the current school year, OUR REC-ORDS SHOW AN INCREASE OF APPROXIMATELY 1,000 PER CENT IN THE NUMBER OF ILLEGITIMATE PREGNANCIES AS COMPARED TO THE 1948-49 SCHOOL YEAR IN THIS AGE GROUP [Capitals mine]."

(Of 190 total pregnancies reported among schoolgirls under 16 between September 10, 1956, and April 10, 1957, 178 were among Negro girls, and 12 among white girls.)

The special report disclosed other findings of particular significance to persons concerned over efforts to force integration of white and Negro students in the District schools. For example:

"The over-all figures for the District of Columbia in the year 1954, insofar as were obtainable, show 3 per cent of the births to whites were illegitimate and 26.3 per cent to nonwhites."

It might be noted in passing that the rate of illegitimacy reported in the District surpasses that shown for Negroes in numerous states of the Deep South.

In looking into the background of the "junior mothers" of Washington, the health service probers found in a study of records available at the Southwest Health Center that 61 of 78 cases came from broken homes, a common characteristic of Negro family life which shows up repeatedly in statistical studies.

"For the most part," the report stated, "they come from large families with a number of children, live in crowded conditions, with a history of separation of parents, common-law fathers or multicommon-law fathers in one family. Some of these junior mothers come from families where this pattern has existed from two to three generations. . . . In discussing the seriousness of the situation, the parents' reaction mostly is one of complacency. . . .

"Certainly, from all indication, an alarming percentage of births in the District of Columbia are illegitimate. In the early part of the 1956-57 school year one school in southwest [Washington] reported over half of the 240 children enrolled were illegitimate."

One further excerpt indicates the moral factor involved in all this:

"Out of the total records of approximately 75 junior-high-school children seen, on only two cases has the girl become legally married to the father of her unborn child. . . ."

For still more light on the Washington "showcase of the nation," note this report from Georgia's Congressman James C. Davis, speaking to the States Rights Council of Georgia, at Atlanta, on Nov. 28, 1956:

"Crime statistics show that throughout the years the Negroes in Washington have committed the bulk of the crimes of violence, although until recently they have constituted about one-third of the population. In 1955, out of 11,072 crimes of violence . . . 9,056 were by Negroes. This is 82 per cent of the total, and the percentage for the last three months of 1955 was 88 per cent of the total.

"Let's look at the District of Columbia health records. A report for the year 1955 made by the District of Columbia Department of Public Health of venereal diseases in children of school age and under, showed 834 Negro children 17 years and under treated for gonorrhea, as compared with 20 white children. Of the 834 Negro children, 10 were under 6 years of age. The total cases of gonorrhea of all ages, children and adults, for 1955 were Negro 10,243, or 97.5 per cent of the total; white 271, or 2.5 per cent. . . .

"Mr. Howard West of the D. C. Department of Public Health testified that in 1955 there were 996 illegitimate babies born to girls of school age in Washington—that is, ages 18 and under. Of these 926 were colored and 70 white; 86 of them were born to girls under 15 years of age, 5 white and 81 colored.

"There were 3,533 illegitimate births of all ages in Washington in 1955, of which 382 were white and 3,151 colored.

"All white births in Washington in 1955 totaled 8,556, of which 382 were illegitimate. The illegitimate white births were approximately 4.4 per cent. All colored births in Washington in 1955 totaled 11,404, of which 3,151, or 27 per cent were illegitimate.

"He testified that it is a close estimate to say that one out of every four colored children in the D.C. public schools is an illegitimate child, and this statement is based on the birth records in his department. . . ."

Is it any wonder, in the light of such disclosures, that proposals for the forcible mingling of Negro and white children should draw such intense resistance from the mothers and fathers of the white children? This parental revulsion of feeling is something apart from the political considerations involved, and constitutes a barrier which for years will prove well-nigh insurmountable in those states where the knowledge of such conditions among the Negroes exists.

Psychologists contend, of course, that race has nothing to do with the prevalence of these undesirable conditions; yet even the jargon in which they make such statements discloses the fact that the practical effects remain the same. Note this observation in a study of *Psychiatric Aspects of School Desegregation*, issued by the Group for the Advancement of Psychiatry in May of 1957:

"Neither delinquency nor communicable diseases are primarily related to race. Both are directly related to the complex social, psychological, and economic forces that form the ingredients of the pattern of inferior status of the Negro. Positive changes on these forces should lessen delinquency and improve the health of Negro children."

That is a hopeful statement, but it does not lessen the fact that those objectionable conditions at the moment ARE linked with the Negro race, and that they will prevail until the race undergoes positive changes in those "complex social, psychological, and economic forces" which make the Negro community what it is. White Southerners are willing, and could be made increasingly eager, to aid the Negro in reshaping his community, but NOT at the expense of white children. That is an intensely practical attitude which might as well be accepted here and now by those who seek to force integration upon an unwilling South.

One of the most disturbing aspects of the picture of illegitimacy is the fact that the ratio is rising instead of falling. It would be logical to expect that the improved standards of education, public health, and earning capacity would tend to stabilize the Negro family, and to improve its level of morality. But on the contrary, the rate of illegitimacy seems to be rising, in the North as well as in the South. Figures already cited for the District of Columbia indicate the alarming increase in illegitimacy in that "promised land."

Equally discouraging trends are in evidence elsewhere. In the city of Charleston, S. C., for example, the rate of illegitimacy had risen to 37.5 per cent of all live births for Negroes in the year 1956. (The rate for white births was 4.6 per cent for 1956, also an increase over previous ratios.)

These distressing statistics are symptomatic of two things, the continuing lack of a community morality among Negroes, and the increasing deterioration of family life with the shift from rural to urban living. As Negroes move from the farms, where behavior patterns are subject to family and church pressures, they find a greater degree of individual freedom in the crowded life of the city. Free from restraints which may formerly have operated upon them under rural circumstances, many Negroes succumb to the promiscuity and sexual looseness of city life, and soon find themselves established in a way of life which is the negation of everything decent, healthy, and respectable.

The wonder is that little sense of community uplift seems to develop with the Negro community itself. And even when it does, it frequently takes a form of segregation itself, as the better educated and wealthier Negroes ease themselves out of the company of the more vicious and depraved blacks and into a social, and frequently a spatial, stratum of their own. Unfortunately, they suffer (in the eyes of whites) from the stereotype which in greater measure reflects the conduct of the very Negroes from whom they themselves have fled.

It is suggested by some public welfare workers of the South that the inability of Negro leaders to work any reformation in the social conduct of their people is due to a Negro lack of confidence in their own leaders. That conclusion may be subject to challenge, but somewhere along the line there seems to be something which obstructs the emergence of any genuine and effective community leadership by Negroes—at least in the sense of social and moral guidance.

Negroes themselves have other explanations of that phenomenon, explanations which lay the blame at the foot of the white man. In his revealing *Saturday Evening Post* articles on "The Negro in the North," (October, 1957) the Negro journalist Carl T. Rowan says:

". . . it is apparent that the proud, responsible Negro will never achieve complete acceptance until he forces society to examine the factors that created the uncouth [Negro] ignoramus and then helps to lift the latter to a more acceptable level."

In support of the contention that Negroes will be as law-abiding, as cultured, and as responsible as the community will allow him to be, Rowan quotes Dr. Mozell Hill, chairman of the sociology department at Atlanta University:

"Negroes have been forced to live together in separate areas . . . they have come to learn and feel that they are different; their life chances and possibilities of full participation in community life are limited. This fact alone accounts for differences in forms of conduct. Thus the chief, and

perhaps only, explanation for deviation in behavior patterns
of Negro families stems from social isolation and its con-
comitants of economic deprivation, emotional frustration,
and cultural starvation."

Implicit in such reasoning, however, is the acknowledge-
ment that Negroes cannot, of themselves, create a community which measures up to acceptable standards of conduct
and culture. And herein seems to lie full vindication of the
challenge posed to the Negro race back in 1912 by Georgia's
Tom Watson:

"The fair test of the Negro's capacity is what he does
when left to depend upon himself."

There is evidence a-plenty of the apparent inability of the
Negro community to do anything for itself AS A NEGRO
COMMUNITY. Real estate developers and landlords of the
South long have complained that investing money in new
and modern housing for Negro families is an extremely hazardous business. They cite instance after instance in which
modern plumbing is wrecked, walls defaced, glass panes
broken, woodwork scarred, and furniture marred or even
destroyed. Bathtubs are used by some Negro tenants as
storage bins for coal.

But one of the most graphic descriptions of the Negro incapacity, or unwillingness, to maintain any standards of
community decency comes not out of the South, but out of
Washington, D. C. Nor is the narrator of this account a
Southerner; he is Rep. Earl Wilson (Republican), of Indiana. These are his words recorded in the *Congressional Record* of June 27, 1957:

"Two years ago . . . the District of Columbia, with financial aid of the taxpayers all over the United States, completed construction of a $677,400 elementary school build-
ing at East Capitol and 55th Streets, N. E. The property,
including a well-equipped playground, covers an entire block.

"Known as the Marion P. Shadd school, it has 26 class-
rooms, auditoriums, cafeterias and all modern facilities.

There are 32 teachers in addition to clerical and maintenance workers. Students total about 1,300, ranging from
kindergarten through the sixth grade. It is an all-colored
school in an all-colored community of modern, spacious
apartments and homes.

"This is one of the finest school plants in Washington or
anywhere else. It is an architectural and cultural landmark,
an institution of which the residents of that Negro community should be very proud.

"However, this beautiful edifice is being destroyed—literally ripped to bits by vandals and hoodlums—while people
of the neighborhood stand by in apparent disinterest. The
Marion P. Shadd school is rapidly becoming a landmark of
shame to the very people it is intended to serve.

"I inspected this school a few days ago. . . . I found
hundreds of window panes broken. Mud and filth have been
hurled against the building. Empty beer cans are scattered
about the premises, piles of filth lie in the doorways, outdoor
electrical equipment and entrance lights broken and destroyed. Three or four windows at the cafeteria end of the
building have been boarded up by the school authorities because vandals break window glass as fast as it is replaced.
Obscene words and crude drawings cover portions of the
neat little frame annex used for kindergarten pupils . . ."

The dismal picture painted by Congressman Wilson
comes as no great surprise to Southerners who long have
noted the general inability of Negroes to establish and maintain even a semblance of community discipline and decency
unless it be superimposed upon them by white authorities.
The picture must come as a shock, though, to those who
have contended that Negroes live in squalor only because
their economic circumstances can support nothing better.
That portrayal is rudely shaken when the Congressman
says the school is located "in an all-colored community of
modern, spacious apartments and homes."

If under such optimum conditions Negroes are so lacking

in pride, in self-respect, and in community consciousness, is it any wonder that white persons shy off from any prospect of integration? And if also those Negroes are unwilling to remain in association with one another in segregated schools, how can they hope that white persons will be willing to associate with them? And if Negroes are not acceptable on their merits, what reason is there to believe they will be accepted by pressure?

The plight of the Negro in this respect was well put by one of their own spokesmen (W. E. B. Du Bois) in these words:

"The Negro of education and income is jammed beside the careless, ignorant and criminal. He recoils from appeal to the white city even for physical protection against his anti-social elements, for this, he feels, is a form of self-accusation, of attack on the Negro race. It invites the smug rejoinder: 'Well, if you can't live with niggers, how do you expect us to?' For escape of the Negro cultured to areas of white culture, with the consequent acceleration of acculturation, there is small opportunity."

Thus Du Bois, who seldom found himself in agreement with Booker T. Washington, gave additional meaning to Washington's earlier advice:

"Let us spend less time talking about the part of the city that we cannot live in, and more time in making that part of the city we live in beautiful and attractive."

There have been other and more recent Negro leaders about the South, and elsewhere, who have had the courage and the perception to tell their fellow Negroes that acceptance by whites requires considerably more than mere legal action.

In February of 1950, Dr. J. A. Long, Jr., of Palatka, Fla., had this to say at the laying of a cornerstone of a new hospital for Florida A. and M. College at Tallahassee (as reported by the Associated Press):

"We are not wanted in white neighborhoods, not always

because of race but often because of risk; not always because
we are slaves but often because we are still asleep; not be-
cause of prejudice but often because we still destroy property; not always because of color but often because of character; not always because we are wanton but often because
we disrespect women. . . ."

Even some of the most outspoken of the Northern publications are beginning to look askance at the incidence of Negro crime. Here speaks the Philadelphia *Evening Bulletin* in
the summer of 1957, when criminal activity by Negroes was
running at an unusually heavy pace in the metropolitan areas
of the North:

"It must be apparent to respected leaders of the Negro
community that much of the manifest animosity against
their race stems from the crimes of violence so frequently
committed by Negro youth. What these disturbed leaders
can do, more than they have attempted, about checking
criminal tendencies which even the police are unable to suppress isn't clear. But the situation challenges their continued
study and activity. . . .

"Welfare workers will say that youthful criminals have
been reared in sub-standard homes without suitable parental supervision. True. But that will not account for the existing condition, which is almost unknown in the South,
whence came the parents of these young criminals in most
cases, if not the criminals themselves. What keeps these
elements under better control in the South? Unfortunately,
the answer is probably fear. . . ."

From the tone of the *Evening Bulletin's* editorial, it is evident that the Philadelphia Negroes have not responded favorably to the type of advice given by one of their own
number, Municipal Court Judge Herbert E. Millen. The one-
time official of the National Association for the Advancement of Colored People had recognized the same problem
more than three years earlier when he addressed these remarks to a Negro audience at Charleston, S. C.:

"My people contribute all out of proportion to their numerical ratio to the crime statistics of Philadelphia. Some 90 per cent of the assault and battery cases are Negroes. If I receive 42 or 43 cases of unwed mothers in the 12 to 14 year bracket, usually 39 or 40 of them are Negroes. Is this because we have lost our sense of moral standards? Are these children naturally immoral? I think not. It is due to a lack of attention by the parents."

That statement challenges the Negro to improve his own neighborhood, to lift himself by his own bootstraps, to establish a reputation for peace and good order which will at once add luster to his own standing and enhance the likelihood of his acceptance by his white neighbors. Unfortunately, the record shows that the average Negro, individually and collectively, manifests an aggressive and argumentative attitude when he sets out to gain equal footing with the white residents of any given neighborhood. An illustration of the contrast between their minority group approach and that of other minorities is recorded in an article published in the June 29, 1956, issue of the *U. S. News and World Report* concerning racial problems of the West Coast:

"Japanese Americans, it is found, want to solve their problems in their own way—through hard work, education and high moral standards, more than by court action or publicity. Already their educational median is higher than that of Los Angeles County as a whole, and their income is considerable above that of the other minorities.

"As a result, many 'Anglo' whites of Los Angeles voice a growing respect for Japanese-Americans—respect that means growing acceptance. And Mexican-Americans are heard to cite the Japanese-American community as an example that their own people should emulate.

"A Mexican-American member of the city council says this: . . . . We are not going to straighten out the problem of discrimination against Mexican-Americans just by holler-

ing about it. What we're after is to do something about it
ourselves—improve our own community, give it a sense of
'belonging,' get the chip off our shoulders."

"A contrasting attitude of militancy and suspicion, officials and others say, often turns up among top Negroes. . . .
One of the best-known white churchmen in Los Angeles
says:

" 'As Negroes become educated, they become more aware
of injustices and discrimination—that's only natural. But
they're inclined to be aggressive and suspicious, and they
hurt themselves by that attitude.' "

The merit of the growing Mexican-American insistence on
group and individual performance is borne out by the example of one of the nation's most famous Mexican-Americans, Federal Judge Harold R. Medina. His youth in Brook-
lyn was punctuated with not infrequent manifestations of
anti-Mexican, or anti-Spanish, sentiment. Yet out of that
practical and personal experience Judge Medina developed
an attitude, not of bitterness, but of determination to make
his way whatever the odds. Note these words of his in *The
Baltimore Sun*'s 1954 series on "This is Prejudice":

"I have the feeling that a whole lot of people who are discriminated against, if let alone and not having constant
agitation, would not get despondent, down in the mouth
and licked. There are lots of things in life you just have to
struggle against, and you have to make the best of it."

Judge Medina gives this formula for combatting prejudice:

"A quiet and persistent way of conducting one's self in
private and public life, without agitation and whining. It's
the way you live, what you do day to day. Talking about it
merely makes it worse."

The Negro suffers also from lack of a good reputation for
honesty. True, there are historical and sociological explanations for much Negro thievery—if so harsh a term may be
used—but nevertheless the Negro stereotype has that reputa-

tion among many of the white employers for whom he (or she) has worked.

Looking far backward, it is easy to see that slaves, who owned nothing they could call their own and who enjoyed little prospect of ever owning anything, would have been hard put to develop a sense of property values consistent with that of their white masters. Things, as such, were to be used, or enjoyed, and since those things generally belonged to the master, and since he himself belonged to the master, then there was no harm done for the one to appropriate the other. The concept of private ownership of property was later in coming, and many a freed slave learned the hard way when he found that what was rightfully his had been shanghaied away by unscrupulous whites AND Negroes who took advantage of his lack of understanding of property ownership and property protection.

Today, something of the old appropriative attitude still lingers among many groups of Negroes. Added to that residual frame of mind is a more modern inclination toward thievery born of economic deprivation in childhood. Youngsters who grow up in squalor and scarcity—crowded into horribly cramped quarters, denied the material and nonmaterial advantages they see enjoyed by white persons—can easily be turned toward theft and its corollary, falsehood.

It is that latter attribute which is so chronically exasperating to the Southern white man and so perplexing and infuriating to the non-Southern stranger on his initial contacts with the Southern Negro. Here again there is a measure of historic justification for the Negro propensity to conceal the truth, but it hardly serves to improve his reputation today. From slavery times forward, the Negro has been the low man on the Southern totem pole—the starting point of suspicion and the terminal point for oppression. Under that situation it was but natural that he should seek to defend himself with what few weapons were at hand. One of them

was words, or lack of words. To this day, there is no finer
actor in the world than the average Southern Negro when
confronted with questions he does not wish to answer. He
can range from outlandish prevarication to simulated ignorance with a display of sincerity which would do credit to
the most accomplished of actors.

Former Gov. Duncan Clinch Heyward, a South Carolina
rice-planter who recorded many a valuable observation of
the times in his book, *Seed From Madagascar,* expressed the
situation in these words:

"Having been thrown much of my life with Gullah Negroes and knowing their natures fairly well, I have won-
dered if they had not inherited from their ancestors a trait
often noticed—that of pretending to misunderstand what
was said to them when it suited their purpose to do so."

The Negro's feigned ignorance or misunderstanding, however, could not and cannot be taken as evidence of any lack
of native shrewdness. Gov. Heyward was on equally firm
ground when he wrote:

"There used to be an old saying among the Low Country
Negroes: 'De buckruh [white man] hab scheme, en de nigger hab trick, en ebery time de buckruh scheme once, de
nigger trick twice."

In similar vein but different wording is the observation of
the Columbia University professor of economics, Dr. Eli
Ginzberg in his book, *The Negro Potential:*

"It must also be remembered that 'dumbness' was a habit
developed by many Negroes, especially in the South, to protect them in their daily dealings with whites."

The instability of the Negro family is another mark
against the race, at least insofar as establishing itself as a
grouping of persons reflecting the social conduct generally
accepted as desirable from the standpoint of community attitudes. The propensity of Negroes, male and female, to
"take up" with each other without regard to the niceties of
marriage or family obligations is so well-known in the South

as to need no documentation. But that free-wheeling sort of family life is not restricted to the Southern Negro, for the same sort of loose living characterizes Negro life elsewhere in the nation.

In his sympathetic study of the Negro, Dr. Ginzberg, includes this observation:

"The family structure of Negroes has long been subjected to serious stresses and strains. Millions of Negroes leave their home communities during their formative years and must sink roots in new and different communities. Many family units are disrupted, temporarily or permanently, by migration. Residential restrictions in the large urban centers of the North are a serious handicap to family life, for they imply poor housing, inadequate recreational facilities, and all other blights of slum areas.

"Moreover, a disproportionately large number of young Negroes are brought up in homes which the father has deserted or in other situations where major responsibility for the continuance of the family unit centers around the mother and her relatives. According to the 1950 Census, over one-third of the Negro women who had ever been married were no longer married or no longer living with their husbands . . ."

Further proof of this chronic family disruption among Negroes is found in a 1957 study of *The Negro Population of Chicago,* by Otis Dudley Duncan and Beverly Duncan. With reference to family heads reporting "spouse absent," they found:

"In both 1940 and 1950 this form of family disruption was reported about four times as often by non-white married males as by white married males, and about five or six times as often by non-white married females as by white married females. . . ."

The shortcomings of Negroes in this realm of community life can be attributed to a combination of causes. Some date back perhaps to the days of slavery when families were forcibly disrupted by the commercial demands of slave-trading. Others reflect the press of modern times and the acute shortage of adequate Negro housing in crowded urban communities. But whatever the cause, the result is that the average, or typical, Negro family lacks many of the characteristics which are counted desirable by the community—family cohesion and stability; family disciplines of manners, of cleanliness, of obedience; personal standards of reliability, dependability; personal goals based on ambition and the desire for self-improvement.

Is it any wonder that white parents are reluctant to undermine their own attempts to foster such habits among their own children, by exposing them to youngsters whose standards are demonstrably lower in almost every respect? Here again, as at almost every turn of the wheel, the comment comes back: Let us do what we can to help improve the lot of the Negro, but NOT at the expense of our children.

Perhaps more to the point here is the unmistakable need for some large-scale self-improvement on the part of the Negroes themselves. Many of the deficiencies noted above can be corrected in whole or in part by determined effort, plus changed attitudes, by the Negroes of the various American as well as the various Southern communities. Here is ample room for "advancement" of colored people, yet one which seems to hold little attraction for the National Association for the Advancement of Colored People.

The professional integrationist, whether Negro or white, does not want either equality or opportunity; he wants merger. Give the Negro equal school buildings (and he has them in most areas of the South now) and he complains that the whites have better instruction. Give him Negro teachers with profuse academic degrees and he complains that the degrees mean little since they were won at Negro colleges and universities. Give him every facility and every encouragement to better himself, and he still admits that he cannot advance his own power and by his own ability.

But instead of seeking to remedy this monumental inferiority complex by the therapeutic treatment of accomplishment, the Negro prefers to seek advancement by agitation. In this approach, he has received great help from federal judges whose soft hearts have been matched by such soft-headed pronouncements as this invitation to self-pity:

"Segregation of white and colored children in public schools has a detrimental effect upon the colored children. The impact is greater when it has the sanction of the law; for the policy of separating the races is usually interpreted as denoting the inferiority of the Negro group. A sense of inferiority affects the motivation of a child to learn . . ."

That lower court expression in the Kansas school suit was picked up by the Supreme Court in its desegregation decision, along with this added comment:

"To separate them [Negro students] from others of similar age and qualifications solely because of their race generates a feeling of inferiority as to their status in the community that may affect their hearts and minds in a way unlikely ever to be undone."

Contrast the social worker concepts of contemporary federal judges with the hard-headed logic of a 1896 Supreme Court which was concerned more with establishing the equality of Negroes before the law than with providing solace for tender feelings. Said the Supreme Court in the Plessy v. Ferguson case:

"The object of the 14th amendment was undoubtedly to enforce the absolute equality of the two races before the laws but in the nature of things it could not have been intended to abolish distinctions based on color, or to enforce social, as distinguished from political equality, or a commingling of the two races upon terms unsatisfactory to either. . . . We consider the underlying fallacy of the plain-

tiff's argument to consist in the assumption that the enforced separation of the two races stamps the colored race
with a badge of inferiority. If this be so, it is not by reason
of anything found in the act, but solely because the colored
race choose to put that construction upon it."

Yet the clamor goes on and on and on. In one of its
propaganda pieces, the American Jewish Congress makes
much of what it calls the "cultural deprivation" of Negroes.
The answer according to the AJC, lies not in generating a
greater intellectual and cultural stimulation within the Negro group, but in integrating the Negroes with whites who
already are "participating fully in the cultural benefits and
social rewards of American society."

The Jewish Congress glosses over such educational materials as schools and teachers and subject matter to lay its
heavy emphasis on the intangibles of "life satisfactions" and
the like. Nor does the American Jewish Congress see much
cause for rejoicing in the admittedly improved economic
standing of the Negro group. Read this and weep:

"Culturally deprived children do not, understandably,
find much compensation or motivation in sheer exposure to
the contents and benefits of public education; the value of
this opportunity is over-shadowed by feelings of inadequacy
and by an inability to relate education to their own realistic
notions of what a segregated culture is like. . . ."

What all this means in plain English is that education has
become secondary; the real mission is race mixing.

Bit by bit, the grand strategy of the integration plan is
making itself discernible, but it is not unfolding at the same
rate in all parts of the nation. In the South, the Negro integrationists and the white submissionists are now saying that
a desire for better education motivates their quest for desegregation. But in the North, where there already is desegregation of a sort, the next step is beginning to take form, as
propagandists declare in so many words that their goal IS

integration, not education. And it must follow, as the night the day, that the next goal is amalgamation, hybridization, or mongrelization, depending upon how plain or fancy one wishes to be in describing the same thing.

10

Agitation Incorporated

Tʜᴇ National Association for the Advancement of Colored People is the *bête noire* of the white Southerner. Few Southerners found fault with the initial purposes and policies of the organization, for advancement of the Negro is a goal to which all can subscribe unreservedly. Through the years, however, the NAACP has supplemented its original propagandizing with pressures which discomfort and disturb Southerners over a broad range of attitudes, with the result that the organization today stands as the symbol of everything the white Southerner detests in the field of race relations. Beyond that, it has come to represent, in the eyes of countless Southerners, a distinct threat to the very fundamentals of American constitutional government and an instrumentality of the Communist conspiracy. The injection of this latter element into the situation presents an interesting development in mass psychology, for it reflects both a willingness to ascribe the basest of motives to an agency which is regarded as an implacable foe of the South, and a tendency to cross-identify Communism and integration, not entirely without reason.

Through the years, dozens of persons—white and black— who have played leading roles in NAACP affairs have also performed services for other organizations designated by Congressional and governmental agencies as Communist or Communist-front. The NAACP has fought back diligently against the "guilt by association" which inevitably has stemmed from every disclosure that its officers, directors, members, or sympathizers have been linked with reddish or pinkish undertakings, but that has been a losing battle in the South. Throughout the entire region, governors, attorneys general, and other public and private spokesmen of substance in the pro-segregation ranks have exploited every discernible connection between the NAACP and Communism. Unhappily for the NAACP but significantly for the Southerner, the integrationist goals of the NAACP and of the Communist Party have been so nearly identical that the Southerner feels fully justified in concluding that "things equal to the same thing are equal to each other."

Consequently, the NAACP has difficulty refuting arguments such as this one from Georgia's Attorney General:

"The racial aims of the Communist Party and those of the NAACP are virtually identical. The Communist program, as reported in the May 26, 1928, issue of the *Daily Worker*, calls for:

" 'Full racial equality.

" 'Abolition of all laws forbidding intermarriage of persons of different races.

" 'Abolition of all laws and public administration measures which prohibit, or in practice prevent, Negro children from attending general public schools or universities.

" 'Full and equal admittance of Negroes to all waiting rooms, restaurants, hotels and theaters.' "

Faced with that sort of information, Southerners listen when Attorney General Cook adds that the NAACP "knowingly or unknowingly . . . has allowed itself to become a part and parcel of the Communist conspiracy to overthrow the democratic governments of this nation and its sovereign states."

More fuel is added to the fire by reports such as this one, published in the Washington *Evening Star*, February 11, 1957:

"New York, Feb. 11—The American Communist Party promised today 'full participation in and support of the all-sided anti-segregation movement in the South.'

"It also pledged to strengthen and broaden 'the battle for the unfettered right of suffrage for all Southerners.' . . ."

But the Communist link, whether real or fancied, is only one of many reasons why white Southerners despise the NAACP. They can see at first hand the continuing agitation of NAACP spokesmen, nationally and locally, for racial integration. They can witness the disruption of amicable relations in countless communities throughout the South where white men and black men got along peaceably together before the NAACP began pressing for integration of the public schools. And they have good cause to suspect that much of the political harassment which comes their way from both national parties is due in large measure to the pressures applied on the national level by the NAACP.

Because of all this, white Southerners feel every justification in striking back at the NAACP, as at a mortal enemy, with every weapon at hand. And since the most potent weapon available is the control of state and local government, they have used legislative, administrative, and in some instances, judicial cudgels in beating back the integrationist designs of the NAACP. This fight, obviously, has been made within the Southern states themselves, since the battle could not be carried by Southerners into the NAACP's own strongholds—the metropolitan areas of the North where is concentrated the Negro's political influence.

In passing, it might be noted that neither the NAACP nor

its integrationist allies can expect kid-glove treatment in those areas of the South where Southerners have the capacity of retaliation against integrationist pressures. In the minds of most white Southerners, this is no game to be played with delicacy, but a war for the survival of a civilization.

Beginning with Alabama in August of 1955, state after state in the Deep South adopted measures to curb or to suppress the NAACP. Some of the legislation threw financial roadblocks in the path of the organization, requiring it to pay licenses and solicitation fees. Some called for disclosure of membership records, contributions, and other organizational data. Other acts, or revived enforcement of old acts, required the NAACP to file statements, and in some cases to pay taxes, as organizations subject to restrictive or regulatory conditions. A number of states undertook to prevent the NAACP, either by name or by category, from initiating or sponsoring lawsuits to which it was not actually a party.

Here and there, federal as well as state judges have undertaken to warn the NAACP against attempting improper force in pressing its case for integration. One such warning came in August of 1955 from District Judge Ashton H. Williams, of Charleston, S. C. He roundly condemned the Ku Klux Klan and then made these comments in the course of considering a case in which Negroes sought court-directed admission to a South Carolina white state park:

"This [NAACP] too appears to be a secret organization. Reports indicate that they will resort to any means to carry out their purposes. It must be kept in mind that the rights given to Negroes by the Supreme Court are personal, and no one has a right to persuade them by unlawful threats or otherwise to exercise the rights given them by the Supreme Court . . .

"This organization, along with the Ku Klux Klan, are the real enemies to any progress in the school cases. It is my belief that no progress can be made unless and until both the Klan and the NAACP are wholly eliminated from the picture in South Carolina. This does not mean that the officials of the NAACP cannot advise those who seek their advice. I deny their right, however, to coerce or force anyone to seek in our courts a right he does not care to seek . . ."

The fact that recent NAACP pressures have engendered strong resistance in both the South and the North may possibly be contributing as well to a re-examination by Americans generally of the profuse propaganda which long has characterized the NAACP. From the very beginning, propaganda has been a chief weapon in the NAACP arsenal. It was designed to condition the nation's thinking; to draw attention not upon itself but upon those wrongs and alleged wrongs suffered by the American Negro; and to implant a sense of unease and guilt within the consciousness and conscience of the American white man. Part of the propaganda effort was aimed at whispering into the public's ear that all racial wrongs stem from segregation and that all will be sweetness and light once the two races are integrated. Another part of the propaganda has been shouted into the politician's ear, saying that the Negro vote stands ready to exert its entire influence against him unless he hews to the NAACP line of racial reform. The combined assault has brought about that frame of mind which makes possible such startling developments as a Supreme Court's abandonment of all legal precedent and its adoption of a sociological approach to matters of law.

If there be those who hesitate to charge the NAACP with carrying on a planned propaganda campaign, let them turn to the words of the scholarly mulatto who served as the first Director of Research and Publications of the NAACP. W. E. B. DuBois, who in 1910, founded the NAACP's official magazine, *The Crisis,* and was for 22 years its editor and driving force, says this of the turn of events which led him into the official family of the NAACP:

"My career as a scientist was to be swallowed up in my role as master of propaganda."

Late in life, as DuBois reviewed his changing attitudes concerning the best means of furthering the Negro's cause in America, he wrote: ". . . not sudden assault but long siege was indicated; careful planning and subtle campaign with the education of growing generations and propaganda." This concept grew out of his bitter disillusionment in World War I, prior to which time he had held this view: "The black world must fight for freedom. It must fight with the weapons of Truth, with the sword of the intrepid, uncompromising Spirit, with organization in boycott, propaganda, and mob frenzy." But even then, there was the stress upon propaganda, a stress which has ever been present. Let DuBois speak again on the course of action followed by the NAACP:

"This program of organized opposition to the action and attitude of the dominant white group includes ceaseless agitation and insistent demand for equality; the equal right to work, civic and political equality, and social equality. It involves the use of force of every sort: moral suasion, propaganda and where possible even physical resistance. . . .

"Moreover, until such a campaign has had a chance to do its work, the minority which is seeking emancipation must remember that they are facing a powerful majority. There is no way in which the American Negro can force this nation to treat him as equal until the unconscious cerebration and folkways of the nation, as well as its rational deliberate thoughts among the majority of whites, are willing to grant equality."

The rejection of that last admonition—either consciously or unconsciously—brought about the mid-century eruption of racial friction. Neither the thinking nor the folkways of the nation, and certainly not of the South, were ready in the 1950's for racial commingling, and the effort to force not only equality but integration disrupted the pattern of progress which had been so painstakingly built up through all the preceding years.

Through years of probing and patrolling the entire governmental front, the integrationists found that their best chance

for success lay in those spheres of influence furtherest removed from the untrammelled expression of the public will.
In the face of a nationwide resistance, most especially in the
South, toward pro-integration movements, the NAACP and
its allies turned their guns on the central government, only to
run into another reflection of the popular resistance to race-
mixing. True, the application of political pressure against
non-Southern members of the Congress did succeed in establishing a clamorous if none-too-effective beachhead in the
federal legislature. But very little in the way of pro-integration legislation was actually passed over the sturdy opposition of Southern Congressmen in both House and Senate, and
the quieter but nevertheless formidable opposition of non-
Southern representatives and senators who refused to be
stampeded by minority bloc pressures.

Even while working on the elected representatives of the
people, however, the integrationists continued to pressure
the other two branches of the government—the executive
and the judicial. Through years of Democratic occupancy of
the White House, they received substantial lip-service and a
less substantial measure of action aimed at eliminating or reducing racial segregation in the nation generally and in the
agencies of the national government in particular. Presidents
Roosevelt and Truman demonstrated rare ability in persuading the NAACP and its like-minded associates that the Democratic administrations and the Democratic party (on a national basis) were the best political friends the Negroes and
other minority groups could have. The result was that those
minority votes swung solidly behind the Democrats and
stayed there for years. Not until Republicans finally got back
into power through the personal popularity of General Eisenhower did that picture begin to change.

Meanwhile, the integrationists had been learning with
gratification that the federal judiciary, notably the Supreme
Court, was increasingly willing to strike down racial barriers
wherever they existed. These federal judges, insulated by life

tenure from both the people and their elected representatives, proved able to accomplish by judicial decree what could not be done by legislative action—that is, to alter the Constitution of the United States so as to make it fit the new and liberal concept of personal liberty. It should be remembered that the Supreme Court at this critical stage of American history was a peculiarly political body, comprising individuals whose experience, qualifications, and claims for reward were political, not judicial. The well-known Washington columnist, Ray Tucker, had this to say on that score in May of 1954:

"Let it be remembered that every single man on the Supreme Court was a politician before he became a black-gowned jurist, and that every single man was appointed for political reasons."

The susceptibility of these politically-appointed and -motivated judges to the incessant propaganda of the integrationists was demonstrated in their astounding reliance upon sociology and psychology, rather than upon established law in reaching their decision. Reasoned judicial thought could never have produced an opinion incorporating statements such as this:

"Whatever may have been the extent of psychological knowledge at the time of Plessy v. Ferguson, this finding [that segregation tends to retard the educational and mental development of Negro children] is amply supported by modern authority."

The modern authorities cited by the Supreme Court included an array of sociologists and psychologists, at least one of whom was directly affiliated with the NAACP, and many of whom had earned the scrutiny of the House Un-American Activities Committee. Also among them was the Swedish sociologist and economist, Dr. Gunnar Myrdal, whose massive study of the Negro in the United States, *An American Dilemma*, incorporated the foregone conclusions of the NAACP-connected social scientists and researchers who did his field work for him. Thus the Supreme Court was thrice ex-

posed to the persuasion of NAACP propaganda: in the legal
arguments advanced before the Court; in the "authorita-
tive" sociological writings upon which the Court leaned in
reaching its decision; and in the integrationist atmosphere
created in the upper levels of the federal government by the
unceasing political pressures built up by NAACP propaganda.

The cumulative effect of all this caused the Warren Court
not only to reverse the venerable "separate but equal" doctrine, but, in effect, to repudiate words which the Court had
spoken as late as 1952. In the case of Beauharnais v. Illinois,
the Supreme Court had said this:

"It is not within our competence to confirm or deny claims
of social scientists as to the dependence of the individual on
the position of his racial or religious group in the community."

The real essence of the Supreme Court's desegregation decision drew this revealing observation from the Committee on
Social Issues of the Group for the Advancement of Psychiatry, writing in a booklet entitled *Psychiatric Aspects of
School Desegregation:*

"Perhaps not since the Declaration of Independence has a
public federal document stressed the importance of personal
feelings as an item of political consideration. The Supreme
Court decision was in part based on personal, psychological,
and sociological data showing that segregation constitutes a
psychological and personal handicap."

Back of this culmination of NAACP propaganda was long-
term adherence to a consistent theme, always the secret of
successful propaganda. In this particular instance, the theme
has been: "Integration is good; segregation is bad," and that
refrain has been woven with skill and imagination into every
conceivable fabric of American life. It has been repeated
thousands upon thousands of times, fastening upon the

American public like Socrates' gadfly, "all day long and in all places . . . arousing and persuading and reproaching you." The good-versus-evil theme is preached a hundred ways:—"Integration is Christian; segregation is unChristian"; "Integration is democratic; segregation is undemocratic"; "Integration is American; segregation is unAmerican." The pattern is an effective adaptation of Adolf Hitler's dictum:

". . . all effective propaganda has to limit itself only to a very few points and to use them like slogans until even the very last man is able to imagine what is intended by such a word."

Just such strategy as this has been followed religiously (the term is well-advised here) by the integrationists, chief among whom is the NAACP. They have managed to achieve a substantial degree of brain-washing among non-Southerners who necessarily rely upon mass news media for their information concerning the South and its problems. With consummate skill, compounded out of a blend of moralistic persuasion and politico-economic pressure, the NAACP crowd has succeeded in selling its point of view to most of the individuals and corporations which control the mass media of the nation. As a result, the NAACP cause is aided and abetted almost automatically, whereas anything at variance with that cause is given short shrift or is invalidated by editorial and reportorial devices which adroitly destroy or debilitate the capacity of uninformed readers to comprehend the truth.

Perhaps even more pernicious than any distortion of the truth, however, is the complete omission of the truth. So long as only one side of a controversy is presented to the public, it is hard for the public to realize that there is another side. As a consequence, the attitude develops that there is no real racial problem at all, and that merely a handful of recalcitrant, ignorant, and misguided individuals stand in the way of wholesale racial intermingling in the South. Only the sheer intensity of Southern resistance to enforced integration has been sufficient to gain notice in the non-Southern press, radio, and television, and even then only in hostile tones and connotations.

Nevertheless, even the unfriendly reporting of such resistance serves the purpose of manifesting the determination of Southerners to continue their fight. Furthermore, it discloses a dogged spirit of pro-segregation sentiment even in the face of a propaganda barrage which inevitably has had some effect in the South as well as in the rest of the nation. Southerners of emotional gullibility had begun to doubt the validity of their own beliefs in some instances, but many of these now have been brought up short by the ferocity of the integrationist effort. And as for the general run of white Southerners, so inured have they become to the hostile propaganda and distortions from the North that they have developed conditioned reflexes which automatically raise warning signals of disbelief and disgust when propaganda reaches them through press, magazines, radio, television, or other media.

Nevertheless, magazines on the market today somehow manage to depict segregated groups as patrons of the various commodities advertised by photograph or sketch in their colorful pages. Perhaps the professed scorn of segregation which is reflected editorially, and frequently reportorially, in this segment of the press is not shared by those whose economic interests are at stake. The reference here is to those magazines which circulate primarily in the white market, for there is a degree of integration in the advertisements which appear in the Negro press and periodicals. But even here, the "integration," if it can be so termed, exists only to the extent that there are a growing number of ads which use Negro models in an obvious bid for the Negro dollar. Certainly there is nothing reprehensible about that, for the Negro dollar is a big dollar and represents a market well worth cultivating. The irony of it all is that the very firms which underwrite or contribute to integrationist enterprises so heavily will not mix the races in the art work by which they seek to sell their products.

As a matter of fact, the chief purveyors of integrated art are the Negro publications, which obviously take great delight in featuring photographs of whites and Negroes, preferably of both sexes, in intimate association. Many of these very same photographs, which in the one instance are aimed at gratifying the Negro reading public, often are reprinted in the most extreme of the segregationist publications as visual warning to white readers of "what's going on" in the integrationist world.

But the mass media are not the only devices of communication by which the integrationists disseminate their propaganda. They keep up a steady outpouring of race-mixing "literature" in church journals and other religious publications, in scientific and pseudo-scientific periodicals, in professional and semi-professional journals, and in the verbal flow of discussion which eddies about in the sociological, religious, political, and educational circles of the land. And in every instance, full advantage is taken of recognized propaganda devices.

Irrespective of whatever effect all this propaganda may have had in the North, its very nature, coupled with the NAACP's militant forcing of the integration issue, has, in the Deep South, defeated its own purpose. Instead of keeping pace with community willingness to accept Negroes into schools and other areas of activity, the NAACP has pushed and prodded to the point where a wholesale reaction set in, surprising even the NAACP officials themselves in its intensity. As an illustration of how badly the NAACP misjudged the temper of the white South, note this optimistic observation from Clarence Mitchell, head of the NAACP office in Washington. Back in October of 1951, when the South Carolina and Kansas school desegregation cases were first under consideration by the United States Supreme Court, Mitchell hazarded this guess as to the probable effect if the Court were to outlaw segregation:

"The whole thing would go well. There would be no problem. I get around quite a lot in Southern communities. The South more and more is getting into a mental state where it knows that segregation must go in almost everything. With this attitude, segregation sort of fades away."

But neither the NAACP nor the Supreme Court were willing to wait for segregation to "fade away," and they sought to hasten the process with court-directed integration. The net result (foreseeable to all but the integrationists) was a solidifying of opposition and a hardening of resistance. Had they followed the advice of the much-scorned Supreme Court of 1896, they could have turned the 1950's into a great working expansion of that earlier Court's formula for developing interracial amity and equality: "natural affinities, a mutual appreciation of each other's merits and a voluntary consent of individuals."

In rejecting such an approach to interracial amity, the NAACP turned to a frontal assault of such intensity and intemperateness as to work a severe setback to the cause of integration. Had the NAACP stopped short for a time after it had won its major victory on May 17, 1954, and its lesser victory a year later, there might well have been a gradual, if unenthusiastic, acceptance of the Supreme Court's decision in large areas (but not all) of the South. But once again the extreme integrationists took charge of the situation and, in 1955, began bombarding the South with school integration petitions demanding prompt and positive steps toward the admission of Negroes into white schools. The immediate consequence of this was an upsurge of reaction against integration.

White Southerners who had been floundering in a welter of indecision and confusion suddenly were presented with rallying points. They came face to face with the threat of integration as petitions were filed and as "deadlines" were pompously announced by NAACP officials. The subsequent postponement of deadline after deadline reflected the effectiveness of the opposition which crystallized, once the integrationists had erected specific and identifiable targets for that opposition.

When the NAACP held a legal conference at Dallas in late June of 1954, Chief Counsel Thurgood Marshall announced that September of 1955 was the target date for ending segregation in all public elementary and high schools throughout the United States. That goal was still in sight, or at least it was professed to be, when the NAACP held a Southeastern conference in February of 1955. At that meeting it was declared: "We are not alarmed by those state governments which have adopted amendments to state constitutions and by other means are seeking to circumvent the Supreme Court's decision."

But when September of 1955 rolled around, the South was still solidly segregated except for its fringes, and Marshall was writing in the *Southern School News* that "we intend to continue to push toward integration in most areas of the South by not later than September, 1956."

By December of 1955, however, NAACP officials were admitting that conditions in Alabama, Florida, Georgia, Mississippi, and both Carolinas were "particularly discouraging." In each of those states, and in Virginia as well, official resistance was stiffening rather than weakening, and the attitude of the white people bolstered the formal pro-segregation stands of the various states. Two months later, in February of 1956, the NAACP predicted that lawsuits would be filed "by June 11" in every one of the eight states of the Deep South. That prediction was not borne out by subsequent developments, but statements continued to be made that further litigation was on the way.

As for the NAACP itself, it is only now being repaid in kind for its years of indulgence in political pressure, propaganda, and solicitation of federal backing against the states of the South. For too long, white Southerners took little notice of the organization. That lack of attention served the NAACP well by permitting it to go almost unnoticed about its business of building political and propaganda alliances which in recent years have begun to pay off handsomely in the form of federal court capitulation to NAACP litigation. While Southerners were defending segregation on a legal basis, grounding their arguments in the Constitution and in court decisions, the NAACP cleverly was using each court as a forum and a platform from which to expound and publicize its integrationist propaganda, thereby setting the stage for an ultimate change in the law by reasoning which was not itself predicated upon the law.

But since the NAACP elected to fight with the weapons of pressure instead of persuasion, it should not now complain when similar weapons are turned against it.

Not only has the NAACP disdained securing the friendship of the white race in the South; it seems deliberately to have set about alienating whatever friends it may have had among that race. Here is a sample of the vitriolic language which has driven white Southerners into well-nigh unanimous opposition to the NAACP and everything it stands for. Listen to the late Walter White, NAACP's longtime executive secretary, crow over the Supreme Court's desegregation decision at a regional NAACP conference held at Atlanta. The report comes from the Associated Press and is dated May 23, 1954:

"If I had the skill of an artist I would build a picture of the nine justices of the Supreme Court and of decent Americans, both Negro and white, marching forward with heads high and shining eyes toward democracy. Far in the rear I would picture three or four pathetic and diminutive figures weeping and screaming 'I won't let it happen.' The little figures, of course, would be labelled Byrnes, Talmadge and others of the shrinking minority for whom they speak . . ."

This seeming determination of Negro leaders to foment racial discord rather than harmony, even where the peaceful course would have been the easier to follow, has been evident in other times and places. Two significant events in Charleston, S. C., illustrate the point.

In early 1954, two dramatic groups in Charleston began joint planning for the local production of *Porgy and Bess*, the Charleston-centered play by DuBose and Dorothy Heyward. Mrs. Heyward granted full rights without royalties in order to help promote the local enterprise, and the Dock Street Theatre group (white) began active work with the Stage-crafters (Negro) for a production which would use a cast of local Negro talent. In February, the president of the Stage-crafters, a Negro insurance man named A. J. Clement, Jr., proposed that the problem of audience seating be met by "splitting the auditorium exactly in half from gallery to orchestra." That suggestion was received favorably by the white group and preparations moved forward. Tryouts were conducted and rehearsals were begun.

Two weeks thereafter, Clement, who also was then president of the Charleston branch of the NAACP, abruptly announced that the Negro cast would not play unless the audience were completely integrated as to seating. In the face of South Carolina laws prohibiting such mixed seating at places of amusement, the only recourse left was abandonment of the entire project.

Less than six months earlier, Charleston had experienced another incident which savored so much of a "put-up job" that it brought sharp criticism from a number of Charleston Negroes, just as did the *Porgy and Bess* episode.

On October 19, 1953, a Navy directive against segregation became effective at the Charleston Naval Base. With respect to eating facilities, that meant that an upstairs dining room in the cafeteria building became accessible to both races, instead of to whites only. When the first group of about 15 Negroes entered the formerly all-white area after the desegregation order, they immediately split up by obvious pre-arrangement and went individually to some 14 separate tables so as to achieve maximum integration with such white persons as they could find.

That provocative conduct subsequently was defended by the State NAACP President James M. Hinton in these words:

"I think Negroes will act like human beings. When the cafeteria was opened [to mixed patronage] had they seated themselves around one table, it still would have been segregation. So the obvious thing to have done, as they did, was to spread out in the cafeteria so there would be integration."

In passing, let it be noted that there has been little integration achieved in the "desegregation" of the Naval Base cafeteria. White patronage fell to, and remained at, a fraction of what it had been. White workers arrange to patronize the establishment when Negroes are not present, or stay away altogether.

The action of the Negroes on that first day, however, drew adverse comment not only from white persons but from some Negroes as well. One wrote *The News and Courier* to describe their conduct as being that of "hoodlums." Obviously, not all Negroes subscribe to either the NAACP principles or to its practices.

One outspoken Negro who did not endorse the doctrine of early and enforced integration was W. R. Farley, founder of the Goodwill Radio Hour and Goodwill Youth Council of Southland, Inc. His sentiments were published in the *Orlando Morning Sentinel,* of Florida, and subsequently reprinted in the *Congressional Record* of July 13, 1955. These excerpts are taken from that source:

"I think all will admit that the Negro race has come a long way in a short space of time. The most dangerous point in the general progress of the Negro race now is the fact that he is being misled by many agitators who would have him believe that he has caught up with the fellow who was several hundred years ahead of him. Give my people, the Negroes, time and they will run a good race, because they have it in them. They may not get ahead of the winning horse, but they will run an honorable race. . . .

"We, the Negroes of the South, with the goodwill and help of our many white friends, are creating our own social standards, our own way of living. If given time, we will create a standard of distinction and goodwill so effective that others will seek it also. What is needed now is time, education, training and a little more real Christianity, living what we preach."

In South Carolina, a native South African who came to the United States in 1903, received a master's degree at Fisk University, and who has been a school principal and preacher for 36 years, has publicly repudiated the NAACP. P. B. Mdodana was unsuccessful in his 1956 effort to present a resolution condemning "pressure groups" at a convention of Negro school teachers, but he later made public excerpts from the blocked resolution. It sought to have the Negro teachers' association, which he said he helped form, record itself as "opposing pressure groups, declaring our racial pride, voicing our appreciation to the taxpayers who have provided the necessary equal facilities for our schools and as voicing our opposition to those who are relentlessly bent on bringing about the so-called integration of races in the public schools of the South."

But such segregationists within Negro ranks get short shrift from the NAACP, which is determined to press for full integration irrespective of the wishes of those Negroes who do not want to force the issue. This militant and openly intolerant attitude was bluntly stated by Thurgood Marshall on the heels of the Supreme Court's desegregation decision. From Atlanta, Marshall was quoted by the Associated Press as saying that Negroes who prefer segregation "represent themselves alone and can't deter the program. . . . Negro leadership is in NAACP and we won't worry about the small minority. We are not going to let them get in our way."

Since that time, it has become abundantly clear that Negroes who speak out for segregation, or who otherwise run counter to the NAACP's integration program, occupy a precarious position within the organized Negro community. In February of 1956, the Fort Gaines *News Record*, of Georgia, reported an incident in which a young Negro principal had been threatened and forced to leave the community after advising Negroes to "forget integration" and concentrate on community up-building. Harrison E. Lee made the mistake of telling his fellow Negroes to "forget integration and remember that we yet have not learned how to pool our resources and build even a recreation hall for our children. . . . We haven't learned how to take our children to Sunday school, how to cooperate with our local school administrators and our school board, with our school teachers, with our ministers, and even with our state laws. We still want that which we either do not deserve or that which we are not ready for."

In Mississippi a few weeks later, a series of newspaper articles in which a Negro college professor censured the NAACP provoked a walk-out of students from the college and brought down upon his head the wrath of Negro integrationists within and without the state. Professor Clennon King, a native Georgian with a bachelor's degree from Tuskegee and a master's degree from Western Reserve University, spoke out bluntly and critically of the NAACP's emphasis on agitation and its indifference to racial tension, to Negro crime, and to the opportunities for Negroes to raise themselves through their own economic efforts. The series of articles he published in the *Jackson State Times* brought him threats of bodily harm or death from Negroes who resented his criticism of the NAACP. The episode gave positive proof of just how intolerant are those who complain most noisily about intolerance from the other side of the segregation argument.

Even more important in the long run is the manifest desire of the NAACP to achieve full integration without regard to the place of residence of the school children affected. The ultimate goal is not education but integration *per se,* and en route to that goal the NAACP and its partners in propaganda mean to bring about integrated housing as a device for mass blending of the white and black components of the community. Already that pattern is beginning to take shape in New York, with the backing of such leading white liberals as ex-Sen. Herbert H. Lehman.

North Carolinians can look forward, in their turn, to the same demands for an accelerated integration program extending far beyond the admission of a few Negroes into schools as a symbol of token integration. The very life of the NAACP is dedicated to all-out integration, for from its very inception, the organization has operated on the thesis, in its own words, that "the task of the NAACP has been to wipe out racial discrimination and segregation."

Nor can there be any hope that a pattern of "voluntary segregation" can be achieved so long as the NAACP controls the Negro community. Unless the rank-and-file of peace-loving Negroes take the play away from the militant NAACP leaders, the aims and objects of Southern Negroes will continue to be expressed in terms such as these, used by a group of Negro educators meeting in Hot Springs, Ark., in November of 1954:

"We regret that some public officials have sought to persuade Negro educators and other leaders to evade the [Supreme Court's] decision by agreeing to voluntary segregation. This cannot be decently done; and such persons who agree to this will not be respected even by the officials seeking such commitment or compromise of principle."

In January of 1957, there came a "Statement to the South and the Nation" from 60 Negro leaders from 29 communities in 10 Southern states, attending the Southern Leaders' Conference on Transportation. That statement said, among other things:

". . . no matter how great the obstacles and suffering, we urge all Negroes to reject segregation."

The manifest inability of the NAACP to achieve a satisfactory degree of integration through its present tactics is apparent not only in the South but elsewhere in the nation. Even in areas such as Detroit, Philadelphia, New York, Washington, and other metropolitan areas where the Negroes have obtained almost everything they seek by way of anti-segregation legislation, there still continues to be racial strife with a frequency and intensity virtually unknown in the present-day South. There still is friction in the North whenever black people seek to force their way into white social groups, whether those groups be concerned with schools, housing, recreation, or otherwise. If the goal of the NAACP is interracial amity, then some other approach to the problem needs to be tried. The one now being employed is not working.

11

Mixing the Races

THE white Southerner's concern over race relations is in substantial measure a concern over sex relations, for the sexual factor lies just beneath the surface of any discussion of integration. Back of this preoccupation is a complex of reasons, both rational and irrational, which makes it impossible to raise the prospect of integration without raising the specter of intermarriage, or of interracial sexual relations. Perhaps more than any other single factor, this apprehension has solidified white resistance to integration, and has remained fixed in the face of every effort to discount its validity or relevance.

The NAACP, with good cause but with poor effect, has tried mightily to dissociate itself and its program from any hint of promoting intermarriage, but its best efforts have done little to dislodge the fear from the minds of Southern white men and white women.

The Southerner is not too much concerned over the relative merits and demerits of races in general and the black

211

and white races in particular. With or without the backing of anthropologists, he finds complete repugnance in the idea of any mixing of the races, and that is one of his fundamental objections to racial integration in the public schools. There is a fierce pride of race among Southerners who have come by such an Anglo-Saxon concept either by heritage or by adoption, and that pride countenances no adulteration of the white family stock.

The intermarriage potential within a fully integrated society is something Southerners do not wish to risk, even if their fears were subsequently proved to be groundless. The chance is too great a one to take, for if intermarriage on a considerable scale were to result, there could be no effective turning back by the time the mistake were discovered. Racial admixture, or "mongrelization" as it is denominated in the South, has a snow-balling effect. Once started, it grows of its own momentum and resistance to its acceleration becomes harder and harder. The same analogy pertains to the moral involvements, for there would result inevitably a relaxing of moral objections to hybridization, once hybrids themselves were present in appreciable numbers among the policy-setting social group.

NAACP officials, integrationists, and high-minded "moderates" say that racial intermarriage need not accompany race-mixing, but there is ample evidence among the writings of sociologists, including a number of Negro sociologists, which validates the fear that Southern whites have of amalgamation. For example, Edward B. Reuter, formerly of Fisk University, is steadfast in his contention that wherever contacts have occurred between the white and colored peoples in the modern world, amalgamation or biological union of the races has resulted. In his section on "Race and Culture" in the College Outline text, *Principles of Sociology*, Reuter says: "In all places where divergent peoples have come into contact for a period of time they have produced a hybrid offspring. . . ."

Countless instances of this interbreeding occurred during World War II and in the occupation years which followed. Wherever Negroes went in uniform outside the United States, they promptly established sexual relations, legally or illicitly, with such women as welcomed their company, or with those whom they forced to submit to their desires. As one brief illustration, the U. S. Army disclosed in November of 1957 that it was reassigning to non-Southern military posts some 30 Negro soldiers of the Second Armored Division who were bringing white German brides back to the United States.

The subject of racial intermarriage draws some interesting observations from the well-known Negro scholar, Professor E. Franklin Frazier, of Howard University, in his book, *Race and Culture Contacts in the Modern World*. He notes that the assimilation of Negroes into the Brazilian population was facilitated by "the mixture of the races and the absence of barriers to intermarriage. In this sense, amalgamation may be regarded as a forerunner to assimilation."

Frazier also quotes this from Adams' work, *Interracial Marriage in Hawaii:* "In short, if intermarriage is legally permitted and socially approved as between two or more peoples they are sure to become one people, one in social inheritance and one in ancestry and race."

With respect to the United States, Frazier sees prospects for an increasing incidence of racial admixture. Referring to the emergence of new peoples and new cultures through the fusions of racial groups in multi-racial communities, he says: "Even in the United States, where the mixing of whites and Negroes slowed down after emancipation, the urbanization of the Negro and his rise in economic and social status are accelerating racial mixture. The absorption of the Negro will scarcely change the physical character of the population but the cultural influence of the Negro, especially in music, has left its imprint on the new American culture that is evolving."

Despite the efforts of the NAACP to avoid or suppress references to the possibility of intermarriage, the subject crops up occasionally in the unguarded remarks of Negroes identified with the organization. One instance of this occurred in late August of 1955, when a Negro lawyer of Columbia, S. C., linked with the NAACP as a legal counselor, said that "once the two races are integrated, intermarriage is the natural consequence."

Speaking in an interview with an Orangeburg newspaper reporter, Albert A. Kennedy said:

"I won't speak for the NAACP on the intermarriage question but I will give my personal opinion. I was an ex-soldier and during the war I saw countries where there were no Negroes. Relationships were carried on between two parties concerned and if two people wanted to carry on it was their business. Intermingling can't be regulated by the state."

Kennedy said intermarriage had not been discussed at the NAACP meetings he had attended, but he added: "I am sure the NAACP knows that once you integrate it is the natural consequence."

Kennedy's remarks brought a blast of editorial reaction from South Carolina's white press and a prompt disavowal from the state NAACP president James M. Hinton. Terming Kennedy's comments "most unfortunate," Hinton said that the remarks "did not represent the program of the NAACP or any of its national or local officials. . . ."

Another frank Negro expression concerning intermarriage came to light in *The Pittsburgh Courier* when that Negro publication took exception to Dr. Norman Vincent Peale's advice to a Negro girl against marrying a white boy. As quoted by the Rev. G. T. Gillespie, president emeritus of Belhaven College, in a vigorous exposition of "A Christian View on Segregation," the newspaper stated this:

"It is not possible to have people of different races, nationalities and religions living together, working together and playing together and bar them from marrying. Intermarriage is as necessarily Christian as interfaith and interracial education. We will have to have desegregation in that area of life, and it has already begun to move heavily."

What might be taken as the official position of the NAACP on the subject of racial intermarriage was voiced by its executive secretary, Roy Wilkins, in an Associated Press interview published on April 8, 1956. Addressing himself to the charge that integration will make for intermarriage, Wilkins said:

"Our answer is that the incidence of intermarriage in states that don't outlaw it is infinitesimally small. People who bring up the question make a basic assumption which is fantastically wrong and insulting. They assume that white people are ready and waiting to marry Negroes and Negroes are ready and waiting to marry whites, and that only laws now restrain them.

"The question of intermarriage is a private matter between two individuals. We are neither for or against it . . ."

Wilkins' statement is open to challenge on several points, but even if it is acknowledged that the number of interracial marriages still is small, their incidence among prominent Negroes is sufficient to give basis for the supposition that the Negro's desire for a white mate is significant whenever circumstances place whites and blacks in the same social stratum. Statistics in such instances are less meaningful than are the mixed marriages of such well-known Negroes as singers Herb Jefferies, Lena Horne, and Billy Daniels; Musician Sidney Bechet, and the late Walter White, long-time executive secretary of the NAACP—to cite only five such unions mentioned in a single magazine article of 1951.

But aside from these legal interracial unions, there have been far too many instances of illicit or improper sexual relations between whites and Negroes in areas, or under circumstances, where normal barriers have been dropped. Press reports in recent years have documented occurrences of "widespread sex orgies between white girls, Negro youths and perverts" in Milwaukee; of so prolonged and persistent a sex affair between a white girl and Negro youth in Indiana that the courts were required to break it up; of killings stemming from episodes in which Negro servicemen danced, or sought to dance, with white women; and of riots and near-riots precipitated by inflamed emotions provoked by the wild abandon of "rock-and-roll" dance sessions attended by both races.

Northern police officers can verify such incidents, and can vouch for the disturbing effect of mixing whites, blacks, and primitive music. One veteran Southern radio man whose "disc-jockey" experience qualifies him to comment has made this observation:

"The smartest thing the Negroes ever did [in promoting integration] was taking over Tin Pan Alley."

Unfortunately, there seems a strong measure of feeling among the lower classes of Negro men that integration, or even the talk of integration, means a lowering of the bars which heretofore have kept them distant from white women. The feeling is not new, as witness this 1904 statement by the perceptive Southern writer, Thomas Nelson Page, in his book, *The Negro: The Southerner's Problem:*

"As the crime of rape of late [Reconstruction period] years had its baleful renascence in the teaching of equality and the placing of power in the ignorant Negroes' hands, so its perpetuation and increase have undoubtedly been due in large part to the same teaching. The intelligent Negro may understand what social equality truly means, but to the ignorant and brutal young Negro, it signifies but one thing: the opportunity to enjoy, equally with white men, the privilege of cohabiting with white women. This the whites of the South understand; and if it were understood abroad, it would serve to explain some things which have not been understood hitherto."

One evidence of the truth of Page's premise is the alarming and continuing pattern of assault and rape of white women by Negro men. Unfortunately for the cause of scientific fact-finding, the Federal Bureau of Investigation does not include among its statistics a report of the victims, as well as of the offenders, in rape cases. Nevertheless, the records of arrests for rape show Negroes to be far and away the worst offenders. The annual *Uniform Crime Reports* of the FBI for 1956 show that Negroes commit almost one-half of all rape in the United States, although they comprise only about one-tenth of the nation's population. Of all arrests for rape in 1956, totalling 4,591, Negroes were involved in 2,043. These figures, incidentally, are not all-inclusive, for they reflect arrests only in 1,551 cities with more than 2,500 population.

Social scientists attribute the proclivity of Negro men to assault white women to a variety of psychological factors. Among them is an alleged sense of retaliation against the white race, at its most sensitive point, for the many wrongs done to Negroes, and more particularly to Negro women. Less discussed by sociologists but more understandable to the Southern white is the fact that Negro men obviously find white women desirable. The undeniable fact that lightness of skin is equated with desirability gives full support to the contention that the admission of the Negro man to the company of white women places him quite literally in the happy hunting ground.

Southern police officers can and do attest to the fact that a great number of Negro men, especially those who have been in foreign countries while in the armed forces, habitually carry snapshots or other photographs of white women, some taken with Negro men, and some, perhaps with the same men, showing the women in various stages of undress or compromise. The more belligerent Negroes, or those speaking in drunkenness, defiantly proclaim their real or fancied conquests of white women (and generally suffer unpleasant consequences thereby).

The impulse toward sexual gratification on the part of Negro men generally is a matter of common knowledge among both races in the South, and seems to be accepted by both—with this paramount qualification: Negro men must never cross the color line. The fear of swift, certain and severe punishment hangs sword-like over the head of the Southern Negro who entertains thoughts of consorting with a white woman, and white Southerners firmly believe that in the absence of that deterrent fear, there would be no restraining of Negro men.

Here again there comes into evidence the lack among Negroes of the force of community public opinion, and of the restraints of self-discipline and self-control. In the absence of such factors, the Negro man requires an exterior discipline to keep him within the confines of acceptable conduct. Added to the official deterrents is the widespread realization that there is among white men what amounts to universal agreement that an all-inclusive protective mantle shall be maintained around all white women. This collective determination to safeguard white women from black men formerly was evidenced in the mob psychology of lynch crowds. Some of the thinking persists today, in more legal and less violent manifestations, in the white Southerner's insistence upon strict enforcement of laws barring interracial contacts, by whatever means accomplished.

In all fairness, however, it must be acknowledged (although it will displease many a Southern white) that the wrongs done white women by Negro men cannot equal, at least in number, the great wrongs done Negro women by white men from the days of slavery until recently. Bereft of any real protection from their own men and denied (until recently) any measure of legal protection, Negro women have been victimized by white masters and white men for generations. The lasting and visible proof of this is the presence in our midst of considerable numbers of Negroes of mixed blood. A number of anthropologists, among them Professor Melville J. Herskovits and Ales Hrdlicka, report surveys which show that as many as 70 out of 100 Negroes can lay claim to one or more white ancestors.

That astoundingly high ratio seems due primarily to the incidence of concubinage during slavery days, when extra-legal sex relations with slave women on the part of slave-owners and/or their sons was tolerated, although not applauded. The birth of every mulatto child of such a union tended to accelerate the diffusion of white blood into the Negro race, since the fate of the mulatto in this country always has been to be forced into the lower rather than the higher level of parentage.

There seems little scientific evidence at hand on which to base an accurate estimate of the numbers involved, but it is obvious that a number of half-breed Yankees were left among the Southern Negroes in the wake of marauding Federal troops who ranged the South under the command of William Tecumseh Sherman and other despoilers of the land.

Since those days, interracial sex affairs have become increasingly frowned upon by both whites and Negroes of respectability, and there is substantial agreement that the numbers of children stemming from such unions are decreasing. Whether this reflects a real lessening of sex relations between the races or merely a reduction in the children resulting from such relations may be debatable, but Southern feeling supports the first view.

Maurice R. Davie, in his 1949 study, *Negroes in American Society*, says:

"Both Negro and white observers in the South are agreed that direct infusions of white blood through illegitimate relationship is on the decrease. The two races are not in such intimate contact as they were in earlier days, especially during slavery, and public opinion in both races has become increasingly opposed to interracial immorality. Moreover, the changed status of the Negroes has made them less subject to sexual exploitation. Significant also is the advancement of the Negro, such as his improved economic and educational condition and his development of a more stable family life, which has been a powerful factor in the decline of extra-marital interbreeding. Whereas the role of mistress to a white man was once highly desired, entailing economic security and a measure of prestige within her own group, today colored women who consort with white men are declassed. Miscegenation, like illegitimacy, is heavily tabooed, especially among middle and upper class Negroes."

Today, the question is of interest to white Southerners, for the reason that the Negro insistence for race-mixing seems now to have an inordinate degree of federal government support. Southerners agree that public opinion has brought about a reduction in interracial promiscuity, but they lay most emphasis and most dependence upon formal racial separation as the factor most responsible for diminished sex relationships between whites and Negroes. The separation of the two races into divided social groupings has kept social contact at a minimum, and correspondingly has lowered both the incentive and the opportunity for line-crossing in sex relationships. The oft-cited contention that racial intermarriage is at a low ebb, even in communities where there is no racial segregation, overlooks this fact: where true integration prevails, Negroes are present in such small numbers as to be statistically insignificant, whereas in metropolitan areas where Negroes do comprise large numbers, residential and social segregation still keep the races widely separated. There is, therefore, no real yardstick with which to measure intermarriage in a fully-integrated situation (in the United States) where whites and blacks are both present in substantial number.

Since white Southerners for the most part have a revulsion against cross-breeding with Negroes, they vigorously oppose the elimination of barriers which have proved effective— either of themselves or in combination with other factors—in inhibiting intermarriage. Their fears are given expression to some degree, albeit in rather fancy language, in this excerpt from a pamphlet on the *Psychiatric Aspects of Desegregation:*

"If and when there is a shift in the direction of integration, this would show itself as a shift toward greater mutuality and breadth of shared experience between whites and Negroes in their total relationships, including psychosexual components. One might expect, therefore, that if there were eventual Negro-white integration, there would also be a shift from a preponderance of illicit interracial unions to the fuller, more enduring legalized unions of marriage . . ."

Southerners will argue the degree of biological mixing which now goes on between the races, but they will agree with the psychiatrists' conclusion that a trend toward integration would likely be accompanied by an increase in the "shared experience . . . including psychosexual components." And that is something they do not wish for themselves or for their children.

In this respect, as in the case of purely biological factors, the scientific findings are of less real importance than the popular attitudes with respect to evolving satisfactory adjustments between the races. What is true frequently is not as influential as what people think is true. Since the great mass of Southerners think the races are anthropologically different, the problem must be tackled from that point of view. And of equal import is the fact that the white man's concept of the Negro is as much social as anthropological. The proof of that attitude lies in the numerous Southern statutes which label an individual a Negro even though he may be three-fourths white by descent and totally white in appearance.

The social identification of the Negro carries weight in any discussion of intermarriage. As Professor Otto Klineberg, of Columbia University, has pointed out: "If there is general objection to miscegenation the effect upon the individual may be unfortunate . . . it is clearly the attitude toward hybrids, not their biological makeup, which determines their place in the community." The half-breed (having dubious standing with both races) has a powerful dual incentive to continue cross-breeding: to avenge himself for a wrong done him without his knowledge or consent, and to add company to his own category of half-castes by further propagation of persons of mixed blood. A further stimulus is cited in this extract from Reuter's *The Mulatto in the United States:*

"The desire of the mixed-blood man is always and everywhere to be a white man; to be classed with and become a part of the superior race. The ideal—the center of gravity—of the hybrid group is outside itself. The ideal of beauty, of success, of all that is good and desirable is typified by the superior race."

Many a Negro seems to feel that what impedes his progress and blocks his acceptance in the general social structure is his color and the reputation associated with that color. Of course, that particular factor is beyond the control of mortal man, be he segregationist or integrationist. The race-mixers ultimately may be able to "remedy" that situation through several generations of interracial breeding, but even that unpalatable solution cannot change the present circumstances of color differential. Thus far, not even the most rabid South-baiters have accused Southerners of being responsible for the color of Negroes.

Yet the color barrier exists, North and South, East and West, perhaps in varying degrees of intensity; but nowhere are its effects completely unnoticeable. For better or for worse, for now or forever, the Negro is stamped with a hue which sets him apart in terms of appearance if nothing else. And because of that badge of distinction, there is a tendency of white persons everywhere—not only in the South—to lump all Negroes in one homogeneous group in their thinking. That natural propensity, neither admirable nor avoidable, is accompanied by another manifestation of human weakness: the inclination to assign to any obviously different group all those undesirable characteristics which are reflected by individuals within that group.

The soldier who errs in uniform transmits his error to the account of all men in uniform. The Hebrew who draws criticism upon himself draws it likewise upon Jews everywhere; yet those who attain favor usually are given a non-Jewish identification in the eyes of their contemporaries and of succeeding generations. The theologian, Dr. Reinhold Niebuhr, has an apt summation of that trait:

"We regard a criminal within our own group as just a criminal, but if he belongs to another race or religion, we are inclined to consider him typical."

So it is with Negroes, and particularly so in times of emotional stress when racial consciousness is at a peak. Because the Supreme Court subscribed to the NAACP contention that the school segregation issue is a "class action," there immediately arose a class consciousness on the part of the resistant whites as well as of the insistent Negroes.

The upshot of the Supreme Court decision was the pitting of class against class, of white against Negro, rather than individual against individual. The inevitable result was what has aptly been termed a "massive deterioration" in race relations. Many individual relationships still remain cordial, although a good number of these have suffered, but the greatest break-down has come in group attitudes. It is understandable, even if not commendable, that the average white Southerner today is prone to attribute the instances of Negro crime, corruption, or mischief to the race rather than to the individual. Consequently, every misdeed by the black man is seized upon by the white man as added justification for keeping the races separated.

The persistence of the Negro-stereotype propaganda, however, is by no means due solely to the wishes or the actions of the white Southerner. There are many supposed "interpreters" of the Negro race who refuse to look at the achievements of the race, preferring to dwell sadistically on the real and fancied abuses suffered by black people in America. Ben Burns, former executive editor of the Negro magazine, *Ebony*, tells an interesting and revealing story in this regard. When the celebrated French photographer, Henri Cartier-Bresson, asked to be shown about the Negro areas of Chicago on a pictorial mission, the Frenchman was sublimely indifferent to the many physical manifestations of Negro progress visible on every side in the form of buildings, homes, schools, and the like. Instead, all he wanted to see—and to photograph—were slums. That obsession drew these comments from Burns as he recounted the experience in the March 8, 1956 issue of *The Reporter*:

"But I could not but fume inside at the thought that poverty and despair was the prevalent portrait of the Negro and here was the highly original Cartier-Bresson in the same rut . . .

"I recalled that in two trips to Europe I had often been amazed by the number of stereotyped beliefs about Negroes. In Paris the most mediocre of Negro entertainers were enjoying prosperity such as they had never known back in the States as Frenchmen flocked to see and hear these 'exotics' from America.

"These stereotypes could be amusing until one sat at a sidewalk cafe and listened to Negro expatriates bemoaning their status back home. Drawing G.I. Bill of Rights checks or author's royalties from America, they stayed in Paris until their last cent was gone. Then unable to find any kind of decent employment in Paris—because most Negroes in France do only the most menial kind of labor—they had to return to their terrible homeland to take good jobs as social workers or newspapermen."

The self-pitying Negroes of whom Burns speaks are among those who reflect an almost fascinating psychology of white consciousness and a striving for "whiteness" not only in culture, but actually in color and color corollaries such as hairdress, habits, and other distinctions normally associated with the white race. There are, of course, numerous coal-black Negroes who by reason of racial pride or by manifest force of circumstances have nothing but scorn for their lighter-skinned, part-white brethren, but in general the Negro seems to lay heavy emphasis on lightness. In many respects, his quarrel is not so much with the white man as with the Creator. The Group for the Advancement of Psychiatry dwells briefly on the phenomenon in its booklet, *Psychiatric Aspects of Desegregation:*

"Psychiatrists and social scientists are aware that Negroes develop their own hierarchies of status based on how close skin color approaches white and how close social and sexual standards approach the supposed white middle-class standards. It is well known how much money and time many Negroes feel driven to spend on cosmetics, deodorants, clothes, and automobiles in efforts to break away from the destructive devaluing self-concept which they have developed as the result of childhood guilt and shame."

These color distinctions—discriminations, if you please—among the Negroes themselves are quite apparent even to the casual observer who takes care to look and listen for them. A Negro maid who served this writer's family for a number of years was part white, although not distinguishably so, and had nothing but scorn for a coal-black Negro policeman to whom she invariably referred as a "soot ball." Also revealing was the local Negro beauty contest which sought to select "Miss Fine Brown Frame." Then, too, there are the names of Negro magazines such as *Sepia, Tan, Bronze Thrills,* and the like, leaving one to marvel that such pure black connotative titles as *Jet* and *Ebony* could survive. In all these magazines, photographic stress in "glamor" pictures always is on the light-skinned Negro who more nearly approaches the generally accepted white standard of pulchritude.

Erasure of color, therefore, would actually be more to the Negro's liking than erasure of the color line. In August of

1949, in *Look* magazine, Walter White wrote hopefully of a chemical which had potentialities for changing black skins to white. The NAACP official, who was himself only about one-sixty-fourth part Negro, regarded the chemical, mono-benzyl, as having the capability of doing "more for race relations than any other scientific discovery to date."

The significance of White's article, and in his "passing" reference, lies in the obvious belief that blackness must be eradicated if Negroes are to achieve their goals. Here is further evidence that amalgamation looms large among those goals, for the stress is not placed upon development and improvement of the Negro race as a distinctive, black race, but upon its absorption—by chemical or biological means—into the white race.

12

The Academic Arena

THE pattern of public school segregation in the South is most seriously threatened from without by those who seek to destroy the system by federal pressure, but there are also forces within the school establishment itself, North and South, which are at work toward integration. The suspicion that a sprinkling of Southern educators favored race-mixing was confirmed in the aftermath of the Supreme Court's desegregation decision of May 17, 1954. True, most of these educators retained enough caution to tread lightly and speak softly in their respective Southern communities, but a fair number began to expound their theories in various professional publications, notably those affiliated with the National Education Association. Southern laymen who were concerned with the attitudes of their school officials found evidences of defection in such periodicals as *Educational Leadership*, the Journal of the NEA's Association for Supervision and Curriculum Development. And as for the NEA itself, its pro-integration proclivities had long been evident.

The surprising thing to Southern laymen was the failure of Southern school men and women to champion the cause of the South at the various NEA-sponsored meetings. Either through timidity and intimidation, on the one hand, or through agreement with the NEA program on the other, many Southern delegates have remained silent or acquiescent in the face of anti-Southern declarations by the NEA.

For example, at the NEA convention in New York City shortly after the Supreme Court's decision had been announced in 1954, only Mississippi and South Carolina voted against adoption of a resolution which stated: "The principle embodied in the recent decision of the Supreme Court of the United States with regard to racial segregation is reflected in the long-established provisions of the platform of the National Education Association."

Even more ominous to the South, however, was the NEA's issuance of a fat and insidious little publication entitled *Leaders' Guide to Use and Study of Materials on Intergroup Education.* Like similar educational publications which promote the cause of race-mixing in public schools, the booklet lost some of its effectiveness through use of high-faluting trade jargon which rendered it well-nigh incomprehensible to laymen. And, fortunately for the South, laymen still control the affairs of government (and of education) on this regional level.

Throughout its 106 pages, the *Leaders' Guide* hammers away, as best it can with its sponge-like phrases, against any concept which might hold dear such old-fashioned ideas as racial purity, natural affinity of like-minded and like-cultured individuals, and parental concern over children's associations. The galaxy of cooks who prepared this recipe for interracial mixing would stir all peoples in all places, most especially the young people, into one bubbling cauldron and simmer the mass down to an even-textured blend devoid of distinctive color, culture, or flavor. As praiseworthy examples of such sociological hash-making, the booklet points pridefully to Brazil, Hawaii, and France, with the strong implication that the United States should proceed promptly in remaking itself into the mold of those areas.

To bring about that much-sought-after result, the educators and sociologists who compiled the *Leaders' Guide* want to work primarily through the schools of America, and secondarily through other community forces. In this latter respect, the booklet declaims: "It is important that the local leadership have a sensitivity to the problems and an understanding of the interrelatedness of the forces which play upon the community life."

The fact that such sensitivity and such understanding might make for continued segregation in the South seems never to occur to the pundits of the NEA and of the American Teachers Association (essentially a Negro group), who concocted the recipe for race-mixing. Everything which smacks of continued allegiance to social customs must be cast aside: "Each succeeding generation has tended to accept the established pattern of behavior as a part of its social heritage." That, according to the NEA-ATA brain trust, is bad.

"We recognize," say the two authors of the pamphlet's foreword, "that for many persons who have grown up under patterns of discrimination and who have come to accept certain practices as natural and inevitable, it is difficult to relinquish the habitual attitudes and behaviors which support these practices. We have learned, however, that both attitudes and behaviors may be changed through re-education, if the desire and the will are strong enough. We also know that customs and traditions may be changed in the direction of achievement of desirable practices when circumstances upon which they have developed are altered or when persons make up their minds that new and improved ways of doing things are needed."

Manifestly, what the NEA-ATA do-gooders have as their goal is a mind-changing operation on those persons who prefer to choose their own associates, or to supervise the associations of their children. Note this:

"Considerations of race, creed, color, nationality, economic position or other arbitrary distinctions which tend to develop divisive, differential, and discriminatory treatment have no place in America's educational system."

One of the truly alarming revelations of the *Leaders' Guide* is the astounding extent to which pro-integration literature has been built up in recent years. Dozens upon dozens of publications are cited, either by text or by bibliography, which dwell incessantly upon the desirability of enforced brotherhood and racial commingling through varying degrees of coercion. And because the vast majority of these socio-educational works generally employ double-talk and high-sounding camouflage for the black and white of race relations, it is worthwhile noting this revealing statement—one which tips off the reader to the phraseology employed in the constant effort to brainwash the segregationist:

"The growing literature in the fields of 'group dynamics,' 'race relations,' 'intercultural education,' and 'adult education' contains a wide range of suggested techniques ranging all the way from individual catharsis . . . and group restraining devices, to conventions and legislation."

On another educational level, here comprising members of Phi Delta Kappa, a professional fraternity of men in education, there seems a general acceptance of the inevitability of integration—the only question now being how the Supreme Court's decision can best be put into effect. A special desegregation issue of the *Phi Delta Kappan* (May, 1956) opened with this editor's note:

"It is our belief that eventually the matter of desegregation will reach the point where educators will be told, 'O.K., we're through fighting, now *you* tell us what to do.'"

Many of these professional publications in the world of education, and a considerable proportion of the other propaganda disseminated by the integrationists, make much of the premise that school children themselves have little or no objection to integration. Here is a sample of the NAACP exposition of that theme, embodied in a little pamphlet entitled *It Can Be Done:*

"In the difficult months ahead, it is to be hoped that authorities in charge of integrating public schools will impress parents with the need for letting the children work out their new associations for themselves. Desegregation tends to become a problem chiefly because of adults."

That sort of reasoning pre-supposes that children know better than their parents the sort of education they should have, and the sort of associations they should form in obtaining that education. The NAACP argument might as well ask the question which obviously goes along with the paragraphs just quoted: "Why bother with parents?" Does that mean that the youngsters should simply be dumped into an educational grinder where they make their own rules, presumably under the benevolent guidance of the NAACP, the Northern integrationists, and the Southern submissionists?

Most sociologists, perhaps even those trained and retained by the NAACP, will concur in the statement that a fundamental purpose—perhaps the ultimate purpose—of education is to transmit the culture of a society. That being true, then it follows naturally and obviously that there is a definite and deliberate relationship between a given culture and the educational pattern aimed at perpetuating that culture. How foolish it would be to let the children determine their own culture pattern, since they have neither the experience nor the judgment upon which to base intelligent decisions! But their time will come; and if, in later life, they want to modify or drastically revise their culture or their educational system, then they can use their influence to accomplish the change.

In the meanwhile, they will have learned from their own experience and observation that there *are* racial distinctions which cannot be ignored except at the peril of unpleasant consequence. "It is a false philosophy," says Robert M. Mac-Iver in *The More Perfect Union*, "that denies the differences between groups, and it is a misguided program that in the name of our common humanity seeks to instill the belief that these differences are either negligible or nonexistent. Genuine cultural differences exist all about us, and all men set store on their own culture. To minimize these differences is no solution of the problem of inter-group relations, and the teaching that propounds it is rejected by the discerning student."

Nevertheless, there are those in official position within educational, governmental, social and other areas who think it advisable to pretend that color distinctions do not exist. They remove all reference to race in personnel records, eliminate such references from application blanks, and avoid it in statistical studies. By doing so they apparently hope that the problem, thus ignored, will go away, or that at least they themselves will not be subjected to harassment which grows out of racial contrasts or comparisons.

Psychologists term this attitude a "denial of difference," and look upon it with mixed emotions. Some, whose identification and sympathy lie with Negro groups, recommend the elimination of racial references on the supposition that the elimination will constitute a defense against some forms of discrimination, or against public exploitation or disclosure of unfavorable aspects of the racial group. On the other hand, there are those (as in the Group for the Advancement of Psychiatry) who contend that "knowing the child's race, like other factual information about him, such as his age, sex, and health, can enable schools to better recognize and meet whatever his special educational needs may be."

Another theme recurrent in the race-mixing literature is the argument that "integration will work if the people want it to work." Such a statement carries the obvious to the point of asininity. Anything will work where the people want it to work. Any form of social structure, whether segregation or integration; any form of economic structure, whether capitalism, socialism, or communism; or any form of political structure, whether democracy, monarchy, dictatorship or otherwise—any of these will work where there exists "the will to comply" with whatever directive or authority sets up the particular pattern.

It is only when a sociological, economic, or political pattern is sought to be forced on a people against their will that resistance and non-compliance develop. And that is precisely the situation in the South today. The white Southerners want no part of any arbitrary rearrangement of their educational and political structure, and they will resist having it forced upon them. In the face of this determined resistance, based upon attitudes and experiences which the non-Southerner has never had, the many suggestions which come to the South smack of almost unbelievable naïveté. In their remote sections of Yankeeland, with backs turned to or eyes averted from the segregated Negroes and Puerto Ricans in their own midst, the Northern integrationists look piously Southward and expound advice as lacking in sense as it is in substance.

For example—and no isolated example it is—there is this typical statement in a *Christian Social Relations Bulletin* (Feb., 1956) of the Council of the Diocese of New York of the Protestant Episcopal Church:

"Basic to a calm discussion of the decision is the further fact that the Court did not order immediate integration. The Court recognized the differences between the situation in the States the deep South, the middle South, and the border States. Keeping these differences in mind, the Court ordered integration 'with all deliberate speed,' and remanded enforcement of the order to the Federal district courts . . . There is no need for the people of the South to fear the use of force by the Federal Government in States where an honest effort is being made to implement the decision."

Somehow, these good brethren of the North cannot get it through their heads that in the States of the Deep South there is *no* "will to comply," nor will there be made "an honest effort . . . to implement the decision." The white Southerners of these states will fight to the bitter end to prevent or forestall integration, and it is utterly foolish to talk of "a will to comply."

Through the years, Southerners of both races have evolved a pattern of peaceable and practicable accommodation, based on what had been a growing respect and regard for each other. Through the attrition which comes with time, the wall separating the two races was beginning to sink a bit, and here and there bricks were falling from its edges as traffic across the wall increased. And that was all right; but once the wall itself was threatened with sudden destruction, Southerners rushed to its defense and its repair. Today, the wall is higher and stronger than it had been in years, and all because of the onslaughts made against it.

It rankles the Southerner that all this disruption has been occasioned by Northerners whose moralizing is equaled only by their hypocrisy. In all their moral rectitude, the non-Southern integrationists preach the brotherhood of man and the abolition of color bars. Yet in their day-to-day living they find it expedient and no doubt comforting to follow what might well be termed "the great white way" of life, for themselves and for their children.

A prime example of this colossal hypocrisy occurred at Columbia University. In the face of an influx of Negro and Puerto Rican children into the public school attended by many children of the University faculty, an appreciable number of these faculty parents arranged to have their children attend private schools elsewhere. Russell Maguire, the editor of *The American Mercury*, brought the situation to light in a June, 1957, editorial sharply contrasting the preachments and the practices of Columbia University faculty members with respect to school integration. He charged that faculty members who could afford to do so were sending their children to other schools in order to avoid participation in what Maguire termed "the great social experiment."

"The great advance of the integrated school," Maguire wrote, "which liberal Columbia has so long advocated has routed the Columbia liberals almost to a man."

No such admission was forthcoming from Columbia University, however. When the University was asked to comment on *The American Mercury* editorial, this is what came back by way of an answer from the associate provost of the University:

"University faculty members set high educational standards for their children, as you would expect. The problem for them has not been caused by students being Negroes or Puerto Ricans but by the socio-economic composition of the group and what this means in practical terms for the educational process. Some faculty members have withdrawn their children from the nearest public school and have sent them to private schools. Others have moved into the suburbs partly for educational reasons and partly also to get their children off the streets and for the obvious advantages of suburban living. On the other hand, many faculty children still attend the school . . ."

All of which shows that there is substantial agreement in the thinking of Northerners and Southerners, liberals and conservatives, concerning the rearing and education of their children. The chief difference seems to lie in the language employed by way of explanation or justification for what remains, by whatever name called, "segregation." The Southerner, who recognizes from history and from his daily life that Negroes comprise a cultural group distinct from the whites, simply deals openly with the problem by separating the two groups frankly and above-board on the basis of race. The Northerner, backed into a corner by his own hollow preachments of racial brotherhood, bases his case for segregation on terms such as "socio-economic composition."

All over America, parents are coming face to face with the question of how best they can protect or improve the educational environment of their children. In the Deep South, where racial separation is still the custom of the community (the Supreme Court to the contrary notwithstanding) that question is being answered by increased emphasis on improvement of both white and Negro school facilities—separately. Along the Southern border, uneasy efforts are being carried on to blend whites and Negroes in a joint educational process. And in the "integrated" North, many a white parent is finding that his only escape from educational problems lies in the direction of the private school. Especially is this true in New York, where the entire school populace is being threatened with forced feeding of integration by school authorities and pressure groups.

The problem of providing an adequate education for the nation's children is a difficult enough undertaking at best without having it compounded by racial and "socio-economic" complications. The task of financing education poses a terrific problem in itself, as the South knows from hard experience. In the long, bitter pull since the tragic days of the Reconstruction Era, the South—despite its longtime status as the nation's Number One Economic Problem—has taxed its impoverished people at a higher rate in proportion to per capita income than the states of the North have taxed their wealthier people in the cause of public school education. That is largely true even today, for a look at the records will show that Southerners still contribute a larger share of their income to education than do taxpayers in any other section of the country. Yet the smart alecks who play with statistics can always come up with some hard and fast figures which show that, on a dollar-for-dollar basis, the

South is not measuring up to the rest of the nation in school spending.

Prime examples of the relative efforts of the Northern and Southern states to meet the educational needs of their people are reflected in graphs in the Ashmore report, *The Negro and the Schools,* published by the University of North Carolina Press on the eve of the Supreme Court's desegregation decision of 1954.

States such as Louisiana, North Carolina, South Carolina, and Arkansas, for example, were among the lowest-ranked 10 states in per capita income in 1950, but were among the top 10 with respect to the relative effort being made to finance public schools. Specifically, Louisiana stood 40th in rank for per capita income, but in 3rd place in per cent of total personal income spent on public schools. Similarly, North Carolina ranked 43rd in income but 5th in effort; South Carolina stood 46th in income but 10th in effort, and Arkansas ranked 47th in income but 9th in effort.

Quite the reverse was true for the wealthy states of the non-South. Delaware, which had the nation's highest per capita income in 1950, stood 45th among the states with respect to per cent of income spent on public schools. New York, which is addicted to self-adulation and South-baiting with respect to public education, ranked 3rd in per capita income but 43rd in percentage of that income which was spent for public schools. And so it went with Connecticut, 4th in earnings, 40th in educational effort; and with Illinois, 5th in per capita income, but 41st in per cent of income spent for schools.

But if the public schools of the South have suffered through the years from lack of finances, they have not languished for want of attention, nor have they lessened their status as major elements of Southern life. The public schools, in the minds of most white Southerners, are woven into the social fabric of the community, and indeed into the family pattern itself. Schooling is not an objective activity carried on impersonally between mature individuals. It is an experience in personal living which is caught up closely with the very formation of growth patterns and psychology.

The two federal judges who upheld the "separate but equal" doctrine when the famous "Clarendon county case" of South Carolina was moving through the lower courts, had a clear grasp of the Southern attitude when they had this to say:

"Education at this [public school] level is not a matter of voluntary choice on the part of the student but of compulsion by the state. The student is taken from the control of the family during school hours by compulsion of law and placed in control of the school, where he must associate with his fellow students . . .

"In formulating educational policy at the common school level, therefore, the law must take account, not merely of the matter of affording instruction to the student, but also of the wishes of the parents as to the upbringing of the child and his associates in the formative period of childhood and adolescence. . . . If public education is to have the support of the people through their legislatures, it must not go contrary to what they deem for the best interests of their children."

The Supreme Court itself unwittingly called attention to one of the fundamental reasons that white Southerners do not want racial integration in the public schools when it said that education "is a principal instrument in awakening the child to cultural values, in preparing him for later professional training, and in helping him to adjust normally to his environment." The white Southerner finds no fault with that statement, despite its source, but his emphasis and his fear hinge about the words "culture" and "environment." Whether mistakenly or not, and the Southerner does not regard his attitude as mistaken, he wants his children to absorb the "culture" and preserve the "environment" which reflect the social traditions of white society in the South. Without regard to the superiority of one culture over the other, it is manifest that they are different—and there are few white Southerners who want their children to undertake the experiment of bridging the gap.

The breach is wide between the races, despite assertions of the equality cultists that native ability disregards color lines. Be that as it may, the fact remains that in the here and now of Southern history, Negro children have measurably lower standards than their white contemporaries in terms of academic standing, intellectual background, personal hygiene, and morality. It can be, and is, argued that this situation exists through no fault of the Negro (the point is debatable), but such a contention is somewhat extraneous. The hub of the matter is that the white parent whose responsibility includes implanting proper standards in his children will not readily yield to a situation wherein his children would not only be exposed to, but in countless instances immersed in, a group having lower standards.

It takes no hydraulic engineer to realize that the linking of two reservoirs of different levels necessarily means the lowering of one to bring about the raising of the other. The application of that rule to the field of integrated education is being tried in the schools of Washington, with consequences which have alarmed some of the very individuals who so diligently undermined the dikes which formerly kept the racial reservoirs separate. But all that is Washington's business, and if the residents of the District of Columbia want it that way, or if they prefer to desert the city in droves while the nation's capital becomes ever-increasingly a black metropolis, then so be it. The darkening face of Washington distresses Southerners, as perhaps it does Americans elsewhere, but that is a problem for the federal government to solve, since the District is federal domain.

The vast sociological experiment of forced integration in the New York schools, inhuman though it may appear to Southerners, is really no concern of theirs. If the hybrid population of that great melting pot wishes to bring the amalgam to a quicker boil by stirring the ingredients furiously, then Southerners will stand by in silent wonderment, but they will not interfere.

But in New York, as in Washington, school administrators are learning the hard way that mixing the races in public schools is not a way to save money, at least not in areas where sizable numbers of different races are present. One of the more specious arguments advanced against separate schools in the South has been the contention that it requires duplication of facilities, with consequent duplication of costs. A case can be made out for that argument in a few places, but only in those relatively rare instances where a handful of Negro students have been transported considerable distances to Negro schools, or where separate schools have been built for small numbers of Negro pupils. But by and large, in the Deep South areas where resistance to integration is strongest, there is little or no added cost because of segregation, and for this reason:

In almost every part of the South where segregation is practiced, there are sufficient Negroes in residence to warrant the maintenance of a separate school for them alone. It is not a question of duplicating facilities, but of trying to keep pace with the need for burgeoning enrollments of both whites and Negroes. If Negroes were brought into the white schools today, or vice versa, then some of the presently enrolled students would have to be displaced. There is no surplus space available in the schools of the South, and the only way to make room for Negroes at schools which are now white would be to withdraw some white students and send them elsewhere—if the "elsewhere" were available.

True, there may be some duplication of effort and expense in the realm of school bus transportation, for the consolidation of smaller schools into larger ones means that the tiny neighborhood school has virtually disappeared. Consequently, white students may ride past a Negro school to get to their classes, and so might Negroes be carried past white schools en route to their classes. That cost, however, is relatively small in comparison with the overall school budget, and it is one which is borne cheerfully by the white taxpayers.

Furthermore, if that argument is really intended to be valid, then why is it not applied to the New York situation? There, integrationists urge the transporting of white children away from their own neighborhood simply in order to distribute them among Negroes or Puerto Ricans. Here is an instance which runs directly counter to what the courts have held; which would do precisely what the courts have said should not be done: discriminating against children solely because of their race. This process, which may or may not be swallowed by New Yorkers, obviously is part of a program for enforced integration, not as a means to the end of improved education, but as an end in itself.

If New Yorkers continue to play at race-mixing with the vast numbers of Negroes and Puerto Ricans who throng into the city, they may soon gain a better appreciation of a major facet of the situation in the South:—that in many a Southern community, the white people, and more especially the white children, are in the numerical minority. Yet the integrationists, who cry for racial admixture in the cause of bolstering the personality development of a Negro minority, do not hesitate to compel the mingling of a white minority with a black majority without any consideration of the inevitable psychological impact upon the personalities of the *white* children.

Indeed, there has been a monumental indifference on the part of the race-mixers concerning the likelihood of adverse psychological effects upon *white* children. This uncocern may be due in part to the Northern integrationists' ignorance of the human numbers as well as the human nature involved in Southern race relations. If Southern communities had as few Negroes to contend with as do the vast majority of non-Southern communities, then there would be no problem of consequence—and little reason for worry over psychological reactions from bringing a handful of Negro children into what would still be a predominantly white class or school. But the reverse of that would frequently occur in much of the South, where integration would bring a sprinkling of white children into what would be an overwhelmingly black group. Even the most rabid integrationist should be able to foresee the fears, tensions, apprehensions, and anxieties which inevitably would arise in the white child's mind, and to understand that these would seriously disrupt the psychological balance of the child's personality.

Unfortunately, there are integrationists who do see that problem in all of its dimensions, yet who still persist in demanding race-mixing at all costs. Their attitude is a sociological perversion of Farragut's battle-cry, revised to read: "Damn the consequences; full speed ahead!" Their goal obviously is integration, not education; and their concern is solely with the Negro, not the white, child.

Within this group are psychologists who appear more preoccupied with "improving" the mental health of "disadvantaged" minority groups than in preserving the mental health of majorities which prefer the continuation of association within their own group. It is quite understandable that the professional psychologist's interest would be stimulated by social disruptions which would afford him a vast proving ground for experimentation and research. But it is equally understandable that the average white parent has little inclination to offer up his own children as guinea pigs for sociological experiments which may or may not work out successfully.

In all fairness to the psychologist, however, it must be admitted that he has been able to dredge up some plausible motivations for the conduct of integrationists. For example, a pamphlet of the *Psychiatric Aspects of School Desegregation*, published in May of 1957 by the Group for the Advancement of Psychiatry, contributes a paragraph which seems singularly significant as applied to the conduct of numerous apostate Southerners:

". . . a person unable to adjust to the customs and authority of his community may adopt the values and attitudes toward desegregation of a group outside the community and thus satisfy a vengeful motive against the local community. Or someone who believes himself to be an underdog in his own family may vigorously take up the side of the underdogs in the community when he is really mainly serving his own needs."

Despite the community disapproval of what the integrationists or the moderates have to say in the South, there has been little freezing of expression. The proof of that assertion lies in the very quantity of "liberal" views which have poured from the pens of those Southern writers who find a ready Northern market for their tortured portrayals of a benighted South. Less famous persons, however, do find it frustrating to talk of integration or moderation when their neighbors refuse to listen to them, or even to accord them an audience.

Out of this community rejection comes much of the foolish prating of integrationists and submissionists about "freedom of speech." What they want is not actually freedom of speech, which they have in abundance, but freedom from verbal and social retaliation from others who choose to exercise their own freedom of speech.

The right of freedom of speech carries with it no compulsion on the part of listeners to agree with such speech, to heed it, or to refrain from speaking against it. Nor does it carry immunity from reaction which might be stirred up by such free-speaking. There are few places in this country where a man cannot have his say, openly and publicly, in person or in print. If, however, he chooses to say things which run counter to the sentiment prevailing in his community, then that is his decision. It is up to the individual to determine in his own mind whether he can best fulfill his chosen role in society at any given time and place by keeping his mouth shut, by speaking discreetly among friends and acquaintances, by speaking openly from all available platforms, or by putting his feelings in print for broader and more lasting dissemination of his views.

Yet when others say individually or collectively to the free-speaker: "We do not like what you say; we do not like you for saying it, and we will have nothing further to do with you,"—then up goes a great outcry of denial of freedom of speech. There is no denial; there is simply the matter of action and reaction; nevertheless, earnest lamentations have arisen in many quarters. For example, note these words from a 1957 report of the Council of Christian Relations of the Presbyterian Church in the United States, approved by the 1957 General Assembly of that denomination:

"A congressman is not reelected, a school teacher faces investigation, a health officer is dismissed, a journalist is forced to leave the community, a man suddenly loses his credit, and a minister loses his congregation—all because they exercised their right to speak freely."

Such things have happened in the South; they are happening today, and they will continue to happen—all because individuals of their own volition choose to speak out against the community pattern of segregation. If the Presbyterian councilmen want an answer to their apparent quandary, they provide it themselves when they say within the same paragraph which includes the above quote: "Freedom of speech includes the right to register one's opinion through the medium of voting." That single sentence should remind the Presbyterians that people vote as they please. If their representatives in Congress adopt positions which displease them, then why should the people be constrained to continue voting for such Congressmen? And besides voting, people can register their disapproval in many ways, as integrationists are learning to their dismay.

Those who prate of "human relations" would do well to understand more of "human nature." Friendships, associations, business connections, political ties, and virtually all the social links which bind individuals together grow out of like-mindedness. One man strikes up a friendship with another because they find common enjoyment in common pursuits. A businessman does his buying and selling partly on the impersonal basis of dollars and cents, partly on the personal basis of mutuality of interest or of identity. A newspaper subscriber, given a free choice, buys the paper which more nearly reflects his own point of view and which provides him with the news content he desires. Even the churchgoer singles out that denomination or that church within a denomination which he finds most appealing to his personal predilections. And in all these pursuits, the individual, by himself or in concert with others, has the right to form his own affiliations or to change his affiliations.

The freedom of speech preachments are cited with great frequency and persistency in the educational world, along with demands for "academic freedom," but here again the arguments lack consistency. If a Communist-minded professor is afforded complete impunity to harangue his students or the public, then does not the exercise of that freedom deny to the college president his freedom to maintain a loyally American institution?

What Communism has been to the rest of the nation, so integration is to the South—something so undesirable, so foreign to the domestic way of life, so fraught with danger to present and future generations that it is fought on every front, including the educational. Complaints arise, more by indirection than direction, to the effect that college professors and educators generally are afraid to voice any opinion contrary to that prevailing in the community where they happen to be located. Without attempting to establish any positive link between Communism and integration, there is nevertheless an analagous connection in that Southerners consider integration as much a threat to their way of life as Americans generally think of Communism as a threat to the American way of life. Under such circumstances, it is easy to understand why pro-integration statements draw prompt rebuttal and resentment from Southern audiences in whose midst they are made, or from Southern taxpayers and school boards whose beliefs may be flouted by educators with opposing concepts of educational values.

Sometimes, the "freedom of speech" situation takes a reverse turn, as when segregationists are denied their opportunity to speak. One such occasion was recorded in November of 1954, when Dr. Channing H. Tobias, NAACP board chairman, arranged the suspension of an NAACP meeting at which speakers were to include W. Bryant Bowles, then head of the pro-segregationist organization known as the "National Association for the Advancement of White People." Bowles had been invited to speak at the conference by the Peekskill branch of the NAACP, which was serving as host for the gathering, but neither state nor national headquarters had been so informed. When Dr. Tobias learned of the scheduled address, according to an NAACP press release, he "took immediate steps to suspend the scheduled meeting and issued a directive that 'under no circumstances' should Bowles . . . be permitted to address an NAACP meeting."

Dr. Tobias explained his stand in these words:

"Freedom of speech does not require us to make our platform available to a man in custody of the law as Bowles was at that time or to one who openly incites violation of the law of the land as interpreted by the U. S. Supreme Court. Bowles is opposed to everything for which we stand."

In similar vein were the protests against the appearance of Georgia's Attorney General Eugene Cook at Yale University in 1955. When the Georgia official was invited to give "The Southern View of Segregation" at a meeting sponsored by the Conservative Society, six campus groups immediately protested against his being allowed to speak unless someone spoke in opposition to his views at the same occasion. The groups were the Yale Chapter of the NAACP; the John Dewey Society; the New Haven Civil Liberties Union; the Yale Hillel Foundation; the Yale Christian Association; and the Young Democrats of Yale.

Freedoms, in the final analysis, are relative things, and are "rights" only to the degree that their exercise by one group does not infringe upon the freedoms of another group. In the field of race relations, a freedom to integrate is an automatic denial of the freedom to segregate, and vice versa. Race-mixers in the South have been denied freedom to integrate because Southern communities have not been willing to give up their freedom to prefer segregation. They still are not willing to do so.

They will resist to the bitter end any attempt to integrate the public schools, and then, if force of federal arms brings them to the point of capitulation, many will withdraw their support of the public schools themselves. It may be difficult for the non-Southerner to conceive of so determined an attitude, but hosts of white parents throughout the Deep South are in complete agreement with the statement made in March of 1951 by the then governor of South Carolina, James F. Byrnes:

"If the court changes what is now the law of the land, we will, if it is possible, live within the law, preserve the public school system, and at the same time maintain segregation. If that is not possible, reluctantly we will abandon the public school system."

13

The Black Shadow of Politics

T HE political structure of the United States has degenerated to the point where its control lies in what might be called, with apologies for this necessary distortion of a noble concept of government, the "concurrent minority." We are, in effect, rapidly approaching the opposite extreme of that state of political tranquility which John C. Calhoun envisioned as the natural consequence of rule by his "concurrent majority." For, instead of having the various elements of the American community united in a common undertaking to promote the welfare and progress of the whole, with each of its individual parts assured of protection against oppression or maltreatment at the hands of the others, we have achieved a state of balance between the two major political parties wherein an imbalance can be effected by a numerically insignificant portion of the populace. Thus, what Calhoun feared as the tyranny of the numerical majority actually has evolved into an even more distressing tyranny of the numerical minority.

This state of affairs has evolved, perhaps inevitably, from a combination of circumstances which characterize the American government. The emergence of the two-party system had its inception in an understandable difference of policy and governmental philosophy between segments of the population which gravitated together out of political like-mindedness. Then followed a consolidation of power in the hands of the relative few who came to control the machinery of the respective parties, whether overtly or covertly. Simultaneously, out of the natural propensity of American citizens to "choose up sides," a situation developed wherein each of the two major political groupings achieved a virtual parity of strength in many areas of the nation. One exception was the South, where the regional heritages tended to bind the people together in a common bond of sympathy with one party and of hostility to the other.

But, with the achieving of comparable political strength between Republicans and Democrats elsewhere in the nation, and more especially in the big states with many electoral votes, self-serving politicians realized that those electoral votes could be tipped into one party basket or the other by the simple expedient of maneuvering the uncommitted minorities which were chiefly concerned with their own special interests.

Out of this realization on the parts of both the politicians and the leaders of the minority groups came this control by the concurrent minority. In city after city, and state after state, there gradually were developed combinations of racial, religious, and occupational minorities which together provided political schemers with the means of influencing the outcome of elections on local, state, and national levels. And since the consuming interests of these minority groups transcend the broader considerations of the general public welfare, it became a simple function to manipulate such groups as voting blocs. Appeals to their minority consciousness and promises to serve their minority interests did the trick. And just so long as the major parties remain in positions of relative political balance, the minority combinations can be employed as the balance of power to tip the scales— and the votes—to whichever of the major parties caters most abjectly to the minority demands.

The concurrent minority, therefore, thrives upon discord and disunion. Instead of promoting a harmony which would bind together diverse elements of the majority in the joint and amicable exercise of political control, the militant minority bloc—in order to preserve its own influence—seeks to pit one faction of the majority against the other. Only thus can the minority retain its status as the balance of power, and exercise its disproportionate power to bargain and to intimidate. It naturally follows that the concurrent majority and the concurrent minority are in fundamental and continual opposition to each other—the first making for peaceful coordination of effort with the aim of political tranquility, the second making for incessant agitation with the view of forestalling and thwarting any likelihood of agreement between the majorities.

An essential ingredient of this sort of political chicanery is the exploitation of class consciousness, a development which came to full flower under the nurturing care of the late Franklin Delano Roosevelt and his Democratic strategists. Beginning in 1936, the Rooseveltians devised the effective vote-getting scheme of appealing for support on the basis of racial, ethnic, religious, economic or other special grounds. By assiduous and insidious propaganda, coupled with effective ward-heeling on the low level and "fireside chats" on the upper, the New Dealers succeeded in compartmentalizing the electorate. Thus, to millions of Americans, the overriding consideration for political loyalty came to be not so much the question, "What is good for the nation?" but "What is good for me, as a Negro, or a Jew, or a Pole, or a labor union member, or a government worker, as a member of a special class?" The obvious disservice to the nation in the promotion of such class consciousness stood as no obstacle to the vote-minded politicians who were willing to sacrifice the national interest to their own selfish desires for perpetuation in office.

When the Democrats' 20-year tenure came to an end through a popular revulsion of feeling enhanced by the attraction of a personable national hero campaigning under the opposition banner, the political pattern had become crystallized. The Republicans, once in office, promptly adopted the same shabby tactics of the Democrats. After an initial appeal based on the fundamental American doctrines of states' rights and local self-government, the Republicans soon turned their attention to the cultivation of minorities.

Of all these minorities, the one most responsive to specialized appeals and concessions is the Negro group. But whereas the Negro was in large measure attracted to the Roosevelt banner by promises of economic as well as racial betterment, the present-day concern of the Negro seems almost solely based on color-consciousness and a burning desire (at least on the part of Negro leaders) to eliminate segregation. This contention is borne out by this observation from Louis Harris, a poll-wise researcher whose appraisal of election polling was inserted in the *Congressional Record* of July 23, 1957:

"As of 1952, there seemed little question that the Negro group would continue to go more heavily Democratic in the future. The oldtime Republican base among Negroes seemed to have nearly evaporated; the combined civil rights-New Deal base among Negroes seemed nearly monolithic. Nevertheless the dramatic events of desegregation under a Republican administration produced wholesale shifts among Negro voters in 1956. The cause is clear: the Negro group is today almost wholly absorbed with a single issue, and the Republicans have convinced many that their chances are greater under their leadership, and that the

Democrats must be punished unless they set their own civil-rights record straight."

The Negro realization of the political strength inherent in the bloc Negro vote is evident from numerous statements on the subject. As just one sample, take this editorial expression from the *Journal of Negro Education* (Summer, 1957), a document which should be required reading for every student of politics and every Southern voter:

"At the present time, over half (54 per cent) of the potential Negro voters are found in the . . . 11 Southern states. The remaining 46 per cent are found in the other 37 states, comprising about 6 per cent of the potential voters in these states. Despite its relatively small size in these 37 states, however, the Negro vote has a significance considerably greater than its numerical strength would suggest. In some of these states the Negro vote constitutes the potential balance of power between the two major parties, and in closely contested elections could be and often is a decisive factor."

A look at the presidential election of 1948, which was a reasonably close contest in terms of popular votes cast for Republicans and Democrats in the non-Southern states, bears out the fact that the Negro vote frequently is the determining factor. James Reston, *New York Times* political writer, is authority for these revealing statements:

"In 1948, for example, President Truman carried this state of Illinois by 33,612. The Negro vote for him in Chicago alone was in the vicinity of 90,000.

"In that same election, the Democratic majority in California was 17,865, and in Ohio it was 7,107. In both of these states, as in Illinois, the Negroes gave the Democratic party far more than the number of votes needed to win. . . .

"The Democrats carried California, Illinois, Ohio and Wisconsin in 1948 by a margin of less than 5 per cent of the vote cast. In these same states, the Negro vote was decisive. . . . Similarly, the Republicans won New York, Pennsylvania, Michigan and Maryland, among other states, by a margin of less than 5 per cent in 1948."

Over a still broader front, there were in 1948 at least 11 states in which the percentage of non-white (for the most part, Negro) population exceeded the percentage of votes which divided the two major parties. In listing those 11 states, it is significant to note the number of electoral votes held by each, since the Negroes, by tipping the scales one way or the other, can effectively determine which party gets the entire electoral vote of a particular state. The states, with electoral votes shown individually are:

New York, 45 votes; California, 32 votes; Pennsylvania, 32 votes; Illinois, 27 votes; Ohio, 25 votes; Michigan, 20 votes; New Jersey, 16 votes; Indiana, 13 votes; Maryland, 9 votes; Connecticut, 8 votes; and Delaware, 3 votes.

Taken collectively, this means that concerted bloc voting by Negroes in those 11 states could influence a total of 230 electoral votes, a situation well calculated to give Southern politicians the shudders, and non-Southern politicians a terrific incentive to cultivate the Negro vote. That staggering total of electoral votes is reason enough for Democrats and Republicans alike to court Northern Negroes in preference to Southern whites, who at best could muster only about 128 votes if they carried all 11 of these Southern states.

The fact that the Southern states, in the last two elections, have begun to break away from their traditional allegiance to the Democratic party makes the balance of power even more delicate. In the years immediately preceding and following the 1956 presidential election, Southerners have seen evidence aplenty that the pre-1952 Republican overtures for Southern support (although still maintained as window-dressing) have been supplanted in large measure by outright and, in Southern eyes, outrageous bids for Negro support. The 1956 split of the Negro vote showed that much Negro support could be enticed away from the Democrats by promising and giving more racial concessions.

The partially successful recapture of the Negro vote
stimulated the Republicans to even greater efforts and
aroused the National Democratic Party to equally great
efforts to appease Negro political demands. Democratic
concern over the situation was heightened by remarks such
as this one from Henry Lee Moon, public relations director
for the NAACP, writing in the *Journal of Negro Education:*

"The 1956 election also thrust into the forefront the most
serious problem confronting the Democratic Party. It is the
issue of liberalism. By now it must be clear that the party
can succeed nationally in normal times only as a liberal
party. And it cannot be a liberal party as long as it attempts
to embrace with equal fervor Senator Eastland [of Missis-
sippi] and Senator Herbert Lehman [of New York]. . . .
The time has come for the party to make a choice. It must
decide whether to seek to be a national party based upon
liberal principles or to sink to the level of a provincial
political clique dedicated to the perpetuation of the myth of
white supremacy."

This NAACP refrain draws echoes from prominent "liberal" Democrats who find it politically expedient to excoriate
the South and Southern Democrats. Sen. Paul Douglas, of
Illinois, labels the Southern wing of the Democratic Party
"the greatest handicap which we [Democrats] have in the
North. The superiority of Northern Democrats to Northern
Republicans is so great that were it not for the Southern in-
cubus we would win sweeping victories. . . ."

But if Southerners find hostility within what has been
their own political party, they find little incentive to align
themselves with a Republican Party which now stands
naked and unashamed as the suitor of every Negro and
minority bloc vote which is available for love or money. A
positive evidence of this inclination on the part of Republicans appears in the May, 1957, issue of their political
propaganda sheet, "Straight From the Shoulder." Under

the heading, "Nationalities Groups Swing to Republicans," appear these statements:

"Long-range results that can be of increasingly important political significance can be looked for in the 1956 swing in racial and minority groups to the Republican Party. . . . Look at the record in Chicago, for instance. In the past Democrats have counted strongly on their majorities among Chicago's large numbers of Polish, Irish and Italian voters, as well as those of Jewish faith and large numbers of Negroes. The shift to Republican candidates was apparent in the senatorial contest as well as in the Presidential race. . . . The Republicans will concentrate in 1958 on increasing the power of the break-through of what generally has been considered a usually invincible Democrat position."

What could be called a forerunner of that statement came on May 21, 1954, a press release from the Republican National Committee, which said: "This week's historic decision by the Supreme Court of the United States, eliminating segregation in public schools, is typical of the healthy climate-of-equality that prevails in President Eisenhower's administration. . . . The Eisenhower Administration put itself squarely behind the nonsegregation case with a brief by Atty. Gen. Herbert Brownell, Jr., before the Supreme Court."

While this brazen maneuvering for minority votes goes on in the North, the East, and the West, the white citizens of the South find themselves in the unenviable position of serving as the target for abuse from both national parties. There is ever-increasing exasperation in the South with the major parties, but with it is a sense of frustration stemming from the South's inability to adequately defend itself against these politically-motivated attacks.

Nevertheless, there remain hosts of Southerners who feel earnestly, if none too optimistically, that the states of the

South have more in common with each other than with either national party. Bound together by their joint adherence to "States' rights, constitutional government, and racial integrity," these Southerners reason that only by collective political action can they protect themselves against exploitation by both Democrats and Republicans. Thus arises the recurring consideration of "third party" movements.

This "third party" talk in the South is not born of any desire to break up the traditional two-party pattern of American politics. It stems, rather, from a sense of political desperation on the part of the Southerner who finds no haven in either national party. *In extremis,* he turns to thoughts of a third party which might more closely represent his political philosophy. Even as he does so, he fully realizes and half-admits the hopelessness of his efforts; yet there still is the fight to be made for a return to constitutional government of the sort relished by Southerners. Since the ultra-liberal third party movements of the non-South have tipped the American political pendulum far to the left, then a conservative third party movement, rooted in the South, might help swing it back to the right. That somewhat forlorn hope was the motive behind many a third party Southern vote in 1956. The failure of that attempt left the Southerner where he had been before—beleaguered and belligerent, without regional leadership or a regional plan, floundering in a welter of political indecision made the worse by his fear of further capitulation to Northern labor-liberals and minority blocs by both parties.

There is a tendency in much of the South to balance off one party against the other in terms of centralism and racial integration, and thereafter to vote, with no great enthusiasm, for presidential candidates on the relative merits of the individual men. This frame of mind contributed heavily to the Eisenhower victory of 1956. Four years earlier, there had been a somewhat different attitude on the part of

Southerners who departed from the traditional Democratic ticket. In 1952, the dissident Democrats rallied behind the Republican nominee, not because he was a Republican, but because he was General Dwight D. Eisenhower and because he talked a brand of states' rights which made good listening to hosts of Southern Democrats. Yet within four years, they had occasion to re-appraise what they had heard, and to re-assess Eisenhower the General, and Eisenhower the Candidate, in the light of Eisenhower the President.

Southerners are hard put, for example, to reconcile President Eisenhower's 1956 plea for federal aid to education with this 1949 declaration made while he was president of Columbia University:

"I firmly believe that the army of persons who urge greater and greater centralization of authority and greater and greater dependence upon the federal treasury are really more dangerous to our form of government than any external threat that can possibly be arrayed against us. . . ."

And in the light of his later advocacy of "civil rights" legislation by Congress, how could Eisenhower's 1948 testimony before the Senate Armed Forces Committee be consistent?—

"There is race prejudice in this country, and when you put in the same organization and make live together under the most intimate circumstances men of different races, we sometimes have trouble. . . . I do not mean to say that I have any final answer to the problem, and I believe that the human race may finally grow up to the point where it will not be a problem. It will disappear through education, through mutual respect and so on. But I do believe that if we attempt merely by passing a lot of laws to force someone to like someone else, we are just going to get into trouble."

In similar vein, there were the words of Candidate Eisenhower on the subject of Fair Employment Practices legislation, voiced in 1952 at Abilene, Kansas:

"I don't believe we can cure all of the evil in men's hearts by law—I really believe we can do more by leadership and by getting states to do it than make it a federal compulsory thing."

And to Southerners, among Southerners, he said this to a vast audience of South Carolinians at Columbia in September of 1952:

"Freedom's greatest threat today is too much government too far away from the people."

Utterances such as those led many a Southerner to throw off his Democratic vestments in the hope of donning a new mantle of states' rights tailored by a revitalized Republican Party. This was no quick-change act, however, for the patchwork Democratic robes had been chafing and galling Southerners for years. The longing for restoration of a meaningful doctrine of states' rights within the national administration persuaded hosts of voters throughout the South, and throughout the country, to cast their lot with the national hero who voiced their own innermost political convictions.

Eisenhower's profession of states' rights sentiments attracted not only the attention but the support of Southerners, but not long thereafter came the grand disillusionment as the Republicans set about trying to out-do the Democrats in catering to customers among the Negro and other minority groups in pivotal states outside the South. Administration spokesmen argued before the Supreme Court that racial separation in the public schools should be outlawed. And when the Court, under the leadership of what Vice President Nixon termed "a great Republican chief justice," rendered the sought-after decision, the Republicans promptly took credit for it. They culminated their drive toward centralized government in 1957 with passage of a "civil rights" act and with the President's ominous and dictatorial dispatch of armed combat troops into Little Rock, Ark., to carry out the school integration ordered by a federal district judge.

All these things, and especially the troop episode, brought a sharp halt to Republican growth in the South, a meaningful defection of several Southern Republican leaders, and an about-face from gullible Southern Democrats who had swallowed the Republican line.

To the accompaniment of "we told you so" recriminations from Southern Democrats, independent Southerners once more were convinced that the Republican Party's real preoccupation was with the Negro, even to the exclusion of the Southern white man. Here again, a hundred years after the Republican Party had been conceived out of a political passion against further extension of the power of slaveholding states, was new justification of the 1854 label applied by Democrats to adherents of the then-new party: "Black Republicans."

That initial antipathy toward the Republican Party was intensified, indeed well-nigh petrified, by Republican Party policies and practices preceding, during, and following the War Between the States. It was during the third quarter of the Nineteenth Century that the Southern states were welded together into Democratic unison by a jointly-shared bitterness against the Republican Party. That bitterness had multiple sources, for it was quite obvious that the Republicans in Congress sought not only to "reconstruct" the South governmentally, but to establish and perpetuate a broad, black base of Republican voting strength among the newly-freed slaves. Coupled with this joint effort was the humiliation suffered by white Southerners, who saw their lives, lands, and liberties mismanaged by black and white Republicans whose corrupt deeds are imprinted not only on the records of government but on the minds of Southerners.

It was at this juncture of American history that Southerners crystallized their persistent belief that the Republican Party was the party of the North and of the Negro, with the corollary belief that the Democratic Party was the party of the South, and most assuredly the party of the Southern white man.

So tenacious did this belief become that Southerners simply refused to tolerate any thought of forsaking the Democratic Party, even in the face of evidence that the later behavior of the party and the preachments of its non-Southern leaders were running increasingly counter to the basic political principles which motivated most Southerners.

Except for the odd overtones of religion and prohibition which marked the 1928 presidential contest and threw five Southern states into the Republican column, the South remained solidly Democratic. And by 1932, the five errant states (Florida, North Carolina, Tennessee, Texas, and Virginia) were firmly back in the Democratic fold, there to remain for twenty more years.

Other factors came into the picture during the 1930's under the adroit management of the master politician, Franklin D. Roosevelt. When the Democrats, under Roosevelt, sought out and captured the Negro votes wherever they could be found, Southerners remained steadfastly Democratic. It was Roosevelt who succeeded in the seemingly impossible task of holding together beneath the Democratic circus tent such diverse elements as the Northern Negro and the Southern white man, the liberal of the North and the conservative of the South, the big city boss of the Northern metropolis and the tenant farmer of the Southern crossroads.

And, during the same days of Roosevelt's New Deal and later under Truman's Fair Deal, when the Democrats courted and caught the affection of the liberal and labor groups, conservative Southern Democrats maintained their allegiance to the party label, although with mounting attempts at face-saving through condemnation of "Northern

Democrats," differentiated from "true Democrats" of the South.

This blind loyalty to the party label was understandable, if not fully rational. There was, as has already been recited, the stigma attached to the mere word "Republican"—a stigma growing out of the waging and the aftermath of the War Between the States.

But there was also a long-standing and, for many years, a valid reason for Southerners to stick to the Democratic Party. During the years when the two major parties were distinguishable by platform and by principle, it was the Democratic Party which championed those causes dear to the hearts of Southerners—causes such as states' rights, low tariffs, and free trade. And, more philosophically, there was the Southern sense of political identity with Thomas Jefferson—as opposed to the Hamiltonian frame of centralist mind ascribed to those who came later to be known as Republicans.

But, even as Roosevelt had wrought his political miracles, there began to be vague stirrings of discontent among a few Southerners who wanted stricter adherence to the Constitution, more insistence upon the sovereignty of the states, and less catering to the mounting demands of shrill minority groups in pivotal states.

From the high tide of Democratic strength in the South (1936), then, there was a gradual, almost imperceptible, lessening of fervor on the part of Southern Democrats for their national party. The overwhelming percentages by which Democrats were accustomed to carrying the Southern states in presidential elections began to abate somewhat, although there seemed no accompanying rise in the Republican vote.

In South Carolina, for example, a corporal's guard of dissident Democrats calling themselves "Jeffersonian Democrats" refused to endorse a third term for Roosevelt in

1940, and cast their meager handful of votes (fewer than 2,500) for Wendell Willkie. Four years later, the dissidents, now tripled in number, again repudiated the national party's selection of another term for Roosevelt, and this time voted for Virginia's Sen. Harry F. Byrd under the banner of the "Southern Democrats." In that same year of 1944, other disaffected Democrats throughout the South opposed the Rooseveltian-New Dealish course of the national party, but without much success. In Mississippi and in Texas, anti-New Deal factions sought to deny electoral votes to the national party, but, significantly, NOT by supporting the Republican Party.

At that stage of Southern politics, not even the irregular Democrats could bring themselves to vote Republican in anything approaching sizeable numbers. Yet the rift between the Northern and Southern wings of the Democratic Party was steadily widening. In late 1947, with the report of President Truman's Commission on Civil Rights, and in early 1948, with Truman's civil rights message to Congress, the breach widened further. The more the Truman administration and Northern Democrats clamored for civil rights legislation, the stiffer became the Southern resistance, both in Congress and within the state legislatures of the South.

Southern and non-Southern Democrats converged on Philadelphia in 1948 for the national Democratic convention in an atmosphere charged by friction and subject to spontaneous combustion. The mixture was ignited on the floor of the convention when an aggressive civil rights plank, drafted by a minority group of the platform committee, was adopted by the convention. It was shortly thereafter that the entire Mississippi delegation, accompanied by a portion of the Alabama delegation, walked out of the convention in protest against the then-obvious determination of the party to cram a strong civil rights plank down the throats of the Southern delegates.

Later, after life-long Democrats of the two deep South

states had walked out with tears in their eyes and sadness in their hearts, Charles Bloch, of Georgia, took the rostrum to warn the convention:

"I say to you Democrats of the North, of the West, and of the East: You shall not crucify the South on this cross of civil rights. . . . We do not propose to return to that tragic era of Reconstruction."

The delegations from South Carolina and Louisiana remained in the convention, but within a matter of weeks they had joined ranks with Alabama and Mississippi in repudiating the national Democratic Party and its presidential nominee, Harry Truman. In those four states, the Democratic Parties proceeded on the assumption—indeed, the declaration—that the state parties were autonomous within themselves, linked to the national party only by tradition and by label, but not bound irrevocably to follow the national lead in all matters, certainly not in one so offensive to the South as the proposed overriding of states' rights with federally-imposed "civil rights."

As the vehicle of protest, the Southern Democrats organized "The States Rights Democrats," hoping to solidify the entire South behind a presidential and vice-presidential ticket comprising then Gov. Strom Thurmond, of South Carolina, and the late Gov. Fielding Wright, of Mississippi. But, despite the fervor of the states' rights movement in parts of the South, it became apparent then, as it has been apparent before and since, that too many politicians had too much at stake to jeopardize what to them seemed a priceless political appellation—"Democrat." As a consequence, in all the South, only the four states which led the fight (and wherein State Democratic Parties supported the States' Righters) deserted the national party. They gave the Thurmond-Wright ticket 38 electoral votes and an independent-minded elector of Tennessee added the 39th on his own motion.

Thus failed the effort to throw the presidential contest

into the House of Representatives, which would have been the case had the Southern defections denied Democrats and Republicans alike the 266 electoral votes necessary for election. But even so, the attempt came closer to realization than is generally supposed. Had North Carolina and Texas joined ranks with their sister Southern states, the election would have been thrown into the House. What would have happened there is problematical, but certainly the South would have been in a powerful bargaining position.

The picture had changed by 1952, partly because of disappointment over the failure of the independent movement of 1948 to influence the presidential contest, and partly because of what seemed a sincere Republican bid to gain support in the South. That latter factor was made all the more effective because the Southern appeal was voiced by a national hero, General Dwight D. Eisenhower, who towered above the Republican Party (at least in the eyes of Southerners), and whose words were accepted at face value by hosts of Southerners.

It was due almost entirely to Eisenhower's personal appeal to Southern voters, and to his seemingly genuine espousal of the principles of state sovereignty, that four Southern states left the Democratic ranks. This time they were Florida, Texas, Tennessee, and Virginia, none of which had forsaken the national Democrats four years earlier for the States Rights ticket.

In 1956, because the growing disillusionment with the Eisenhower administration was offset by a lack of confidence in the Democratic ticket of Adlai Stevenson and Estes Kefauver, those same Southern states, with the addition of Louisiana and Kentucky, once more supported the Republican nominee and gave their electoral votes to Eisenhower. By 1957, however, most of the Southerners in all those states wished they could take back those votes, for both Eisenhower and the Republican administration had given clear, cruel, and unmistakable evidence that their concern for the South was a thing of rags and tatters, torn to shreds while they courted the Negro minority blocs of the Northern pivotal states. The Republican advocacy of a vicious "civil rights" bill in the 1957 Congress set the stage for wholesale defections from GOP ranks in the South; and the curtain rang down with President Eisenhower's ordering of combat-ready Regular Army troops into Arkansas to force integration at Little Rock's Central High School.

One factor which undoubtedly contributed to this cold-blooded decision to sacrifice the white South as a potential source of Republican strength was the surprising split of the Negro vote in 1956. Up until that year, the national Democratic Party had profited from the completely anomalous situation wherein Southern whites and Southern blacks had both supported the Democratic Party—despite that party's obvious exploitation of the racial issue as a means of garnering Negro votes in the North. But when election returns showed the Republicans that Negro votes could be weaned away from the Democrats on the sole grounds of granting racial concessions, the die was cast. The real goal of the Republicans became the Negro vote, North and South; and the aspirations of white Southerners to build up a Republican Party went down the drain.

There was some faint hope in the South that the split of the Negro vote might foreshadow a greater spirit of political independence among the Negroes themselves, but dispassionate analysis and political surveying indicate that the Negroes were in 1956, and presumably will be for some years to come, primarily responsive to voting appeals thrown their way in terms of racial considerations. That response promises even greater catering to Negroes on the part of both Democrats and Republicans. The big question left with the white South is whether to try to recapture Democratic Party control and re-orient the party along more Southern lines, or to establish a third party which

would reflect constitutional conservatism (especially embodying states' rights) in the hope of becoming an influential or controlling factor in presidential elections.

Within the next few years, white Southerners may find
themselves facing the necessity of deciding whether they
will seek to make their Democratic parties distinguishable
on a basis of principle, or whether they should create another political organization based on principles which will
be meaningful. This assumes a continuation of the present
alignment and tactics of both national parties, but there is
some small hope that the whole political picture may be
changed for the better.

Since political pressure is in chief measure responsible
for the tensions which surround the problem of race relations, it follows that whatever will remove that pressure
will likewise lessen the tension. The greatest single con-
tribution to the removal of the pressure would be the revision of American elective practices so as to deflate the
inordinately and improperly exalted role of minority groups,
especially that comprising Negroes.

As matters now stand, such groups are capable of influencing the outcome of elections on all levels from local to
national, in areas where the two major parties are of the
same relative strength. In the all-important presidential
elections, for example, the entire electoral vote of any given
state goes to the candidate and the party which wins a
majority, no matter how slim, of the votes cast for presidential electors in that state. That means in numerous instances
that the votes of millions of Americans are literally forfeited
by the action of minority groups in tipping the scales one
way or the other.

As one graphic example, the Democratic Party in 1944
received only 39.2 per cent of the total vote for presidential
electors in the State of New York. The popular vote was

2,479,000 for the Democrats against 2,988,000 for the Republicans. But the American Labor Party cast 496,400 votes for the Democratic presidential electors and the Liberal Party added 329,200 votes for the same electors. As a result, the Democratic electors pulled ahead of the Republicans with 3,304,600 votes to 2,988,000. Thereby, the Democrats got 100 per cent of the state's 47 electoral votes. In effect, 825,600 Labor and Liberal voters completely nullified the votes of almost 3,000,000 Republicans, whose ballots counted for nothing in that year's presidential contest.

What needs be done is to adopt some plan whereby the votes of every major party will bear some weight in determination of the national outcome. This would require a readjustment of the electoral college system. Of the several proposals which have been advanced for effecting this change, these two have received most favorable consideration, although neither has yet won sufficient strength in Congress to be adopted:

1. A plan whereby a state's electoral vote would be apportioned among leading presidential candidates according to the popular vote cast for such candidates within the state. Referring to the 1944 picture in New York, as cited above, such an arrangement would mean that the Democrats would get 39.2 per cent of the electoral vote since they got that percentage of the popular vote.

2. A plan whereby presidential electors would be elected by Congressional districts or other special districts, with two electors elected from the state at large.

Adoption of either of these plans would result in each party's standing on its own feet and carrying its own weight in presidential elections. There would be no balance of power reposing in the hands of minority blocs, at least not to the extent which now prevails, and the major national parties could tailor their political approach to the will of the majorities instead of the minorities. Furthermore, every citizen would be assured that his vote would count for something, and not be cast aside by virtue of a scales-tipping minority vote.

Yet for all their professed adulation of "democracy" and "majority rule," the politically astute leaders of the NAACP have no desire to give up the thoroughly undemocratic leverage Negroes now exert through their "balance of power" status in critical states. Accordingly, they can be relied upon to fight tooth and nail against any revision of the electoral college which would force every political entity to stand on its own feet and wield only so much influence as its numbers warrant.

Here's how Roy Wilkins, NAACP executive secretary, reacts to proposals that a state's electoral vote be divided in proportion to the popular vote received by presidential candidates within that state:

"This would mean that the Negro voters concentrated in Cleveland, Columbus, and Cincinnati, Ohio, would no longer be able to swing Ohio's Electoral College total behind one candidate. Similarly, the influence of Negro voters in New York City would be cut down, as would that of those in Philadelphia, Pittsburgh, Indianapolis, Detroit, Chicago, and Los Angeles. . . ."

Southerners, whether individually or collectively, by private action or by governmental action, do themselves and the South a disservice by denying to qualified Negroes the right to vote. No case can be made out for a denial of that right to any citizen who meets the requirements set forth by impersonal, impartial, and color-blind law. In truth, the refusal to permit Negroes to vote is in substantial measure an admission of incapacity to out-maneuver them in the give-and-take of political warfare. It is a sort of admission that, without chicanery, the white people cannot exercise their own suffrage in sufficient concert and with sufficient acumen as to carry the day in their own behalf, if an issue resolve itself into a matter of purely racial appeal.

If, as will be argued, the Negroes will vote as a bloc when it is to their racial advantage to do so—then there is nothing to keep the whites from voting as a bloc. Every state has the right and the duty of safeguarding the caliber of the entire electorate by establishing whatever standards it desires, so long as those standards are fair, constitutional, and nondiscriminatory on the basis of race or sex. State legislatures which are so lacking in political courage as to avoid setting high standards deserve whatever harassment comes their way.

14

The Myth of Moderation

Tʜᴇ myth of moderation which receives so much sanctimonious approval from the North when advocated by the liberals of the South warrants a closer examination than it has thus far received. First of all, it is virtually impossible to arrive at a point of moderation between two such diametrically opposed sets of circumstances as segregation and integration. Neither can exist in the presence of the other. The well-intentioned peacemakers of the North and South who counsel "moderation," therefore, embody this basic flaw in their reasoning: There is no basis for compromise for those, on both sides of the issue, who think in terms of principle alone.

Philosophically, the matter of integration, like that of pregnancy, leaves no middle ground. Segregation and integration are absolutes—and as such are mutually exclusive. Therein lies the fallacy of the seemingly reasonable argument of the NAACP. Individually and in groups, spokesmen for that militant organization have made much out of their professed willingness to "sit down and work this thing out." Here is one such expression of the "get together" attitude, incorporated in a statement drafted by nearly 100 Negroes who met in Hot Springs, Ark., in October of 1954, five months after the Supreme Court had handed down its desegregation decision:

"Good statesmanship in a democracy requires that all segments of the population participate in the implementation of the Court's decision, which is of common concern. . . . We are all, Negro and white, deeply and equally involved. Many Negroes can contribute sound, intelligent and statesmanlike techniques for the handling of the inevitable issues."

On its face, that statement, like many others in similar vein, seems plausible and reasonable—until one realizes that implicit in the NAACP attitude and explicit in the statement is the fixed notion that integration is the only thing which can emerge from any given deliberations. The only area left for discussion, therefore, relates to the method and timing of steps by which segregation will be discarded. The "reasonableness" of that approach pre-supposes an acceptance of ultimate desegregation as inevitable —but millions of white Southerners are not prepared to accept that conclusion. They are equally adamant in their insistence that segregation be preserved—at least for those persons who desire it.

Consequently, when the "moderate" calls for sweet reasonableness, he meets with little response from the Southerner. In the mind of the white Southerner, the prospect of integration is repulsive, whether it stem from seduction by the moderates or rape by the extremists. The end product, racial commingling, would be the same in either circumstance, and the Southerner wants no part of it.

The definition of the word "moderate" itself poses a problem, for there seem to be as many versions as there are individuals who lay claim to the designation. For one definition, here are the words of a liberal (what does *that* word mean?) North Carolina editor, C. A. (Pete) McKnight, of *The Charlotte Observer*. Writing in the June 22, 1956, issue of *Collier's* magazine, McKnight says:

"By a moderate, I mean the fellow whose mind is still open to facts and opinions on either side of the segregation issue, and whose emotions are under such firm control that he can discuss the issue with his neighbors and friends calmly, temperately and with some detachment. Moreover, he is a man who would not be averse to seeing limited school desegregation tried in a few selected communities, so that future public policy in his state could be based on facts, and not on fear and fancy."

Such a definition adequately confirms the suspicion of many Southerners that most of the so-called "moderates" are sugar-coated integrationists—quite willing to mix the races so long as it be done without violence on either side. To that extent, the Southern "moderates" differ from the Northern "liberals," many of whom are quite willing to have federal authority exerted to the utmost in an effort to compel unwilling Southerners to integrate the races. But both liberal and moderate seem to suffer from a compulsive social consciousness which confuses legal equality with social welfare.

Some of the native Southerners in this category lash out with such immoderate language that it jeopardizes their own status as self-professed "moderates." One such is Marion A. Wright, who long was president of the Southern Regional Council, and who belabors not only the governors of South Carolina and of Georgia but the entire concept of resistance to enforced integration in terms such as these:

"So when the ideas of evasion or circumvention of a court decision—whether by constitutional amendment, legislative act or the connivance of officials—emerge from the slime in which they are spawned, let us test their right to our acceptance, not by the eminence of their authors, but by our individual standards of what is a right and honorable course for a state to pursue."

Wright, like so many of the messianic moderates of the South, assumes unto himself an omniscience and perception denied to his lesser brethren. Says he: "Indeed, when hearts are searched, the consciences of white Southerners are troubled and ill at ease."

In similar diagnostic vein is this psychoanalysis rendered by a Virginian, Benjamin Muse, writing in *Harper's Magazine:*

"There are many uneasy consciences, and many unhappy people, in the South today. Educated men who speak lightly of abolishing public schools, patriotic Americans who voice contempt of the government of the United States, Christians who flout the teaching of their churches—these do not sleep well at night."

Somehow, Southerners seem as unaware of the mass insomnia which Muse envisions as they are of the categorical inferiority complex attributed to them by Lillian Smith's strange literary fruit in *The New York Times Magazine* of July, 1951:

"Racial segregation has been a strong wall behind which weak egos have hidden for a long time. A white man who feels inferior, who can add up more failures than successes in his public and private life, craves the feeling of superiority which his white skin has given him in our culture."

Whether by calculation or not, these self-styled moderates and liberals are playing with the stuff of history when they take their stands for integration of the races—now, or in the "gradualist" future. Some seem to glory in their loneliness, feeding their egos with self-righteousness and a sense of enlightenment not granted to their obtuse colleagues. Theirs is the self-chosen mission of leading the South out of the abyss of racial consciousness into the bright new world where colors fade and cultures blend.

Although they would be the last to admit it, the so-called moderates have done themselves, the South, and the nation a disservice by their failure to reflect the intensity of Southern resentment and resistance to integration. Whether their writings have been aimed solely toward the North, or whether such professions have simply been seized upon by gullible non-Southerners as reflections of true Southern sentiment, the fact remains that the moderates help create the impression that the South would accept integration, sooner or later, and that "reasonableness" would prevail in Southern reaction to court-ordered integration.

The moderates, who are themselves men of good will, have fallen into a trap of their own making. The "enlightened" circles of their metropolitan associations seemingly persuaded them that the South was ready for, or at least would not bitterly resist, even so great a social change as the intermingling of white and Negro children in the public schools. They were wrong, grievously wrong, and their error was compounded by the very publicity they gave it, North and South. While giving aid and comfort to the integrationists of the North, they were irritating their segregationist neighbors of the South. As a consequence, neither side was prepared for the degree of intense feeling reflected by the other, and the inescapable clashes were all the more painful.

What the moderates cannot understand is that hosts of white Southerners are not in the least willing to accept integration as inevitable, or "to relax and enjoy it." The inevitability of race-mixing in the public schools is something that the majority of Southerners are prepared not only to challenge, but to resist. To them, there is no more basis for accepting integration as inevitable than for accepting Socialism or Communism as inevitable.

To the Southerner, the threat of forcible racial integration has taken on all the aspects of aggression and encroachment upon the entire Southern region. And a regional patriotism, rooted in American patriotism, rises up to resist the threat. The proof of that lies in the numerous, but too-often over-looked, referenda which have given Southerners an opportunity to voice their sentiments on the matter of segregation.

Not all of the Southern states have afforded their citizens the chance of voting on the question of segregation, but enough have done so to give a South-wide reflection of the determination to maintain separate schools. These referenda also refute the idea, so often advanced by the liberals and moderates, that Southern people are being led astray by their political figures. These votes, it should be noted, are those of the people, not of the politicians except insofar as they participated as individuals. The ballots went to whites and Negroes, to conservatives and liberals—in short to the entire electorate which was qualified to vote—and these are the results, state by state:

SOUTH CAROLINA—Nov. 4, 1952—"Shall the Constitution of 1895 be amended so as to repeal Section 5 of Article XI thereof, which reads as follows: 'The General Assembly shall provide for a liberal system of free public schools for all children between the ages of six and 21 years, and for the division of the Counties into suitable school districts'?" By a vote of 187,345 to 91,823, South Carolinians approved the amendment, thereby freeing the hands of the legislature to cope with the segregation problems by statute, without the encumbrance of a constitutional requirement that a system of free public schools be maintained. The favorable vote, overriding opposition from such groups as the Christian Action Council and the League of Women Voters, left the existence of the school system in the hands of the General Assembly.

GEORGIA—Nov. 2, 1954—The question here was on the addition to the State Constitution of an amendment aimed at permitting the establishment, if need be, of a system of "private" segregated schools which could be attended by Georgia children at state expense. The amendment was adopted by a vote of 210,478 to 181,148.

LOUISIANA—Nov. 2, 1954—Louisiana, the only Southern state with its legislature in session at the time the desegregation decision was handed down, submitted the following constitutional amendment to the electorate: "All public elementary and secondary schools in the State of Louisiana shall be operated separately for white and colored children. . . ." The amendment was approved overwhelmingly, the vote being 217,992 to 46,929.

MISSISSIPPI—Dec. 21, 1954—One of the most positive declarations of segregationist sentiment occurred in Mississippi, where the voters approved a constitutional amendment embodying the following:

"The legislature shall be and is hereby authorized and empowered, by a two-thirds vote of those present and voting in each House, to abolish the public schools in this state, and enact suitable legislation to effect the same.

"The legislature shall be and is hereby authorized and empowered, by a majority vote of those present and voting in each House, to authorize the counties and school districts to abolish their public schools, and enact suitable legislation to effect the same.

"In the event the legislature shall abolish, or authorize the abolition of the public schools in this state, then the legislature shall be and is hereby authorized and empowered to enact suitable legislation to dispose of school buildings, land and other school property by lease, sale or otherwise. . . ."

The Mississippi voters endorsed the amendment by a count of 106,748 to 46,099.

VIRGINIA—Jan. 9, 1956—The Virginia vote on segregation grew out of an involved set of circumstances which stemmed from a State Supreme Court decision as well as from the desegregation decision of the United States Supreme Court. The State Court's decision invalidated a 1954 enactment by which the General Assembly of Virginia had sought to provide financial assistance for the education of certain war orphans in attendance at private schools. That development was incorporated into the deliberations of the special legislative session convened in 1955 to cope with the general problem of maintaining school segregation.

Out of that special session came an act which submitted to the electorate the question of calling a special constitutional convention limited to consideration of the pressing educational problems "due to the decision of the Supreme Court of the United States in the school segregation cases."

The act specified that a special election be held at which voters would be asked whether they approved the calling of a convention "To permit the General Assembly and the governing bodies of the several counties, cities and towns to appropriate funds for educational purposes which may be expended in furtherance of elementary, secondary, collegiate and graduate education of Virginia students in public and nonsectarian private schools and institutions of learning in addition to those owned or exclusively controlled by the State or any such county, city or town."

When the question was put to the voters, 208,565 voted in favor of the convention, while 83,289 opposed it. All but eight of the state's 98 counties voted in favor of the convention, with heaviest opposition coming from Arlington and Fairfax counties, both of which are located in the Washington, D. C., sphere of influence.

ALABAMA—Aug. 28, 1956—The legislature of Alabama gave the citizens an opportunity to vote on what came to be known as a "freedom of choice" amendment to the State Constitution, containing this clause:

"The legislature may by law provide for or authorize the establishment and operation of schools by such persons, agencies or municipalities, at such places, and upon such conditions as it may prescribe, and for the grant or loan of public funds and the lease, sale or donation of real or personal property to or for the benefit of citizens of the State for educational purposes under such circumstances and upon such conditions as it shall prescribe. Real property owned by the State or any municipality shall not be donated for educational purposes except to a non-profit charitable or eleemosynary corporations or associations organized under the laws of the State."

The Alabama amendment was adopted by a vote of 128,586 to 80,866.

NORTH CAROLINA—Sept. 8, 1956—A special session of the North Carolina General Assembly incorporated a Constitutional Amendment in the legislative package it enacted to preserve racial segregation in the public schools of that state so long as the residents of any community wanted such segregation. The amendment gave authority to the state to make tuition grants and for local school boards to suspend the operation of the public schools.

The people of North Carolina voted overwhelmingly in favor of the Constitutional amendment, and the legislative plan based on it—471,657 favoring the amendment; 101,-767 opposing it. The vote was favorable in every county.

ARKANSAS—Nov. 6, 1956—Citizens of the border state of Arkansas had three opportunities to register their sentiments concerning school segregation in the 1956 general election. Two of the proposals submitted to them were strongly-worded resolutions of interposition. One of them declared, among other things, that Arkansas had never surrendered to the federal government "the power to regulate or control the operation of the domestic institutions of Arkansas," and pledged the state's resistance to "any and all illegal encroachments upon the powers reserved to the State of Arkansas." That resolution also urged other states to join hands with Arkansas in proposing an amendment to the federal constitution so as to specifically bar the federal government from the regulation of public schools and interference with a state's right to maintain racially separate but equal schools.

The interposition resolution was approved by a vote of 199,511 to 127,360, with favorable majorities in 61 of the state's 75 counties. A second interposition resolution, this one in the form of an amendment to the Constitution of Arkansas and embodying a strong element of nullification, likewise was approved by a vote of 185,374 to 146,064, carrying 48 of the state's 75 counties.

The pro-segregation margin was even more pronounced on the question of approving a pupil assignment law which spelled out in considerable detail the factors to be observed in determining the school in which each pupil should be sent. The vote on this proposal was favorable by this margin: 214,713 to 121,129, with 67 counties approving.

On a completely unofficial and spontaneous note, there arose in South Carolina during August of 1955 a singular development which revealed the concern of that state's citizenry over the threat of integration. At a time when there was much floundering over the state's future course, and when both the NAACP and the Citizens' Councils were becoming increasingly insistent in pressing their respective causes, there came forth from a select cross section of the state's business, agricultural, and professional leadership a statement of principles which delineated the stand of a substantial segment of the state's white citizenry. Out of what was an entirely informal and impromptu enlargement of a small but interested group of South Carolinians, there came into being an extremely loose-knit group labeled by the press as "The Committee of 52."

Actually, the term "committee" was something of a gratuity, for the group met only two or three times, and purposely avoided organizing itself into anything of a more lasting nature. What these men wanted to do, and what they did, was to place on the record a clear and unequivocal declaration of the sentiments they held with respect to school segregation. The 52 came from all parts of the state, and from all walks of life. They represented all shades of political belief, but they had in common these three things: a genuine concern over the segregation problem, an established reputation within their own communities, and a willingness to declare their position publicly.

By individual signature, they subscribed to the following resolution, preceded by the usual whereases:

"1. That the South Carolina General Assembly be urged to declare, at its next convening, the intention of this State to maintain the sovereignty guaranteed to it by the Constitution of the United States, and that such declaration specifically affirm the determination of the State of South Carolina to maintain separate schools for those pupils wishing to attend such schools, and

"2. That the General Assembly be urged likewise to take such steps as may be necessary or desirable to interpose the sovereignty of the State of South Carolina between Federal courts and local school officials with respect to any effort of such courts to usurp state authority in the matter of public education, and

"3. That the preservation of public education and domestic tranquility merits the grave concern of both white and Negro citizens, and warrants their individual and collective opposition to outside forces and influences which would destroy both education and tranquility, and

"4. That we, the undersigned individuals, in the conviction that a clear and present danger threatens the principles of constitutional government, racial integrity, and state sovereignty, do publicly declare our determination to resist that danger, without resort to physical strife, but without surrender of our position."

That declaration by the Committee of 52 carried weight in South Carolina and beyond its borders, not only because of what it said, but because of who said it. Included in the

52 were such men as a retired Chief Justice of the State Supreme Court, a retired Episcopal bishop, a college president, several college trustees, State Farm Bureau and State Grange heads, a former governor, physicians, lawyers, top-flight business men and industrialists, and others whose names were well-known and highly respected within and without the state.

Perhaps even more significant, however, was the response that the declaration received from the general public. When its text and the names of its signers appeared in the various newspapers of the state, along with an invitation for like-minded persons to subscribe their names to the same statement of position, some 11,000 South Carolinians promptly clipped the statement from the newspapers, signed it, and sent it in to a designated address.

But all these demonstrations of a public will to preserve segregation do not mean that there are not those in the South who hold a contrary view. There have been some school men, newspaper editors, welfare workers, clergymen, and citizens at large who have spoken out in opposition against the Southern resistance of the desegregation decision. Their voices have been heard, but they have not been heeded, at least not to any degree which would tend to reverse the adamant hostility to integration. Nevertheless, the very sound of their voices and the appearance of their writings has negated the contention that none but the segregationist dare speak in the South.

In the years following World War I, a few regional organizations came into being with the purpose of promoting interracial harmony, understanding, and appreciation, generally within the framework of traditional racial segregation. Among them were such groups as the Conference on Education and Race Relations, and the Commission on Interracial Cooperation. In those days, a major goal of both white and Negro members of such organizations was the diffusion of knowledge concerning the Negro and of information con-

cerning his contributions, actual and potential, to the South
and to the nation. Understanding and cooperation were the
twin goals of the numerous conferences held by these and
other organizations, and along with those intangible objectives went a good measure of activity aimed at spurring improvement in the educational, occupational, residential, and
cultural facilities available to Negroes.

Some of those goals remain as objectives of contemporary
organizations, but there has been a subtle shift toward integration and toward building a climate of acceptance for
the Supreme Court's desegregation decision. That is certainly true of the Southern Regional Council, which de-
scribes itself as the direct successor to the old Commission
on Interracial Cooperation. The Council was formed in
1944, with incorporators including Ralph McGill, editor of
The Atlanta Constitution; Methodist Bishop Arthur J.
Moore; the late Dr. Howard W. Odum, of the University of
North Carolina; and two prominent Negro educators, Ru-
fus E. Clement, president of Atlanta University, and the late
Dr. Charles S. Johnson, president of Fisk University. Its
long-time director was George S. Mitchell, who also served
as a board member of the now-discredited Southern Conference for Human Welfare from 1944 until his resignation
therefrom in 1947. Mitchell's successor at the Southern Regional Council was Harold C. Fleming, whose description of
the Council follows:

"In essence, the Council's approach rests on the belief
that every Southern state and most Southern communities
have people of both races who can work together as equals.
Through their efforts, we believe the South can adjust to the
legal changes now required and ultimately achieve a society
in which racial distinctions will be eliminated from public
life. We see our role as that of encouraging and assisting
with information and professional services the people who
feel this way. . . ."

The Southern Regional Council is somewhat sensitive to

any "misidentification" which links it with the Southern
Conference for Human Welfare (although there was some
overlapping of membership among the higher-ups of both
organizations) or with the Southern Conference Educational Fund, an integrationist organization which grew out
of the Southern Conference for Human Welfare after that
agency came under the guns of the House UnAmerican Activities Committee. Here is how Director Fleming, of the
SRC, differentiates the organizations:

"There is a current [1955] disposition in some quarters to
confuse the Southern Regional Council with the Southern
Conference for Human Welfare. Actually, the two organizations had quite different origins and approaches. The
SCHW was organized about 1938. It operated with a great
deal of fanfare and, I believe, engaged freely in political activity. . . . It formally dissolved, as I recall, in 1949, though
it had been inactive for several years prior to that. The
Southern Conference Educational Fund is the successor in
fact to the SCHW, having been initially established as the
tax exempt wing of the Conference."

The real nation-wide angel of the integrationists has been
the Fund for the Republic, a well-heeled organization set up
in 1952 with a $15,000,000 hand-out from the Ford Founda-
tion. It makes only a passing stab at being objective in its
approach to the problem of race relations. Back in May of
1956, when the Fund began issuing a periodical *Bulletin*
describing its operations in the field of civil liberties and
race relations, it noted somewhat sanctimoniously that the
Fund was proceeding in the belief that conflicts of interest
"will be resolved mainly by getting at the facts and debat-
ing the clash of principles in which the facts are entangled."
Since that initial issue, however, nothing smacking of a "debate" has ever crept into the *Bulletin* or into the Fund's
other publications. There is no "debate" in the Fund for the
Republic's manifest attitude on the subject, except as perhaps might involve a difference of opinion as to whether in-

tegration should come forthwith or be put off for a little while. Nowhere, and at no time, has the Fund so much as suggested that there might be merit in another view of the situation, and much less has it undertaken to publish any presentation of the segregationist point of view. On the contrary, there has been snide sniping at the Citizens' Councils, at Southern legislatures and public officials, and at Southern white people in general—all in the name of serving "the Republic."

Meanwhile, the Fund had distributed as of June, 1956, the tidy sum of $1,652,250 to a number of associations and church bodies dedicated to the bringing about of the mixture of the races. The Fund's preoccupation with race relations and Negro welfare stems from its professed concern with "the protection of minorities" and "due process of equal protection of the laws." Basically, the Fund itself was established "to defend and advance the principles of the Declaration of Independence and the Constitution," but such parts of these two documents as might involve the rights of the states seem to have been studiously avoided.

15

Toward a Proud Peace

I T IS a fair and practical question to ask now whether anything constructive can be salvaged out of all the unpleasantness which has stemmed from the fight over racial integration. The answer might well be "Yes," a qualified "Yes."

The prospect of improving race relations in the face of intense resistance to integration is admittedly difficult under present pressures and hostilities; yet there are changes which can and should be made, not only for the improved welfare of Negro Southerners, but also for the justification of many arguments used by white Southerners against forced integration.

In any attempt to approach this delicately balanced situation, the advocate of change or relaxation immediately runs head on into a major division of opinion. There are those who contend that any concession whatever will tend to weaken the South's position, to crack the dike of resistance, and to make for an ultimate flooding as the dam

breaks. On the other hand, there are those of equal sincerity
who argue that SOME abridgments of the adamant segregation pattern MUST be made if the South is to successfully
defend its main line of resistance, i.e., the schools. Despite
these contrary positions, there IS some hope of improved
race relations by virtue of the fact that these two groups
BOTH oppose racial integration in the schools. It may be
that in joint resistance against a common foe they might
find a basis for agreement on certain changes which might
ease the situation, improving the lot of the Negro without
damaging the lot of the white man.

For one thing, there should be some relaxation of both the
legal and the social barriers which obstruct voluntary association of whites and Negroes. Much of the Southern argument against the Supreme Court decision has been based
on the interpretation (whether correct or incorrect is beside
the point) that enforcement of the decision would deny to
the Southern man a freedom of choice as to where his child
should attend school. Along with that has gone an extension
of the same line of reasoning and its application into other
fields—housing, churches, and so on. The essence of the
white man's argument has been this: The individual should
be protected in his right of freedom of association, and correspondingly, of freedom to AVOID unwanted association.

But by the same token, if the Southern segregationist
wants to be free in his determination of associates, so should
the Southern integrationist be free in HIS determination
of associates provided, of course, that such associations are
mutually acceptable, and provided further that the circumstances and conditions of integrated associations are not
such as to endanger the public peace.

Much of the legislation enacted in the Southern states in
both the immediate and the distant past has been aimed
basically at preserving domestic tranquility as well as racial
integrity. This is especially true in the fields of education
and recreation, where indiscriminate mingling of the races

is bound to bring discord and strife. Whatever the future may bring, and whatever may be the judgment of non-Southerners, the governmental agencies of the South are acting wisely when they seek to prevent mass mingling of the races in schools, pools, and parks. And distressing though it may be, the closing of such institutions in many cases would be the sensible alternative to the emotional, social, and physical upheaval which would follow on the heels of forced race mixing.

But where there is willingness to mix, and where such mixing would not jeopardize the public peace nor infringe upon the rights of others NOT to mix, some concessions are in order. Neither the written law of the political agency nor the unwritten law of the social community should stand in the way of whites and Negroes foregathering to confer, to discuss, or even to dine together with each other's consent and cooperation. The fact that such bi-racial activities might be distasteful to a large percentage of Southern whites should not be allowed to stand in the way of the integrationists' exercise of the right of peaceable assembly.

If an area of bi-racial activity can be carved out of the no-man's-land which now separates the two races by law in most Southern communities, there seems no cause for undue alarm. If the South is to protect the right of some (most) white people to move within segregated circles, then in all fairness it should permit other white people to move within integrated circles if that be their wish. For many years to come, the impetus of such movement will have to be from the whites to the Negroes, but the Southern argument against compulsory integration should apply with equal validity against compulsory segregation of those inclined, however mistakenly, toward racial commingling, so long as the rights of all are protected with respect to preference of association.

The white Southerner can contribute importantly to the easing of the segregation tenseness, and to the ultimate adjustment of the racial problem itself, by the simple expedient—the word is used deliberately—of extending to the Negro Southerner a larger and more adequate share of personal dignity and decency. This can be done with loss to neither, and with gain to both. Courtesy requires only intent and effort, and the application of those two in even small doses would repay the expenditure a thousand-fold.

Many a Negro reduces his racial complaint to this basic emotion: "I just want to be treated like a man." There are those, of course, who want much more than that, who want special privilege, who wish to inject themselves into a white society which is not willing to accept them, who wish to break down every racial barrier that can be found, preferably by force—but these do not reflect the broader and more basic desire of the Southern Negro, which is simply to be accorded a better opportunity to make for himself whatever place he can in his community.

This will necessarily mean a revision of attitude on the part of those whites who say, with altogether too much condescension, "I've got nothing against the Negro, so long as he stays in his place." The fact of the matter is that the Negro is entitled to make his own place, and it ill behooves the white man to do other than help his black neighbor along.

This, too, is important: That a mere change of attitude on the part of white Southerners will aid materially in easing racial tensions. A change of attitude does not entail any change of conviction, or lessening belief in the desirability of racial segregation in the schools, and wherever else it may be needed in the particular community. A change in attitude means only that a white man can help himself, his neighborhood, and his Negro associates by simply substituting an attitude of cooperation for the old pattern of condescension.

Along with this must go a measure of insistence that the Negro play his part in what could be a new and improved level of communication. If the Negro genuinely desires to be treated with greater dignity, then his own conduct must be such as to warrant it. He cannot expect to receive dignity along with indulgence. The burden of performance rests finally upon him. He cannot continue in his improvident ways, squandering his relatively small earnings on drink, trinkets, and carousing, forsaking his family when the mood strikes him, "forgetting" legal and moral obligations—and still look for the sort of treatment reserved for more worthy persons.

Many a white man is convinced that the Negro does not have it in him to break off his old habits, to buckle down to the demanding task of becoming a more laudable citizen, to raise his standard of personal conduct to an acceptable level. But the fair-minded white will show himself willing to meet the Negro fully half-way toward the higher level of communication.

In doing so, the white Southerner himself may gain a fairer and clearer picture of Negro capabilities. There is a Southwide tendency among white people to attribute to ALL Negroes those characteristics of the Negroes with whom they habitually come into contact. Since those contacts are for the most part with Negroes in menial or very subordinate positions, there is little awareness among whites that there are Negroes whose capacities and conduct are such as to warrant better treatment from their white neighbors.

As a corollary of improved communication between the two races, with accompanying better appreciation of each other's merits, there should be the offering of greater opportunity to the Negro to participate in both the planning and the execution of programs aimed at community development. It does not require any great amount of imagination on the part of a fair-minded white man to appreciate the resentment which naturally arises among manifestly capable and decent Negroes when they are denied all opportunity to take part in the formulation of policies and decisions which will bear directly upon them. The solidly American slogan of "no taxation without representation" has a bearing here, and Negroes would be something less than Americans if they did not feel the basic unfairness of complete exclusion from the area of community betterment on the grounds of color alone.

A Negro educator of North Carolina, Dr. Marlowe Shute, dean of instruction at Livingstone College, gave brief but penetrating insight to the situation when he wrote, in December of 1955, that Negroes, like other individuals, cherish these wishes:

"(1) The desire to be able to regard himself of real worth and to be so regarded; (2) the freedom and opportunity to develop himself to the limit of his capacities; (3) to participate in decisions by which he is affected."

In the field of race relations, the white Southerner's major shortcoming in recent years has been by way of omission rather than commission. When the Negro complains of having been denied even the outward trappings of dignity and decent treatment, he is justified in very large measure. It is to the discredit of the white man that he has provided no place in the Southern order of things for the colored man who, by his own efforts, has brought himself up to the level of decency and achievement demanded by white society.

Old habits and old associations die hard, and few Southerners outside the ministry and, to a lesser degree, the world of education have seen fit to bring the Negro into their counsels in ANY capacity. Understandably, the capable Negro who KNOWS his own capacity has become resentful of whites who will accord him no recognition of achievement nor any degree of participation in community development, be it segregated or non-segregated.

In all justice, however, it must be recorded that here and there about the South, degrees of recognition and participation were being accorded Negroes in slow but growing measure. A documentation of the bi-racial enterprises being conducted throughout the South in the years immediately preceding the Supreme Court decision presents a surprisingly long list of joint efforts. Yet the list fell far short of what could have been, and what should have been, an effective coordination between the races in every community of the region. Now, unhappily, the list has been cut to shreds by the revival of distrust and animosity engendered by the Supreme Court decision and the subsequent attempts to force integration on areas not prepared to accept it.

Despite the slowness of the pre-decision progress and the set-backs which followed the decision, however, there still remains in the heart of the average Southerner a willingness to see his Negro neighbor move into a brighter spot under the Southern sun. A great number of white Southerners—not all of them, to be sure—would subscribe sincerely to these two statements taken from "A Charter of Principles" on Race Relations approved in 1947 and again in 1948 by the Southern Baptist Convention:

"We shall be willing for the Negro to enjoy the rights granted him under the Constitution of the United States, including the right to vote, to serve on juries, to receive justice in the courts, to be free from mob violence, to secure a just share of the benefits of educational and other funds, and to receive equal service for equal payment on public carriers and conveniences."

One of the blind spots in the make-up of the average white Southerner is his ignorance of the attitudes and workings, and in large measure of the very existence, of a middle class Negro group. Yet these Negroes presumably have much the same outlook on life as that held by the white middle-class: a pre-occupation with education, for themselves and their children; an adherence to strict (or professedly strict) codes of morality; and a consuming desire to be accepted as desirable elements of the community. Because of these feelings, which are judged desirable by members of the white middle class, it comes as a shameful thing to these Negroes who, upon actually attaining such middle-class status, nevertheless are treated as being inferior to the lower class whites who make no pretense of subscribing to the same standards of values.

Unfortunately, at this stage of the game, these able and cultured Negroes are not strong enough in either numbers or influence to set the tone of the Negro community, whether it be located North or South. Consequently, any such community of appreciable size is much more likely to reflect the habits, attitudes, and values of the lower class. And since the lower Negro classes lean noticeably toward licentiousness, there is no strong pressure of community opinion to guide individual Negroes into an acceptable mode of conduct.

It may well be that, figuratively speaking, the Negro in the South now is passing from a prolonged period of civic adolescence into his maturity. The extended length of that growing period has been due both to the paternalistic attitude of the Southern white and to the childish attitude of many a Southern Negro. Just as parents frequently are somewhat bewildered and irritated by the behavior of their own children as they move from childhood into the trying days of adolescence, so have white Southerners been puzzled by the growing restiveness and resentment of Negro Southerners. So also have many white Southerners been unwilling to recognize the fact that the Negro may be "growing up."

One of the chief rallying cries of the NAACP and its fellow travelers is that of "first class citizenship" for the Negroes of America. The catch phrase is appealing and has been used effectively to enlist the support of well meaning persons whose heart-strings are pulled by the caterwauling which constantly arises from the professional champions of the Negro. Without in any way condoning the undeniable instances in which Negroes have been denied some of their rights, not only in the South but in the North and elsewhere about the nation, let's take a look at the reverse side of the coin and see whether the Negroes have themselves earned a catagorical reputation as "first class citizens." In the process, we might learn whether there is not a tendency among Negroes to confuse citizenship with social privilege. Citizenship is a conditional, not an absolute, right. It comes unasked as a blessing to those fortunate enough to be born in the United States, and to certain others under varying conditions, so there is no real credit attached to BECOMING or BEING an American citizen. It generally stems from the accident of birth. But even so, the right of citizenship can be forfeited, or abridged, by misconduct in any of a number of ways, and therein may lie some basis for distinction between "first class" and "second class" citizens.

First class citizenship demands more than the simple payment of taxes and the rendering of obligatory military or civil service as the need arises. It demands a fulfilment of society's unwritten as well as its written responsibilities. It involves a civic consciousness which contributes to community welfare, a code of personal and family conduct which meets the standards of decency and self-respect, and a willingness to participate in as well as partake of the benefits of the social organization.

On the other hand, the citizen may lose his status, or at least his right to vote or hold office, if he is convicted of any of a number of disqualifying crimes. The list varies from state to state, but to list some which appear in many jurisdictions, there are such offenses as "burglary, arson, obtaining money or goods under false pretenses, perjury, forgery, robbery, bribery, adultery, bigamy, wife beating, housebreaking, receiving stolen goods, breach of trust with fraudulent intent, fornication, sodomy, incest, assault with intent to ravish, miscegenation, larceny, or crimes against the election law." (S. C. Constitution).

Conviction of any of those crimes automatically places an individual in the role of a "second class citizen" regardless of race, but there are other offenses which rightfully establish offenders as something less than "first class" citizens. And here again, as in a great number of the crimes cited above, the Negro offends out of all proportion to his numbers and far beyond the limits of provocation. Unfortunately, he has been *permitted* to do so not only through the laxity of his own standards, but by the indulgence of white persons in positions of authority. In far too many instances, white officials have tolerated intra-racial crime and immorality among the Negroes out of a sense of humoring those whose pattern of life differs in such a large measure from that of white persons.

The time is at hand when such indulgence should stop short, for the good of both races. Prolonged tolerance of immorality and criminality among Negroes tends to perpetuate their inadequate social patterns and to threaten the patterns of white neighbors.

Consequently, if Negroes by and of themselves launch an all-out campaign against their own short-comings, they can contribute to several desirable goals at one and the same time: They can materially improve the community standing of their racial group by reducing the incidence of venereal disease, illegitimacy, sexual promiscuity, indolence, and so on; they can demonstrate to themselves, and to the world at large, that they have both the capacity and the will to raise their own standards; they can enlist the support of other groups in campaigns manifestly designed for community betterment; and—this is important—they can virtually disarm their critics who employ the stereotype device against them. A stereotype label is bound to lose effectiveness in the face of statistical proof that it is factually wrong, and many of the charges brought categorically against Negro conduct are subject to statistical appraisal.

All of this pre-supposes that the Negro can meet the chal-

lenge, and to that extent, the suggestion accepts at face
value the assertions of the NAACP and of the modern-day
sociologists and anthropologists who insist that the Negro
race, as a race, is not inferior to the white. Here, then, is an
opportunity for them to prove the truth of that contention,
and to prove it in a manner which can be understood and
appreciated by the layman. They can do so by an unflagging
insistence that their race measure up to community standards. This means that there is a burden of performance and
respectability imposed upon the Negro if he is to qualify as
a first-class citizen in fact as well as in legal standing.

But if the challenge of self-improvement confronts the Negroes themselves, there is much which can be done by the
white Southerners who hold the political and economic reins
of the region.

For one thing, there is a dire need for improved housing
facilities for Negroes. Even the most cursory study of the
Negro shift in population bears out the obvious but virtually
ignored fact that Negroes are moving in great numbers
from the country to the city. This is no new development,
and it shows no signs of either moderating or ceasing in the
near future. Furthermore, it is a massive sort of flow which
cannot be readily stemmed or controlled by appeals to reason or by the raising of obstacles. The impact of these in-
coming Negroes is being felt in city after city throughout
the South as well as in the North, and there is need for both
planning and action to adjust to their influx.

Since few Negro communities in metropolitan areas now
have decent or adequate sections for residence, the continuing in-migration of newcomers has the effect of piling-up
more and more residents into areas of already high population density. With this comes added problems of public
health, morality, crime, and general conduct, to say nothing
of the added demands for educational, social, welfare, and
medical services.

Adequate planning and preparation by both white and Negro business men, real estate agents, community organizations and city officials would make possible an orderly expansion of Negro residents into new areas, and might even make for gradual rather than sudden and hostile displacement of white families. One of the main complaints of white occupants and property owners in a given area threatened by Negro invasion is the abrupt and seemingly inevitable falling of property values once the neighborhood becomes "mixed." That in itself is due in no small part to the fact that the internal pressure in the "containers" of Negro population builds up to such a point that any break-out becomes anything from a spurt to a torrent, rather than a regulated flow. The need for housing is so great that, once access is obtained to other accommodations, there is a veritable deluge of Negroes into such newly-available quarters. A further complication is the fact that these new or once-white quarters frequently demand a higher rental or purchase price than the average Negro family can meet. Consequently, additional families or wage-earners are crowded into the housing units in order to provide a greater rent-paying potential per square foot of occupancy. All of this combines to hasten the conversion of the recently-acquired housing into veritable slums, which depress property values throughout the entire neighborhood.

It seems that cooperation of the type suggested above might meet this situation through the establishment of rigid zoning ordinances which would limit the occupancy of individual housing units, require the maintenance of adequate standards, and in general insure the maintenance of the area on a respectable basis for residential use.

White landlords all too frequently show interest only in draining a heavier financial return from their investment and accordingly fail to maintain their holdings in decent repair. But if these white property-owners can be accused of being niggardly, their tenants in too many instances can be

accused of being "niggerly," to use a word at once offensive
and descriptive. The proper maintenance of housing requires
joint effort by both owner and occupant, and that state of
affairs very seldom prevails in the field of Negro housing.
The landlords complain of Negro irresponsibility in matters
of both finance and household care, while Negroes complain of indifference and callousness on the part of the white
owners. Here is an area in which much work is to be done
by way of persuasion and regulation on the parts of municipal leaders, whether political or not. Intelligent use can be
made here of existing Negro civic groups, and others can
be brought into the field to heighten the feelings of self-
respect and pride of appearance which make for pleasant
and healthful residential areas.

City planning, although anathema by its very title to many
a rugged individualist, nevertheless can play an important
role in helping communities anticipate and solve such housing problems before they reach the acute stage. One major
need in this field is to plan for spatial expansion of Negro
housing areas so as to serve the dual purpose of providing
living space for Negroes without forcing them into white
residential areas.

Today, thousands upon thousands of Negroes in the
"piled-up" slums and ghettos of the North are finding that
their freedom is indeed a serious thing. They find few of the
helping hands, white or black, to which they could turn in
their former rural settings. They are exposed to all the
meanness, the grubbing, the grasping, and the greed of con-
gested urban life, and they frequently wallow in their own
helplessness and ineptitude. For them, competent guidance,
advice, and instruction could mean the difference between
existing and living. Whether the helping hands should be
black or white, or both, and whether they should be provided by the local, the state, or the federal governments,
or jointly by them all, these are questions to be answered
only after more study—but tax monies expended wisely in

this sort of urban demonstration work could well be bread cast upon the waters.

It once could be said in behalf of the National Urban League (originally "The National League on Urban Conditions Among Negroes") that this sort of endeavor was both a mission and a function of that organization. More recently, however, there seems foundation for the suspicion that the Urban League may have become more obsessed with racial integration than racial improvement—just as the NAACP seeks integration as the only means for the "advancement" of colored people.

The race-mixing tendencies of the National Urban League have brought new headaches to that organization, and to other agencies as well. In many Southern and border state communities, adverse reactions to integrationist pressure has provoked efforts to exclude the Urban League from Community Chest and United Fund welfare organizations. In November of 1957, League President Theodore W. Kheel said the organization was in "serious trouble" in some Southern cities, and in lesser difficulties in non-Southern cities of Ohio, Michigan, and elsewhere. He was quoted in an Associated Press dispatch from New York as saying that the Urban League had been forced out of Community Chests in Little Rock, Ark.; Norfolk, Va.; New Orleans, La.; Fort Worth, Tex.; Jacksonville, Fla.; and Roanoke, Va.

Meanwhile, even in areas where the Urban League is not operative, fund-raising drives have been hampered by the dissemination of propaganda leaflets (from the National Citizens Protective Association, of St. Louis) which contend that "Community Chests Support Race-Mixing" through Chest support of Urban League activities and inclusion of Urban Leagues in overall budgets.

But irrespective of the deeds or misdeeds of the National Urban League, there nevertheless remains a vital need for ground-level, pick-and-shovel work among individual Negroes and Negro communities which desperately need on-

the-scene guidance and help in adjusting to new urban settings.

In devising any approach for the reduction or elimination
of discrimination and in judging the likelihood of its success,
we must ask the practical question, "Will it work?" rather
than the ethical questions, "Is it right?" or "Is it proper?" If
the attack on prejudice is hinged on moral considerations,
it is foredoomed to failure, for neither side of this controversy is willing to admit that morality lies with the other.
Even where there seems preponderance of good on the one
side and of evil on the other in any given situation, the application of "righteousness" as an argument for change will
not prove effective, for man's capacity for rationalization is
such that he always can surround his position with reasons
which to him are ethically sound.

If solutions be sought, therefore, in the bounds of probable success, they must be so framed as to be workable without undue surrender of principle or loss of face by either
side. In this sphere of race relations the prospect of establishing and maintaining amity becomes brightest if the point
of friction can be moved away from the mutually-exclusive
arguments for integration or segregation, and thence on to
some other grounds where there is more likelihood of a meeting of the minds. This shift of locus will not please purists
(or extremists) on either side, but it might make for an easing of tensions, an evolving of a better basis for understanding, and a working arrangement which will contribute to
harmony, happiness, and better community cooperation for
both races.

Short of utter amalgamation of the races, a thing utterly
unacceptable to white Southerners, there is no *solution* to
the problem of race relations: there can only be a continual
adjustment and readjustment of relationships. The sense of
race, no less than those of religion or of nationality, is so
deeply embedded in man's nature—both conscious and unconscious—that it cannot be eradicated in the foreseeable

future, if indeed it *should* be eradicated. Some persons, whose impulses can be regulated or whose incentives can be manipulated, may rise above, or descend below, race consciousness, but the masses are not likely ever to shed their recognition of race.

Whatever may be the future of race relations in America, this much seems evident: That neither satisfaction nor peace can come from any coercive mingling of the white and black races against the will of either, and that little hope can be entertained for any assimilation of one in the other. There remains, then, only the prospect of accommodating their differences in a pattern of peaceful co-existence based upon a friendly tolerance and helpful understanding. It is the recognition of racial distinctions, not their denial, which will lessen the tensions and enhance their adjustment.

There is serious need now for a thorough reassessment of the entire picture of race relations—North and South—and for what the phrase-makers might call another "agonizing reappraisal" of the costs and the consequences of the nation's forced march toward integration. The time is ripe for both sides—for all sides—of the several controversies to inventory their successes and their failures. Fresh decisions need to be made in the light of matters as they stand now, and as they seem likely to develop in the near future.

These are some of the questions to be answered before the making of new decisions, or the reaffirmation of old ones, if that be the course taken:

1. Are the people of the East, the West, and the North willing to persist in driving a divisive wedge between themselves and those of the South through endorsement of anti-Southern legislation which inevitably will perpetuate sectionalism?

2. Is the Supreme Court of the United States so convinced of the wisdom of its school integration decision that it will continue to insist upon the sociological upheaval of com-

munities which are being transformed from peaceful neighborhoods into writhing centers of racial conflict?

3. Is the National Association for the Advancement of
Colored People so determined to compel race-mixing that it
cares not for the regeneration of bitter race hatred, which
had been diminishing steadily for years, but which now is
being planted in the hearts and minds of white youngsters
and which will be a scourge to the NAACP and to the Negro
for years to come, not only in the South, but everywhere?

4. Are the two national political parties so base in their
competition for partisan advantage that they are willing to
offer up the white South as a sacrifice to the unreasoning demands of minority blocs in the North, and thereby to drive
white Southerners into a third political party?

5. Is the national government prepared to display to the
world at large an inability to treat fairly with the inhabitants
of one-quarter of the nation, and a willingness to coerce
with military might those citizens whose only fault is their
insistence on preserving their racial integrity and the remaining vestiges of the local self-government presumably
guaranteed to them by the Constitution of the United States?

6. Is organized labor willing to write off the South as a
target for future unionization by continued agitation for
"civil rights" and other class legislation?

7. Are the churches of America so confident that integration is the only Christian answer to the eternal question of
race relations that they will risk driving into other denominations and other associations those equally sincere Christians
who have received no divine admonition to mix the races?

8. Are the Negroes of the land so devoid of self-respect
and pride that they stand ready to admit that their children
cannot develop and improve except in the presence of
the white race?

9. Are the teachers of America prepared to abandon the
precept that learning is enhanced where students share simi-

lar values and backgrounds, and to embark upon the instructional ordeal of teaching discordant groups of dissimilar children?

10. Are the parents throughout the South, or throughout the nation for that matter, ready to surrender all hope of transmitting their own cultural heritage to their children, and to accept an agglutinated cultural compound distinctive only in its lack of all distinction?

11. Are the people of America so obsessed with determination to force integration upon an unwilling South that they will support their federal government in the use of bayonet-studded force to overcome resistance?

And with the posing of those questions, this book winds up on the same note with which it opened:

"If the two races are to meet upon terms of social equality, it must be the result of natural affinities, a mutual appreciation of each other's merits, and a voluntary consent of individuals."

Index

Abolitionists, 12, 125, 131, 134
Addonizio, Hugh J., 89
Advent Christian Church, 106
Adventures of Huckleberry Finn, 54, 55
AFL-CIO, 91, 92
Africa, 142-143, 144
Afro-American, 49, 50
Alabama, 41, 42, 43, 109, 127, 138-139, 146, 193, 203, 262, 263, 277-278
Alexander, James, 57
Alexander, Raymond Pace, 56
American Bar Association, 38
American Broadcasting Company, 51
American Colonization Society, 143
American Council on Human Rights, 93
American Dilemma, An, 123, 197
American Jewish Committee, 90, 116, 117
American Jewish Congress, 93, 113, 114, 115, 117, 118, 119, 188
American Labor Party, 267
American Language, The, 48, 49
American Mercury, The, 234-235
American Negro Slavery, 163
American Resettlement Foundation, 147

American Teachers Association, 229
American Veterans Committee, 90
Americans for Democratic Action, 90, 93
Anglo, Saxon heritage, 2 ff., 212
Anti-Defamation League of B'nai B'rith, 93, 117, 118
Arkansas, 41, 42, 43, 146, 209, 237, 258, 265, 271, 278-279
Ashmore, Harry S., 66, 237
Associated Press, 74, 75, 76, 124
Association of Catholic Laymen, 102
Atlanta, Ga., 157
Atlanta Constitution, The, 282
Atlantic Monthly, 45

Baltimore Sun, 182
Baptist Church, 99, 100, 101, 103, 104, 109, 291
Beauharnais v. Illinois, 198
Bechet, Sidney, 215
Bethune, Mary McLeod, 59, 159-160
"Bible Belt," 95
"Black Belt," 42
Bland, James, 54
Bloch, Charles, 263
B'nai B'rith, 90, 93, 117, 118
Boone, Willie, 57
Borah, William E., 133-134

303